MANEUVERING TEENAGE LIFE

PRINCESS LUKHELE

A GUIDE THROUGH TEENAGE YEARS

HELPING TEENAGERS TRANSITION FROM CHILDHOOD TO ADULTHOOD

Maneuvering Teenage Life
A Guide Through Teenage Years
First Edition, First Impression 2021
ISBN: 978-1-77633-581-7
Copyright © Princess Lukhele
Email: info@progressiveteens.co.za www.progressiveteens.co.za

Layout design & Print by: Inspired Publishing

Published by: Progressive Teens

© All rights are reserved. Apart from any fair dealing for the purpose of research, criticism or review as permitted under the Copyright Act, no part of this publication may be reproduced, stored in a retrieval system or transmitted, in any form or by any means, electronic, mechanical, photocopying, recording, or otherwise, without the prior written permission of the copyright holder.

CONTENTS

Dedication 12

Acknowledgements 13

Preface 14

Goal Setting 15

Township Child Struggle 20

Body Shame 22

Rape 24

Bucket List 27

Drugs 28

Affirmations 32

Turn Your Lemons Into Lemonade 33

The Stomach Has No Window 36

Your Past Doesn't Define Your Future 38

Watch Your Words 40

Positive Self-Talk 44

Self-Care	46
Sports	48
Bullying	51
We Don't Choose Our Family	57
Money & Blessers	60
Studying Further	62
Clothes	64
Heartbreak	66
Speaking Confidence	69
Self Acceptance	72
Relationships	75
Social Media Effects On Teenagers	81
Is Failing The End Of The World?	83
Cyber Bullying	86
Applying In Time For University	89
Learning Money Skills	92
Creating Generational Wealth	108

Letter Of Promise To Self 112

Letter To The Queen 114

Importance Of Abstinence 116

Uzoyizothola Kanjani Uhlele Ekhoneni 118

Nobody Owes You Anything 121

Forgiveness 123

Business 126

Facing Responsibility At A Young Age 132

Gossip, Hate & Jealousy 134

What Story Do You Tell Yourself? 136

Great Things Result When You Refuse To Accept Excuses 139

My Story 143

Vision Board 146

Develop Hunger For Success 151

Diva 154

Careers 157

I Am The Hero Of My Own Life 197

Letter To The King 205

My Dear Son, This Is How To Treat A Woman 211

Boost Your Body Image With Daily Positive Affirmations 215

Fighting Against All Odds 218

13 Things To Teach Your Son About How To Treat Women 223

Boys Are Allowed To Cry Too 226

Responsibility 230

Accountability 234

Respect & Good Manners 241

Time Management 247

Effects Of Poor Time Management 250

Money Management 255

Ways Teens Can Earn Cash 261

Entrepreneurship 279

Honesty 282

If You Can Dream It, You Can Do It 287

Surrounding Yourself With Inspirational People 290

Have A Support System 295

Raising Your Level Of Expectation 298

Eliminate "I Can't" From Your Vocabulary 302

Positive Thinking Phrases To Change Your Life 308

Affirmation Contract 311

Growth Mindset 314

7 Rules Of Life 317

Get To Know The New You 320

Personal Values & Beliefs 325

Count Your Blessings Instead Of Your Struggles 330

Words Of Hope 332

Keep Moving 334

Look For Good In Everything 337

Be An Answer To Someone Else's Prayer 340

Don't Wait For Tomorrow 344

I Can. I Will. Watch Me. 347

What Conversation Are You Having With Your Self? 356

Positive Self-Talk..362

Are You Trying To Fit In?...365

Importance Of Journaling 368

Have Fun, Life Is Short..371

Validate Yourself, Be Good Enough For You 374

How To Figure Out What You Want In Life 377

Your Path, Your Purpose...382

Failing Forward...386

If You Don't Stand For Something, You Will Fall For Everything 391

Be Of Service To Others...395

Vision 397

Self-Doubt 400

Relationship With Money 403

Rethink Money...406

Don't Envy Others 410

How To Stop Being Envious Of Other People 415

Politely Say No 418

How Big Are Your Dreams? 424

Setting Boundaries 428

Focus On What You Can Do, Stay In Your Lane 431

Truth About Dating 434

Let Hope Overflow 440

Young Lady Be Fearless 442

Traits Of A Badass Women 444

Become A Women Of Impact 448

Become A Man Of Impact 452

Personal Development 455

Unleash Your Potential 464

Careful What You Let In Your Mind 466

Starve Your Distractions, Feed Your Focus 468

References 474

DEDICATION

To My late Mother, Lizzie Lukhele, I know you are up there watching and proud of me. I hope this book shows you raised a wonderful woman in me. Thank you for loving and believing in me. You are missed, I love you always.

ACKNOWLEDGEMENTS

I have to thank my dearest son, Owethu, for bringing coffee and water while I was writing this book. I missed out on some fun nights whilst writing this book. Thank you for your patience and loving hugs throughout the process. To my family; the entire crew of Bomhlanti Wendlunkulu, thank you for being my cheerleaders and believing in me. Without you I am nobody.

PREFACE

Working with youth and girls; mentoring and teaching them through my NGO - Handsofluv since 2012, the journey has been a fruitful one with opportunities to guide, coach and mentor the young leaders of tomorrow. This book was birthed through the experiences, lessons and observations while mentoring and counselling the youth in my organization, The mistakes, lessons and experiences of this process led me to believe that not every teenager has an opportunity to have a Miss P or an NGO dealing with Youth Empowerment in the world. I therefore felt that writing this book would give all teens an opportunity to have their own personal guide and accountability partner to assist them through these challenging years of their lives.

Teenagers are the future of our country and this book will ensure that they don't miss important steps and fall and become a burden to society and taxpayers. This book will help teenagers easily maneuver this phase of their lives. It will give parents topics to discuss with their teenagers. We all want our children to be successful therefore we need to offer and arm them with tools and resources to succeed. This book will help us raise strong, confident, and compassionate teens.
The real power of this book is in the concrete, practical advice each chapter offers. Each chapter has a "Teaching Lesson" which reinforces specific concepts for adulthood, as well as a "declaration" section with exercises for them to do.

The book outlines the various challenges teens face in different settings such as home, among their peers in society and at school. It offers practical strategies for helping a teen manage and win. Topics range from career, mental & physical wellness to business to money handling.

This book is for teens and adults looking for an inspirational book that encourages them to reach for the stars. This manual is a guide to growing up and is essential reading for teenagers.

GOAL SETTING

> *"The tragedy of life doesn't lie in not reaching your goal. The tragedy lies in having no goals to reach"* - **Benjamin Mays**

Direction
A goal gives you direction. It gives you something to aim for and direct your efforts towards. It helps guide you to where you ultimately want to be in life.

Setting lifetime goals is like choosing the destination you ultimately want to reach, and then taking the necessary steps to ensure that you end up there, instead of wandering aimlessly through life. You are able to determine where you want to go, and how to get there.

If you can successfully set - and achieve - your personal goals, many benefits await. Even if you do not reach all your goals, just having them can enrich your life in several ways.

Clearer Focus on what is Important
Your goals give you clearer focus on what you believe to be important in life. It is therefore essential, when setting personal goals, that you first think about what is important to you and what you really want to accomplish in life. If you take the time to reflect on your hopes and dreams, your goals will center on what is important to you. You will then, systematically and consciously focus your attention on that. If you do not set well thought out goals, you tend to spend your time doing things that are not important, and do not add value.

The reason most people never reach their goals is that they don't define them, or ever seriously consider them as achievable.

> *"Winners can tell you where they are going, what they plan to do along the way, who will be sharing the adventure with them."* – Denis Waitley

Clarity in Decision making

Setting goals helps you focus on what you want to accomplish, and where you want to be in the not-so-distance future. This perspective helps in decision making. If you know where you want to go, you are in a better position to make decisions that will lead you in that direction. The decisions you make now directly impact how you proceed and what you ultimately want to accomplish.

> *"Your goals are the road maps that guide you and show you what is possible for your life."* - Les Brown

Gives you control over your future

Setting goals helps you take control of your future. Without goals, you tend to drift aimlessly. When you do not have a plan for where your life is headed, you tend to just go with the flow. By setting your goals, you have more control of where you are headed and how to get there.

Writing down your goals and the steps you plan to take to reach those goals, equates to a plan of action for your future. You are able to get perpective and prioritize what you want to accomplish over the next few months or years. This give you a better indication of future success or failure.

Establishing a goal means very little, without a plan to reach that goal. A plan is a step by step, systematic course of action, that guides you to successfully accomplishing your set goal.

Provide Motivation
Goals give you hope and something to aspire to. Having a meaningful goal to think about and envision reaching can be very motivational. Establishing short term goals, and achieving those, goes a long way in realizing your long-term goals. The more short-term goals you are able accomplish, the more you are motivated to believe that you will reach your ultimate goal. Additionally, that motivation and the positivity experienced will help you get over many of the obstacles you may encounter along the way.

Once you have clear written goals your mind starts to focus more on how to achieve those goals. Your mind shifts from just hoping that you will someday be able to do something, to an actual plan of action, and you can start tracking your progress. Even the smallest action, done daily, adds up to big results over the course of time.

SMART

S	Specific - Make sure that the goal is written out as clearly and as detailed as possible.
M	Measurable - Make sure that any metric requirement in the goal is clearly defined and has specific numbers attached to it.
A	Achievable – Make sure that the goal can be accomplished and is not some crazy "pie in the sky" dream - like tripping your salary in three months or losing 50 kilograms in a month.
R	Relevant – Make sure that the goal is worth your time and effort.
T	Time-bound – Make sure that you have a start and end date in place. Also include any specific dates along the way, that are pivotal to ensuring the end goal.

SMART Goal Setting Worksheet

Name: _____

1. What is the goal? _____
_____
_____
_____

2. Why is the goal important?
_____
_____
_____
_____
_____

3. SMART goal checklist

| **S**pecific ☐ | Is the goal clearly written, with no ambivalence? Is it clear who needs to accomplish the goal, and any support they might expect? |

| **M**easurable ☐ | Does the goal answer th questions of how many, how much and/or how often? |

| **A**chieveable ☐ | Can you get the support needed to achieve the goal by the target date? Do you have all the resources needed to achieve the goal? Are the results expected realistic? |

| **R**elevant ☐ | Does the goal make a difference in your career? Is it going to make an improvement in your personal life? Is it going to significantly make a difference to your business? |

| **T**ime-bound ☐ | Does the goal state a clear and specific completion date? |

4. List potential problems that might keep you from completing your goal.
_____
_____
_____
_____
_____
_____
_____
_____

5. Goal Completion date
_____

Action Item: _____ Who _____ When _____

Action Item: _____ Who _____ When _____

Action Item: _____ Who _____ When _____

Student Goal Setting Worksheet

_____

Name: _____   Date: _____

I AM GOOD AT _____   I AM BAD AT _____

_____   _____

_____   _____

_____   _____

What Will I Improve? _____

_____

_____

_____

_____

HOW WILL I MAKE THESE IMPROVEMENTS? _____

_____

_____

IF MY PLAN DOESN'T WORK, WHAT WILL I DO? _____

_____

_____

TOWNSHIP CHILD STRUGGLE

The neighborhood
Rebuilding and Strengthening Low-Income Neighborhoods

The continuing deterioration of many neighborhoods condemns growing numbers of parents and their children to live in high-risk settings. Increasing numbers of adolescents live in neighborhoods characterized by high concentrations of poverty and crime. They are isolated from basic recreational facilities, such as those offered by youth development programs. As young adults, there are few employment opportunities available to them. Furthermore, the decline in income among already low-income households, coupled with discrimination in housing and reduction in construction of low-income housing, has compounded the problems of marginalized groups, particularly black people.

The effect has been to trap a growing number of poor families in dangerous, bleak, and socially disorganized neighborhoods.

Schools in townships
Schools are a fundamental neighbourhood institution that has historically provided the opportunity through which poor and disadvantaged people have gained access to the middle class. Because school funding is tied to neighborhood wealth, the most adequately funded and highest quality schools are not found in the neighbourhoods where the need is the greatest, but instead serve the children whose family and neighborhood environments already equip them with the knowledge and skills needed for success.

Reviving depressed urban areas will require a major commitment from government and the private sector, including support for housing, transportation, economic development, and the social services required by poor and low-income residents.

Strategies for urban revival
Support is needed to rebuild neighbourhood infrastructures, including transportation networks and such basic community services as police, libraries, and parks and recreation opportunities. Affordable housing in inner cities and the fringe suburbs is urgently needed.

In the absence of National governmental support, neighbourhood residents and some local governments have developed programs that highlight different models of intervention. For example, community organizing, and development efforts have resulted in neighbourhood beautification, increased safety, community policing, improved housing stock, and the creation of new services for disadvantaged persons. Most of these efforts have been accomplished on a shoestring budget and have often involved young people in service organizations. These programs suggest ways in which limited governmental funds can have a beneficial impact on communities and the young people who live in them. Improvements in housing, public service, schools, and public safety will require major public-sector commitments.

_____

_____

_____

BODY SHAME

They say I am too tall; I am called a Giraffe. I am afraid to mingle with people. They look at me strangely. I don't fit in. At school I sit alone. I don't speak much because nobody seems to understand me.

I met a white woman a few years ago who told me with that with my height, long legs and brown skin I could be successful in the modelling industry. She even said I have a beautiful smile.

This boosted my confidence. I was excited that someone finally saw me, and thought this body that I was ashamed of, was beautiful. Was this the only compliment I received in my whole life?

My mom never tells me that I am beautiful. She seems angry all the time; it seems as though she regrets having me and my siblings, because she is tasked with the responsibility of taking care of us on her own.

I don't know what a compliment is. All I know is this body of mine attracts attention, but unlike other girls, I seem to attract wrong attention. I feel alone anyone. I need a friend. I just want to be accepted like all the other girls. I just want to being young and happy.

 Solution

We are all unique. God created each one of us with purpose. You are not a mistake. Your body, and all that God has blessed you with physically, has a purpose. You need to embrace it with pride. Listening to other people's opinion of you does not serve you. You are beautiful, and you are enough, just as you are. Only what you think of yourself matters. Therefore, change the story you are telling yourself in your head. All parts of your body are perfect just the way they are. Remember, when you are older and can no longer do the things you wish to do, you will wish for this body, therefore enjoy it, embrace it, love it and own it.

Affirmation:
- From today onward, I choose to love me. I choose to accept and embrace every part of my body.
- From today onward, I choose to be grateful for all my limbs. I choose to appreciate that which God has blessed me with.
- From today onward, I choose to walk with the confidence of a goddess. I am perfect.
- I love my head. I love my hair.
- I love my face. I love my neck.
- I love my breasts. I love my arms and hands.
- I love my legs. I love my butt.
- I love my feet.

RAPE

We have been friends for a long time, in fact we had attended primary school together. We do everything together, and I trust her with my life. One day she met this guy who drives a GTI, and he took us around to cool places–places we could not afford. Usually, they'd buy us alcohol–even though we were under aged–and we'd chill and have a good time, then they would always take us back home. All we needed to do is just be cute, dress up and show up whenever her old boyfriend called. One Saturday they gave us something to smoke. I had never smoked in my life. I do not know what they gave to us, but everything went blurry after one puff.

I woke up the next morning in a strange place, next to one of my friend's boyfriends' friends. My head felt heavy, and my body felt weird. When I asked how I got there, he laughed and said, "relax baby, you are safe." Baby? He called me baby. What did I do? What happened to me?

It turned out, that what they had given us to smoke, was drugs, and it rendered me unconscious after just one puff. The guy next to me said he didn't do anything to me, but I knew something happened to me because my private parts were sore. I felt afraid and anxious.

I was told we were in Gugulethu. I don't even know how we got here, and he refused to take me home.

He kept calling me "baby" and telling me to relax. I couldn't relax, and I start crying because I knew that my parents were going to kill me. I left home of Friday evening, and it was now Saturday evening. They must be worried about me. I am such a fool for going with my friend and smoking things I do not know. How could I? I knew better. The man I was with, still refused to take me home. He told me that I could go home the following day, Sunday. I didn't want to stay there, I felt sick. I wanted to go home. He didn't care that I was crying. All he keeps saying is "Relax baby." It dawns on me that I was raped, but that I cannot even remember anything. How did I get myself into this situation? I knew I needed to escape. When he went out to by alcohol, he didn't lock the shack we were in, and I snuck out - without my shoes. I didn't have any money, but I reasoned that I would find help once I was out of there.

It was 9:30pm, and there were no taxis. I walked the streets, crying. I was alone, cold and afraid. I regretted every decision that brought me here. I just wanted to go home to my parents. I didn't care that I was in so much trouble, I just wanted to be home. An old taxi driver saw me on the street. He stopped and asked me why I was walking alone at night. I explained the entire story to him. He told me that he is father to a 14-year-old girl as well, and that he wouldn't leave me there. Thank God for this kind man. He took me home to my parents in Khayelitsha, who had already opened a case at the police station. Everyone had been looking for me. I was taken to the hospital to check if I was raped, and the results were positive. He had raped me. My friend whom I loved and trusted very much, refused to testify. She said I had agreed to go with that guy. She had been paid to lie about me. I lost the case because they believed that I never contested to sleeping with him. There were pictures of us a drinking together as a group. My friend betrayed me. I wish this nightmare would end. I am hurt. I am broken.

If I had listened when my mom warned me against this friend, I wouldn't be here.

 Solution

Choices always have consequences. They may not be immediate, but the consequences will come. The girl who went through this horrific experience, survived the ordeal. She is now in a different position, and she is a different person. She has more experience and more information. She now makes better decisions with her life. As painful as it is, sometimes God sends hard situations our way, to put us back on the right track.

This sad situation certainly influenced her future decisions. She is now doing her 2nd year as a law student, at UCT. She is wiser and smarter than that naïve 14-year-old. Her friend, however, was involved in a car accident with her older boyfriend a year later, and unfortunately passed away. She never got to finish matric.

Exercise: Discuss in your group consequences that can emerge from such a story and share with the class. What could have been done to prevent situation:

NOTES

_____

_____

_____

Declaration: Make a declaration to yourself, to commit to making wiser choices and smarter decision with your life.

I_____ promise that from today _____(date) I will

1._____

2._____

3._____

BUCKET LIST

What are the 101 things You want to do before you die

A bucket list is a wish list of things and tasks that you would like to accomplish or experience before dying. The list usually contains inspirational goals that you'd like to achieve.

There should be items on the list that are easy to achieve as you grow from adolescence into adulthood. Example: completing matric; getting full-time employment; starting your own business.

List all the experiences and accomplishments that you hope to realize in your lifetime.

Do not be afraid to go wild on your bucket list, this is where you can dream. Do not worry about the how, just jot them down. There is power in writing your wishes down. It has a miraculous way of helping them come true.

Creating a bucket list will help you articulate what you want to explore and help you focus your attention. It further helps in holding yourself accountable to pursuing your dreams. A bucket list is great method to set your life goals and stay focused on making them come true.

Declaration: I_____ set this **Bucket List** on_____
(date) with the intention and belief that I will achieve everything listed on it:

1._____ 2._____

3._____ 4._____

5._____ 6._____

DRUGS

Peer pressure and the brain
Peer pressure can influence teens' choices about a lot of things. New research shows that, when making a decision, teens think about both the risks and rewards of their actions and behaviors—but, unlike adults, teens are more likely to ignore the risk in favor of the reward.

Sipho, a very smart hard-working boy with great school grades in all subjects. He is well-liked by his teachers and his peers. He is a kind, selfless boy, considerate of others. His future is looks bright. He wants to be a doctor when he finishes his university studies. Raised by a single mom, who regularly works the night shift, Sipho is often responsible for the care of his two younger siblings. He must prepare dinner for them and ensure that they do their homework, before putting them to bed. His mother thanks God, knowing that she is lucky to have such a responsible 16-year-old. Most boys Sipho's age are not as responsible as he is. He only has one year left of high school. Next year, he will be graduating to grade 12. His mom has been saving all her money to make certain that he goes to university; she wants the best for her son.

One day, a boy from Limpopo was transferred to Sipho's school. They are in the same class and soon become friends because they both like mathematics. This new boy, Kagiso, starts visiting Sipho's home often and they became close. What Sipho doesn't know is that Kagiso was expelled from his previous school because he was caught with drugs multiple times, on the school premises. His parents moved him to another province for a fresh start. One night while Sipho's mom was working late, Kagiso bought a pack of drugs and encouraged Sipho to try it out. Kagiso claimed that it would help him study and that it calms the mind. Sipho was hesitant at first, but his friend was very convincing and so he tried it. Sipho loved the feeling of being high and how his mind stopped thinking when the drug was in his body. Soon the two boys' smoking became a habit and they started doing it more often. They started bunking school because they were tired and too high to go to school.

Sipho's marks dropped, his behaviour changed, he became aggressive at school and at home. His mom could not understand the sudden change. The school called her to say they were worried something was wrong. They suspected drug abuse because his behavior was irrational. The boys started stealing things from Sipho's home to sell, so that they could buy drugs. Sipho was losing weight rapidly. When his mother finally learnt what the cause of his behavior was, it was too late. Sipho was already deep into cocaine. He failed grade 11 and dropped out of school. He eventually left his home to be a vagabond and live on the streets. His mother never kicked him out. She tried all she could to help him, but her little boy was addicted to drugs and she could not help him. She still keeps his bed made and his books piled the way he left them, she hopes one day he will return and pick up from where he left off. It's been two years and Sipho has still not come home. His mother is now on high blood medication from worrying about her brilliant boy. She blames herself for working all the time and not noticing what was happening under her roof. She prays every day that her son returns home. Her front door is never locked. She says one day he will come home.

Solution:

When you already know the risks, yet you want to impress your friends, do you run the light or slow down and stop? Do you accept a drink or turn it down? Do you go with the crowd or be your own person and impress others with your individuality? What are some ways you could put the brakes on long enough to think twice before deciding to do something you know is risky?

Discuss in the group:
- Is Sipho's mom to blame for this situation?
- What are your views on peer pressure and how can teenagers avoid peer pressure?
- Discuss the consequences of peer pressure, and the different ways teenagers can take control of their choices.

Facts

1. Drug use is always a high risk. Drug use usually leads to other negative outcomes including mental and other illnesses, becoming a school dropout and academic failure; road accidents; unemployment, low life satisfaction and even relationship problems. Drug use exacerbates other already existing problems.

2. Drug use does not only affect the drug user. Often, family and friends are the first to experience the problems caused by drug use. In addition, drug use has serious consequences for society as a whole, **e.g.** in the workplace, schools, on the roads, in the criminal justice system and in the health and social services.

Declaration

I_____ hereby undertake to commit to never use drugs or alcohol. I promise to walk away from situations that involve drugs or illicit activities. I choose to live a drug free life so that I can achieve all my goals and make a better life for myself. I promise to keep my school and my community a drug free place by reporting any prohibited activities around me.

Signature:_____

Signed at_____**on the**_____

What to watch for

The many pressures teens face can play a big part in influencing choices around risky behavior, especially substance use. In fact, most teens use alcohol or illicit drugs to fit in, to cope with an underlying problem, to feel stimulated or to address some combination of these. So, your first step is to understand this and keep a close eye on your teen. In addition to depression, anxiety, substance use and other risk-taking might signal that your teen is struggling with the pressures of adolescence.

Watch for these warning signs:
- Sudden dramatic change in behavior, such as sleeping or eating habits
- Frequent sadness or over-reactions to everyday events and disappointments
- Less interest in activities, absences from school or poor grades
- Problems with relationships or more isolation than usual
- High levels of irritability, hostility or anger
- Bloodshot eyes or confusion
- Unusual borrowing or spending of money, or secretive behavior about belongings and actions
- Self-injury, such as cutting or scratching oneself with a sharp object
- Extreme eating patterns or unhealthy obsession with appearance or weight
- Needing constant support or reassurance

AFFIRMATIONS

The power of affirmation
Affirmations are words spoken by yourself, to yourself, to build up, encourage, instill courage and to make the impossible possible.

Why should you consider using affirmations?
Life is full of negativity, so speaking affirmations towards your life trains your thoughts and mind to think in a positive manner and you demand the universe to listen and bring about that which you desire.

It's important that you have a list of personal affirmations that you say daily. This will help bring your mind to a state of belief that all that you wish to achieve is doable.

At first it might feel unfamiliar and uncomfortable, but if affirmations are done consistently over time, things which you affirm will stars happening in your life. Some may not happen immediately but with time, as you grow into adulthood you realize them coming true.

Below write some affirmations of your own that you will say every morning and every evening.

 **NOTES**

_____

_____

TURN YOUR LEMONS INTO LEMONADE

She grew up in a two-bedroom home, in the dusty town of Ermelo, with her 7 siblings. Just like every teenager, she wanted her own room. A pink room Barbie-themed room. She wished she could have a room to herself, so she could sing and model and invite her friends for a sleep over, and do girly things in. But all that was a fantasy, because she shared the room with her siblings. The tiny government house had 4 rooms, two of which were bedrooms. The main bedroom was used by her parents, and the second bedroom was for her and her siblings. Life was hard and they were poor, and she knew this was not the life she wanted for the rest of her life. She knew she had to be different. She knew it was not normal for 8 people to live in such a small house, so she made it her goal to study hard so she can change her situation. Her dream was to build her parents a huge house. A house big enough that each one of her siblings would enjoy a room of their own. Her parents did all they could with the little they had, to put food on the table and to ensure a roof remained over their heads. They never went to bed hungry because her mom made sure they were fed and ready for school the next day. She vowed, that one day, when she had kids, her children would not experience poverty or hardship the way she did. So, she chose to be different. She chose to be different from her peers. She worked hard at school and was always the first in class. Her parents were proud, they even nicknamed her "Mistress" thinking that she would one day be a teacher, because she would take the children in her community and teach them. She didn't do all the things teenagers, her age did. They would go to discos and have fun, but she was focused on her books. When her friends were dating and out with boys, she was at the court playing tennis. Her friends and peers believed she thought too highly of herself, because she didn't do what the rest of them were doing. You see she had a goal. She had a dream. In her diary she had written a letter to herself that stated: "I will make the change in my family. I will have a degree. I will build a 7-bedroom house for my mom." She knew she could not do that by being ordinary. Her diary also stated that she wanted to study in Johannesburg. She promised herself that she would change, not only her life, her family's lives, but her community as well. She understood that she could not do that by being ordinary. She had to be different, and she was okay with it, because that would bring her closer to her dream. It paid off. She finished matric, went to university and graduated with a bachelor's degree. The first thing she did when she started working was build her mom the home she never had. Today, this young girl from the dusty streets of Ermelo has helped her young siblings go through university. She has embarked on a mission to help young girls like herself, growing up in townships, to follow their dreams. She is a coach, a motivator and an enabler. That girl with just a dream went on to get her master's degree and started her own NGO to help girls realize the power they have within them. To date she has successfully impacted over 1000 girls in townships though her NGO called "Hands Of Love".

Her name is Princess Lukhele founder of BLM, business owner and the author of this book. That girl that grew up in a 2-bedroom house. she took her lemonade and turned it into lemons. Her message is that if she can do it, you can do it too. It doesn't matter what your circumstances are. Life is hard for all of us. Each of us have different stories, different challenges. Yes, life is hard, but we have a choice to take the lemons and turn them into lemonade. What are you going to do with your lemons?

What are your lemons?

1._____

2._____

3._____

4._____

How are you turning your lemons into lemonade?

Action Steps

1. _____

2. _____

3. _____

4. _____

5. _____

6. _____

THE STOMACH HAS NO WINDOW

Her situation at home was tough. They hardly had anything to eat, but her mom tried her best to ensure they go to school fed and that they go to sleep with food in their tummy. She used to eat all this plain food without complaining. She would go to school with iskhokho and was ready for the day like other children. No one could see what is in her tummy. She would study hard and go home. For dinner they would have amathambo (beef bones) with the entire family. This was not the best of food, but it was made with love. All throughout her school career she ate this food. No one could ever tell she was from a poor home.

The good news is that unfavorable circumstances - which we all face from time to time in some shape, form or fashion - are mere moments in time. If endured and persevered through, these moments can be overcome. If we do not lose our hope for better days and are willing to do our part to bring those better days to pass, they will come. You see, the current circumstance does not determine your future.

You do. In the face of adversity or "sucky" situations, the best antidote is to be strong, be encouraged and take active steps in the direction of what we want to see in our lives.

> "No matter what kind of challenges or difficulties or painful situations you go through in your life, we all have something deep within us that we can reach down and find the inner strength to get through them." — Alana Stewart

Ups and downs; rising and falling; rain and shine; joy and sorrow; day and night; - this is life. A series of events, that ebb and flow.

There are many situations in life which we can classify as difficult. A wise thing to do is to be prepared to face the difficult times in our lives. These times usually affect us on a psychological level and could potentially damage our lives.

Being prepared for these times could help us improve how we live our lives. Being prepared to face the challenges is what it means to learn and grow.

The idea is to make the best out of everything life throws at us. Remember, most of these situations are not within our control. So, the logical method to deal with these circumstances is to accept and move on.

Below we discuss about some of the tough situations we come across in our lives and how we can best deal with them.

Lesson
The lesson for us in this is that no matter the cause of the troubling situation, nor its seeming severity, there is a way out for us if we do not let the circumstance overwhelm us to the point where we lose hope and confidence, that this too will pass. Yes, "this", too shall pass.

YOUR PAST DOESN'T DEFINE YOUR FUTURE

Your PAST doesn't define you. What you do NOW defines you!

If you study the habits and traits of highly successful people, and the traits of those we deem average or unsuccessful, it is impossible not to see clear differences in their habits and thinking…

One of the biggest differences lie in thinking and living in the past or planning into the future.

The majority, and by that, I mean the average and underachieving among us, think primarily in the past. "This is what happened to me, and if this didn't happen to me I would be where I want to be today…"
"I should have done this in the past, and now it's too late"
"This person wronged me in the past, and that's why I'm not where I want to be"

The past drags them down, beats the life out of them continuously day in day out.

They don't take responsibility, they don't believe in future because they are stuck in the past, so their past repeats itself in the future….
Over and over again…

The successful ones however thinks only in the now and into the future.
They set goals into the future.
Clear targets to push them forward…
To light their fire within and give them passion for living.

They visualize the results coming to reality into the future…
They see the future reward, not the initial struggle to bring it to life.
Not 'what I have to go through to get there' but 'how will I feel when I get there'!

And the only way to get to the future, to the big reward, is to have powerful action in the now.

In this powerful present moment.

All successful people know that each positive and productive present moment leads to a positive and successful future moment.

The successful usually have had just as tough a past as the average, but their meaning is different.

Rather than play the victim, they get on with life. Rather than dwell in the past, they plan on how they will create a better life in the future. Rather than use the past as an excuse they use it as fuel to drive them wherever they need to go! Use your past as fuel to take you wherever you need to go!

If you ever look back, make sure it is only to drive you forward! Don't blame others for your situation. Rely on yourself to create a new situation.

Your future starts today not tomorrow.
Plan now, live now! Don't you dare let past failures get in the way of your future success! It doesn't matter what happened in the past.

The only thing that matters is what you are going to do RIGHT NOW!

What are you going to do right now?!

WATCH YOUR WORDS

Words are powerful they become your reality.

He grew up in a toxic home. His dad used to beat his mom and verbally abusive her, especially when he was drunk. His father would come home drunk and bring chaos into the home. He would slam doors, curse at him, and tell him how he regretted having him as his child. At the age of 1 5 he had witness so much domestic violence but could not do anything. He was young and afraid. He could not understand how his own father would hurt and abuse the woman he loved. He would sit in his room and hear his mother cry. His father would ridicule her with all sorts of negative names. He hated his dad. He vowed never not be like him. What he didn't realize is that the environment he grew up in affected him both consciously and subconsciously. When he completed matric, he went to university to study engineering. There he met a lovely girl, they dated, and he thought he had met the love of his life. One day he saw her kissing another guy, and although he detested the thought of ever being like his father, he lost his mind and beat the girl badly. Police were called to the scene, and he was arrested. It was only his first year at university and his dream of being an engineer was cut short. He stayed in jail for 8 months, and when he was released, the university banned him from their premises and bursary he had been awarded, was withdrawn. Despite his best intentions, he became exactly who his father was. Today Maanda is a taxi driver. He works for an old man in his street. He never went back to finish his degree. He lives a sad life.

 Solution

You are not the result of your environment.

You cannot choose the family you are born into, but you can choose how you want to live your life. The words you speak hold power. Power to create new possibilities or to close them down. Power to build relationships or to damage them. Power to lift people up or to pull them down. Yourself included. Psychologists have found that our subconscious mind interprets what it hears very literally. The words that come out of your mouth therefore create the reality you inhabit. For better or worse. Unfortunately, it's often the latter as we unconsciously sabotage our success simply by using language that undermines our opinions, amplifies our problems and chips away at our confidence to handle them successfully.

The words that come out of your mouth create the reality you inhabit.

Whatever direction your words lead, your mind, body and environment will follow. If you use positive language about yourself and your ability to learn new skills, achieve your goals and rise above difficulties, then that's what tends to show up externally. Likewise, if you're continually saying things that affirm incompetence, echo hopelessness, nurture anxiety or fuel pessimism, then that will also shape your reality. It may sound fanciful, but over time your world will morph to mirror you It's therefore extremely important to be intentional about the words you use and speaking in ways that empower and expand rather than devalue and deflate.

The truth is that we possess far more power to affect positive change than we realize. Tapping in to that power starts with building self-awareness of where you are using what psychologists call "out of power" language are words.

1. Reframe to what you want

What you focus on expands. So, if you're focused on the negative aspects of your situation, what you can't do, or what you don't want, it only amplifies in your reality, triggering more negative emotions and diverting your energy and attention from taking more positive action.

- If you want more success, talk about your goals and what you're doing to meet your challenges (not about how big your problems are.)

2. Avoid "absolutes"

Words like always, never and impossible can be dangerous and disempowering. Saying that something is "impossible" guarantees you'll never find a way. Just because you have never done something up until now doesn't mean it can't be done.

• Devaluing your opinion serves no-one and deprives every one of the value your perspective brings.

Words are extremely powerful tools that we can use to uplift our personal energy and improve our lives, though we're often not conscious of the words we speak, read, and expose ourselves to. Yes, even the words of others can easily affect our personal vibration. Spend a few minutes with a chronic complainer who uses all sorts of negative terms, and you'll feel your personal energy bottom out. Words have great power, so choose them (and your friends) wisely!

Declaration:

I_____ promise to observe to do the following:

1. Make Words Work: I will consciously harness the power of words for your benefit, start with the ones you're using.

2. No Name-Calling or Self-Criticism: Everyone is doing the best they can at any moment in time with the consciousness they have to work with, including you. Be kind and offer yourself the same empathy and compassion you'd extend to anyone else.

3. Stop All Self-Deprecation: Never make your body, or something you've accomplished, or anything else in your life the butt of a joke. Words have power, and quantum energy doesn't have a sense of humor.

4. Resist Gossiping and Speaking Ill of Others: It's impossible for your words to resonate in anyone else's body but your own.

5. Go on a Negativity Diet: Instead of saying that a meal was terrible say, "I've had better." You've basically said what you wanted to say without putting negative energy through your body—you even used a positive word to do it!

6. Boost the Positive Energy of Words: Instead of saying something like you had a good time at a concert, ramp up the positive energy by saying great, terrific, or fantastic, instead. These feel much better and generate a bigger energetic response in the body.

7. If you have some negative Nancy's in your circle of friends: limit the time you spend with them or find better friends. Negative energy has a way of dragging everything surrounding it in, like a big black hole. Avoid it when you can.

8. Surround yourself with positive, uplifting words: Put affirmations on sticky notes around your home and office that say wonderful things about you, your family, or your goals. Wear clothes that have positive messages or phrases on them. Imagine the kind of positive energy you'll be generating for yourself when you're wearing positivity all day long. As you keep doing these things, you use the power of repetition in a highly effective way for your benefit. You have the power to change your world, and using words consciously is one of the quickest ways to shift the energy you bring into your life.

Signature:_____

Signed at_____on the _____

POSITIVE SELF-TALK

She spoke badly of herself, underplaying her skills. She didn't want to shine or be seen as too much. She spoke negative of herself and her talents so she could fit in. She gossiped, not because it was part of her character but to please her friends. They would gather at lunch time to talk about others. She never had anything good to say about herself or others.

Even when she knew she was good at something she would never it out loud. She did not want to seem self-righteous to her negative friends, who would say even more destructive things about her and others. She didn't stand up for herself because her confidence had been diminished. She didn't like herself. She was not happy with who she was. All the adverse self-talk was ruling her head, her life, her mouth. Her whole world became cynical because of the person she had become inside. Her grades dropped, the level of respect she had for teachers and adults dropped because the pessimism in her head that had taken over. She felt overwhelmed, trapped in a hole of darkness. Her thoughts were destructive. She was lost and she wanted so badly to become the girl she used to be.

 Solution

It's okay to feel good about yourself, and even to compliment yourself on all your achievements, however big or small.
To change the narrative in the heads of your teens, you can start by letting them know why you think they're great and encourage them to talk about what they like about themselves.

This can help develop a positive mindset and spur on motivation. Encourage them to be mindful of their achievements and skills (or even to write them down) as a regular reminder of their strengths.

Task: Write down a list of 10 achievements or skills you are proud of:

1._____

2._____

3._____

4._____

5._____

6._____

7._____

8._____

9._____

10._____

SELF-CARE

Her life was consumed by school and books. She woke up at 6am every day. She bathed, she ate, and prepared for school. School started at 8am, and classes ended at 2pm. She would immediately head home, clean the house, cook dinner, do her homework and when all that was done, she would watch TV until 8pm. She would repeat this same sequence every day until school break. But the cycle began again when schools re-opened. She lived an isolated life – no hobbies and no friends. Most times she felt lonely and misunderstood. She didn't know how to make friends because of her reserved nature. She kept to herself and got good grades because she was hard worker. She lived for school and that was the only thing that kept her going. In all that monotony, she soon became angry at life for not giving her opportunities to do other things. Her school had a sports program, but she never participated because she was shy. The local community hall had drama and dancing classes, but she never participated. Her life was boring and she felt unfulfilled. She could not wait to graduate high school so her life would begin. But just a year later she was diagnosed with cancer, could not walk and was bed bound. It was then that she realized that she had not lived her life, that she didn't take advantage of opportunities when she had them. If she could turn back the hands of time, she would swim. She always liked swimming. She also like netball but she never played. She blamed all her missed opportunities on being shy. As she lay in bed, she made a pact with God, that if He would heal her, she would stop just existing, and start living. She was here for a purpose, and she was determined to have that purpose realized. God, in His great mercy, heard her cry, and gave her another chance. She was healed and she changed her life for the better. She became a new person. Everyone was surprised. She became active, she said yes to everything and enjoyed every moment of her life. She was lucky to be given another chance, and she was not going waste it by sitting on the couch and feeling sorry for herself. She is now pursuing life wholeheartedly. She is on FIRE.

Solution

Self-care is anything that you enjoy doing. The thing that helps make you happy and maintains your physical, mental, or emotional health. It's when you take the time to take care of yourself. It can be simple everyday pleasures like soaking in the bathtub, reading a magazine, or going for a run. It can be bigger things, like having a meal with friends, engaging in a hobby, or playing sports. For families, self-care helps parents and teens deal with the everyday pressures of life in a more positive and rewarding way.

Task: List 5 things you start doing for yourself so you can start living your life and not exist

1._____

2._____

3._____

4._____

5._____

SPORTS

It's a bit unsettling to know that while most teens aged 13-17years old, are physically able, but only about 40 percent of them are active in any sports activity - competitive or recreational. Unfortunately, this downward trend may likely continue because today's young people are being lured into "activities" that require only the movement of a hand, such as video games, social media, or web surfing.

Advantages of partaking in Sports:

You'll be healthier:
Sports require you to move your body, and it's a commonly known fact that exercise is good for your health. According to research, physical activity helps control weight, combats health conditions and diseases, improves mood, boosts energy, and promotes better sleep. The health advantages of participating in a sport far outweigh the dangers of actual injury.

You'll be smarter:
Many studies reveal that playing sports can boost your brainpower. A report from the Institute of Medicine stated: Children who are more active show greater attention, have faster cognitive processing speed, and perform better on standardized academic tests than children who are less active.

This shouldn't be too surprising as exercise increases blood flow to the brain, and blood flow to the brain stimulates brain growth. Plus, playing a sport does require you to think on your feet and strategize, keeping your mind sharp and alert.

You'll learn teamwork and sportsmanship:
In sports, individuals learn to rely on each other and motivate one another to accomplish a common goal. Though individual sports are great, team sports actually do teach you a life lesson: the success of a team — or an organization — depends on how well the players work together. Not even the "star" player can win the game alone.

Sports also teach you to play fairly and to respect the players on the opposing team. Cheating, gloating, and fighting do not belong in sports — or in the professional world for that matter. Sports teach you to put forth your best effort and exhibit honorable behavior whether you win or lose a game

You'll make friends:
When you join a sports team, you will inevitably make friends. Because teammates share so many fun and exciting moments, your friendships should last long after you finish playing. There is also one more perk: most teams traditionally go out to eat after a game!

You'll learn to focus and manage your time:
Sports require time and commitment, but most players usually perform better in school and are more likely to be involved in clubs or community service. How is this possible? Playing a sport requires teenagers to develop two important skills: focus and time management. Focus and time management are crucial traits in people who get things done and accomplish their short and long-term goals

You'll strengthen your college resume:
Though it should not be the main reason to join a sport, it's a fact that colleges and universities do favor applicants who are well-rounded. Playing a sport will not only pad your resume, it will usually tell the admissions counselor that you are disciplined, confident and work well with others.

You'll have an advantage in the workplace:
Not all people who play sports are "dumb jocks." In fact, there are studies indicating that girls and boys who played sports are more likely to land higher-status jobs than those who did not.

According to a study from Cornell University, teenagers who played sports developed stronger leadership skills, worked better in teams and demonstrated more confidence. The study also stated: "Participation in competitive youth sports 'spills over' to occupationally advantageous traits that persist across a person's life."

Task: Pick a sport ... today!
What sport are you going to enroll yourself in from today?
Name 3 sports of your choice:

1._____

2._____

3._____

BULLYING

He came from a very dysfunctional home where both parents drank a lot. He used to watch his dad beat his mom in front of him. By the tender age of 6 years old, Sizwe had already been privy to a lot of violence- both physical violence and verbal abuse - things no child should ever witness. He kept all the pain and resentment inside. He could not save his mom from the physical abuse she endured every day. The anger began building up and his behavior started to change. He was suspended from school for weeks at a time, due to mischievous behaviour and the use of vulgar language; words he learned at home. He was also abused by his father. His dad would beat him for no reason. This man, who was supposed to love and protect him, was just an angry man who hadn't accomplished anything in his own life. He would tell Sizwe that he was good for nothing and accuse his mother of cheating on him. In light of these accusations, he would say that he was not his father, telling Sizwe to leave and go find his father. To deal with this anger and rejection, the boy started bullying other kids. In high school he would take their money, threaten and intimidate them. He became known as the ringleader of the wayward boys who caused all sorts of trouble in the school. Sizwe also began bullying a boy who came from a stable family, who was unfamiliar with verbal and physical abuse. His name was Sanele. He would say bad words to him, and then, along with his friends, they would kick him every day at school. Sanele didn't know how to defend himself. He suffered through the abuse daily, until one day, he just could not take it anymore. He was tired and wanted to stand up for himself. He was determined to stop the bullying and abuse, so he decided to bring a knife to school. When Sizwe and his friends approached him that Wednesday to take his pocket money, and kick him around, he was ready to fight back. When he refused to give them the money, Sizwe slapped him. It was then that he took out the knife just to scare him, but Sizwe did not back off. As leader he could not show fear or signs of being intimidated, he went straight into the knife saying, "kill me, kill me". The knife went straight into his heart, and he died immediately.

Solution

What is bullying: Bullying is a deliberate and repeated act of hurting someone in a physical, verbal, psychological and/or emotional way.

Bullying can include one or more of the following:
- PHYSICAL – kicking, hitting, pushing, hurting.
- VERBAL – swearing, name calling, racial/gender harassment.
- PSYCHOLOGICAL – teasing, spreading rumors, sexual comments, provoking, threatening.
- EMOTIONAL – leaving people out, demeaning comments, manipulating, hurting people's feelings.
- CYBER BULLYING – using technology to bully an individual or group - including internet, email, chat rooms, social media, discussion groups, instant messaging, web pages, or mobile; text or picture messages.

Effects of Bullying:
Bullying can affect everyone—those who are bullied, those who bully, and those who witness bullying. Bullying is linked to many negative outcomes including impacts on mental health, substance use, and suicide. It is important to talk to kids to determine whether bullying or something else is a concern.
Kids who are bullied can experience negative physical, school, and mental health issues. Kids who are bullied are more likely to experience:
- Depression and anxiety, increased feelings of sadness and loneliness, changes in sleep and eating patterns, and loss of interest in activities they used to enjoy. These issues may persist into adulthood.

- Health complaints
- Decreased academic achievement, standardized test score, and school participation. They are more likely to miss, skip, or drop out of school.

A very small number of bullied children might retaliate through extremely violent measures. In 12 of 15 school shooting cases in the 1990s, the shooters had a history of being bullied.

Kids Who Bully Others
Kids who bully others can also engage in violent and other risky behaviors into adulthood. Kids who bully are more likely to:
- Abuse alcohol and other drugs in adolescence and as adults
- Get into fights, vandalize property, and drop out of school
- Engage in early sexual activity
- Have criminal convictions and traffic citations as adults
- Be abusive toward their romantic partners, spouses, or children as adults

Bystanders
Kids who witness bullying are more likely to:
- Have increased use of tobacco, alcohol, or other drugs
- Have increased mental health problems, including depression and anxiety
- Miss or skip school

The Relationship between Bullying and Suicide
Media reports often link bullying with suicide. However, most youth who are bullied do not have thoughts of suicide or engage in suicidal behaviors.

Although kids who are bullied are at risk of suicide, bullying alone is not the cause. Many issues contribute to suicide risk, including depression, problems at home, and trauma history. Additionally, specific groups have an increased risk of suicide, including, lesbian, gay, bisexual, and transgender youth. This risk can be increased further when these kids are not supported by parents, peers, and schools. Bullying can make an unsupportive situation worse.

What measures can be implemented to prevent bullying at school:

- Effective bullying prevention programs
- Anti-bullying programs
- Increase playground supervision,
- Provide clear consequences for bullying
- Teach students who are bystanders to bullying how to stand up for victims so that bullying behavior gains a stigma rather than being socially beneficial.

10 Simple Anti-Bullying Programs to Try
at Your School Playground peacemakers:

1. Ask older students at your school to casually patrol the playground while younger students are on break. Encourage them to reach out to students who may be playing alone or to let teachers know about a student who seems to be struggling. With guidance, older students can help younger students resolve simple disputes. —*Christina C.*

2. Tree notes: If your school has a large tree near its entrance, adorn it with anti-bullying messages. If the notes are abundant, it will become a conversation piece and keep students talking about anti-bullying. —*Yaritza C.*

3. Superheroes: Use a theme for an anti-bullying program. For example, the Pillager (Minn.) PTO ran a campaign called Superhero: Stop Bullying that included a poster and essay contest. Each participant received a button with the Superhero: Stop Bullying slogan. Essays and posters were displayed at school to

promote awareness and photos of prizewinning entries were published in the local newspaper. —*Misty C.*

4. Build strength and confidence: Create a program focused on fitness and athletics, two areas where kids are often bullied. A fun-in-fitness program can bring together kids who are bullied to work with students who can mentor. Together, the kids work on basic skills and teamwork. Not only does it send a message about healthy habits, but it can also boost confidence and self-worth. —*Jennifer C.*

5. Message in a locker: Work with middle school students to write positive and inspirational notes to classmates. Students then slip notes into lockers without being seen. Classmates later find a surprise note that boosts their spirits. It's the act of writing the note as much as receiving one that improves students' attitude toward others. —*Jenny D.*

6. Lunch friends: Try to mix things up at lunch. Select a group of students, such as the National Honor Society members, to sit with different groups of younger students on a regular basis. Students will get to know other students who they wouldn't typically meet. —*Tina C.*

7. Random notes: Create a Random Acts of Kindness board. Start off with a bulletin board with a plain black background. Explain to students the idea behind random acts of kindness. Provide colorful sticky notes to teachers and ask them to write down a note about an act of kindness they observe. Soon the plain, black bulletin board will be a rainbow of colors and each note will provide an idea for another act of kindness. —*Francesca C.*

8. Buddy club: Set up a buddy club made up of a handful of reliable students who can reach out to students who may be new to the school or may be having trouble making friends. —*Mandy S.*

9. Daily reminder: Ask children to participate in the morning announcements at school so they can share a daily message about anti-bullying. One option is to repeat a motto each day, such as "Treat people the way you want to be treated and make it a great day!" —*Shuyue V.*

10. Kind words all year long: Start by having each student pull a name of a classmate from a hat. Each student keeps an eye on their new "friend." At the end of the week, students compose a note with compliments or nice thoughts and deliver it to their friend. The process is repeated throughout the school year and at year's end, each student has a ring of index cards full of inspirational notes. —*Amy H.*

Declaration:
I_____ promise not to be a bully or a bystander for bullying. I promise to assist those bullies by being a friend and finding help for those being bullied. I promise not to tolerate bullying myself because I deserve to be treated with respect. I will stand up for myself and seek help from an adult or teacher when I feel I am being intimidated or bullied.

NOTES

_____

_____

_____

_____

_____

WE DON'T CHOOSE OUR FAMILY

"Being poor drains you of motivation and self-respect and makes opportunities harder to take. How eating crap food and living in a crappy place makes you feel like crap and how hard it can be to break out of that. People who have always been rich have never felt that, so they assume that being poor is just the same as being rich without having money, and that if they were ever poor, they would just work their way out of it while remaining chipper. But it's not that easy, having no money is insidious and it affects your whole outlook and personality. On a more positive note, how once you get some money you have an iron determination to never be poor again, which can make you work harder and better than the rich kids. Being poor can also give you respect for the value of money and stops you wasting it. Also, when I was poor, I was somehow closer to the people who I lived around. We were poor together and we celebrated together with the little we had."

 Solution

It is true that we don't get to choose the family we are born into.

We are born, where we are born out of pure chance. We don't get to choose our parents or our family environment, but we do get to choose how hard we're willing to work in order to make the best of what we're given.

We came into this world as blank slates and were shaped largely by those who took the responsibility to feed, shelter, and raise us. Our life course was set in motion by those we called our parents or guardians.

The quest for love and happiness begins in childhood where the close bond between baby and mother is instinctive, overwhelming, and based on survival. The kind of loving we receive influences the way our brain is wired and helps form our character. It has an impact on the choices we make in our teenage and adult years and the sort of relationships we forge.

Hardships experiences make you stronger

If you approach negative events with strategies like those mentioned above, you can develop 'hardiness' which will make you even more resilient in the future. This hardiness "enhances performance, leadership, conduct, stamina, mood, and both physical and mental health by giving people the courage and capability to turn adversity to advantage." Negative experiences may hurt, but they are contributing to an even better you!

Turn your lemons into lemonade

I like the idea of turning lemons into lemonade. It seems that there are a lot of things we can do to transform difficult, even painful situations into opportunities for growth, learning and love.

Life can sometimes be unbelievably beautiful, with everything coming together to create a moment of pure, unadulterated bliss. Life can also be pretty awful at times, with situations being incredibly unfair and heartbreaking.

The difference between someone who's a victim and someone who's a survivor is the ability to take the crappiest moments in life and turn them into fertilizer.

When we can use these painful times as fuel for our personal growth, we can move through any type of difficulty with grace and resilience.

Resilience

Resilience is the ability to transform adversity into the opportunity for positive growth and change. When we're more resilient, we don't have to fear the painful moments in our lives because we know that we'll come out of them transformed.

Life's worst times can turn us into a better person if we let them. We simply need to put on the apron of the alchemist and focus on transforming not lead into gold, but life's bitter lemons into delicious lemonade.

Promise to self

I may not have chosen the family I was born into, but I am grateful to be alive, God knows why I am in the family and situation that I am in. I choose to embrace it and be look on the bright side of life. I choose to turn my obstacles and challenges into success. Every day I choose to strive for a better life than I have now. I use my hardships to push me to greater strength. I choose to be a survivor not a victim. I will come out victorious and work hard to turn my families lives around as well.

Signature:_____

Signed by:_____on the_____

NOTES

_____

_____

_____

_____

_____

_____

_____

_____

_____

MONEY & BLESSERS

He is, what we commonly refer to as a "blesser". He gives me money to take care of myself. Look at me, I look amazing. My clothes are impeccable, my hair and my nails are perfectly styled. I know that he is married. His wife called the other day. I am scared, I am hurt, but I cannot stop. I must maintain this lifestyle. What will people think of me when I have no clothes? He takes me places. We go to nice hotels, and fancy joints. His BMW smells new, and when I am with him, I feel attractive and wanted. Yes, he thinks he owns me; yes, he speaks aggressively to me, and yes, there are many times when I don't want to have sex, but I don't know who I am anymore, and I can't stop.

I also have a boyfriend my own age, and we are sexually active. I do have sex with both of them -without a condom- but I no risk in that. I know about HIV but it's not for people like me. Is it?

 Solution

In South Africa, older men who have significantly younger woman as girlfriends, are called "blessers". This, because they "bless" their young girlfriends with money and other material goods. Young women in townships date blessers for a chance at a better life and to escape poverty. Blessers provide expensive gifts and a lot of money and sometimes luxurious trips in exchange for sexual favors or for company. In poverty-stricken communities, multiple relationships between older men and younger women bring a high risk of HIV infection.

The South African government manages the biggest HIV treatment program in the world, currently providing antiretroviral pills to more than four million infected individuals. HIV study centers have found, that of women older than 30 in rural areas, approximately six out of every 10, have HIV.

Women of this age are infecting men of about the same age with HIV. This is the very age group of men most likely to be "blessers". They have become the bridging population, transmitting HIV from older women to younger women. They are a very effective bridge because they usually don't know they have been infected.

It is important for children to be grateful for what their parents offer them because they are doing the best they can to provide for them. Teens need to understand the dangers and pitfalls that come with acquiring a "blesser".

Promise to self
I promise to respect my body
I promise to love myself enough and not run after material things. No matter how hard life may be, I will work hard to earn my own money and live the life I want to live.
I promise not to give my body to underserving people.
I promise to date my age and choose my partner wisely when I am old enough to start dating.
I promise not to be a home wrecker and destroy other people lives and families.
I promise to behave myself so that I don't contract diseases.

Promise made by:_____on the_____

STUDYING FURTHER

I am in grade 12. I am happy, and I am excited, but I am also scared. I know this is where my education stops. I've worked hard, studied hard, sacrificed a lot to be here. But my parents have no money, my dad doesn't have a job, and my mom drinks all day. My future looks bleak. Staying here in the township with no education scares me but what can I do? It is what is. I will let it be.

Solution
Do not allow hard circumstances to determine your future. You need to rise above them. Hardships are part of life but allowing them to bring you down does not serve you. Your home situation does should not cripple you, but it should push you to think outside of the box and look at resources, networks, connections and people that can assist you to reach your goals. Feeling sorry for yourself and having a pity party will keep you in the same situation. Instead stand up and start looking for ideas that can help you get to the next level.

There are lot of scholarships, bursaries and internships that you can apply for that will help you achieve your dreams. You need to apply to as many institutions as possible instead of waiting for a miracle to present itself. Ask mentors and coaches that can direct you and connect you to people wo can assist you. Help is there but it won't come to you, you need to go out and find it.
Ask for help.

What are you going to put in place now, that will ensure you are not stuck after grade 12?

List resources you can use to ensure that you study further:

1._____

2._____

3._____

4._____

5._____

6._____

7._____

8._____

9._____

10._____

CLOTHES

Outside of my school uniform, I can literally count all the clothes I have. I have a T-shirt that everybody knows that I wear practically every weekend, and the same pair of jeans. Everybody knows that I am poor; everybody knows that I have no clothes, and my mom is not even trying.

I hate her! This is all her fault. I hate this life. My best friend lent me her T-shirt last week. But when I saw everyone staring, I knew she told them all. I feel like a fool among my friends. My life is a mess. I can't take this anymore.
I just want to be beautiful and have enough clothes and have a house I can invite people to.

Facts
Low-income children caught up in their parents' economic struggles experience the impact through unmet needs, low-quality schools, and unstable circumstances. According to statistics. children as a group are disproportionately poor: roughly one in five live in poverty compared with one in eight adults. (US Census Bureau 2014).

Many of these children struggle academically, do not complete high school, and have spotty employment as young adults

- The future achievement of ever-poor children is related to the length of time they live in poverty. Persistently poor children are 13 percent less likely to complete high school and 43 percent less likely to complete college than those who are poor but not persistently poor as children.

- Parental education is closely related to the academic achievement of ever-poor children. Compared with ever-poor children whose parents do not have a high school education, ever-poor children whose parents have a high school education or more than a high school education are 11 and 30 percent, respectively, more likely to complete high school. Residential instability is related to lower academic achievement for ever-poor children. Everpoor children who move three or more times for negative reasons before they turn 18 are 15 percent less likely to complete high school, 36 percent less likely to enroll in college or another post-secondary education program by age 25, and 68 percent less likely to complete a four-year college degree by age 25 than ever-poor children who never move.
- Living in a multigenerational household does not improve outcomes for ever-poor children. However, persistently poor children in multigenerational households are more likely to complete high school enroll in post-secondary education, and complete college.

Unfortunately, the same, and worse could be said of South African children.

Declaration: I promise not to allow peer pressure and fashion to derail me from my purpose in life, whether I have nice clothes or not, I choose to focus on working on my bright future.

Signature: _____

Signed by: _____ on the _____

HEARTBREAK

He said he loved me. He said I was beautiful.
I believed him.
I loved him. I could see our future together. I believed I was going to marry him. He followed me around, called me, texted me often. Wow! I was so in love, I couldn't study. I couldn't stop thinking about him. He was my one and only, so when he asked me to sleep with him…. Initially I didn't want to, but all my friends were doing it. I was the only virgin at school, and I did love him, I agreed. He took me to an empty shack, kissed me, undressed me and had sex with me. He made me a woman. He said we would live "happily ever after". But then it was already three days later, and he hadn't called, which was unlike him. I grew worried. I saw him at school, but he acted like he doesn't know me anymore. His friends are glaring at me, and eventually I found out I was just a prize-it was a competition. He didn't love me.

I was so stupid! I can't sleep. I can't stop crying. I feel used, I feel stupid! Why me? He just used my body for his pleasure. It was never love.

8 steps that help fix a broken heart

1. Understand what's happening in a heartbroken brain
Brain studies have shown that heartbreak is like withdrawal from drugs. You become obsessed: obsessed with the person you love or obsessed with figuring out what went wrong. When you obsess, play memories of them over and over in your head, look at photos, and try to contact them, you're getting your 'fix'. That's what makes it so difficult to stop doing those things, even when you want to.

2. Cut off social media
Even if just for 2 months. Now this is a hard one especially for teenagers but to block your ex on WhatsApp and unfriend them on Facebook, even if it's just for a short time.

Call it a "No-Contact" month. Don't push it. It's not an easy thing to do. But you can suggest it and tell them it's a really powerful way to get over someone faster. They can even let their ex know that they are going to try a no-contact-month if that helps.

3. Get rid of the reminders
As much as possible encourage your teen to remove or hide all the reminders of their ex. They can make a box or file if they want to with photos etc. but getting them away and out of sight will make recovery much easier. Of course, if they are at school with their ex then there will be reminders that they can't get rid of, but they can be limited.

4. Make a list of why they weren't perfect
Idealizing your ex and how amazing they were is a common reaction to heartbreak. Everything about them becomes SO perfect: their smile, the way they talked, that birthday when they were so thoughtful…

5. Get a sense of closure
We can waste a lot of energy going over and over the question "what went wrong?" but it just holds us in our heartbreak. e either need to accept the reason the ex- gave or make one up to get closure. It ended because you were not emotionally available. Not because you are not good enough. It ended because he/she wasn't mature enough for a long-term relationship. Not because they're not pretty enough.

6. Fill in the voids

All of them. Moving on involves finding ways to replace the gaps that the ex-left. Going out with friends, or meeting new people, starting a new hobby, exercising, having fun. Support your teen in getting outside and getting active with friends.

7. Don't try to be friends

It's not easy to get over an ex if you are still trying to be friends. Teens usually say they want to stay friends, and they might have to if they are in the same social circles or same classes at school, but it does drag the heartbreak out longer in general. So, if it's possible, encourage that "no-contact" month.

8. Distract your brain

Because your teen now understands what's happening in their lovesick brain, they can control it a bit. When they feel themselves obsessing, or going over old memories of their ex, encourage them instead to redirect their focus.

SPEAKING CONFIDENCE

How we communicate impacts many areas of our daily lives. Aside from perfecting your command of the language, it is important to build your confidence through other means to help you adapt quickly to your new surroundings.

Learn to be Yourself
Authenticity over perfection. Remember, when it comes to public speaking, no one expects you to be perfect. People are meeting a human being, not a robot. Don't be afraid to speak because of your accent. Embrace your accent and background, especially during interviews and networking events it can be a huge icebreaker and lead to awesome conversations after. Mention your country, your journey and if you think you need help, ask for it! If something doesn't go as planned, embrace it. Make fun of yourself. A little self-deprecating humor never hurt anybody. Start to see your "weaknesses" as opportunities. It's also very empowering to see someone on stage admit and laugh at themselves because something didn't go as planned.

Use Humor to Build your Self-Esteem
Become a funny, confident public speaker by taking an improv or comedy workshop. Stand-up comedy can help you overcome the fear of public speaking by using humor as the primary tool. It can help you become a persuasive speaker, improve your presentation skills, and develop self-confidence - especially if you have an accent! A workshop like the Public Speaking Through Comedy Workshop can teach you tips and techniques on public speaking and how to use humor to turn mistakes into opportunities.

Practice! Practice! Practice!

Practice reduces stress and increases your confidence. The biggest reason why people get nervous at interviews or presentations is because they didn't practice. For a 5-minute speech, we recommend rehearsing at least 20 times (without notes) 48 hours prior to the event. It sounds like a lot, but it's only 1 hr. and 40 mins. of your time. You owe it to yourself to dedicate the time you need to perfect your delivery. Make sure you practice enunciating key words that are hard to pronounce. And if you just can't get the right pronunciation, try a synonym that is easier for you to say! After the 10th time practicing, you'll start to see the speech evolve into a version that is more "YOU". Your speech will sound more authentic, you'll start adding body language, different voices, pauses, among other things. But unless you have it written out and you practice many times, it will not improve significantly.

Point Out the Elephant in the Room

It can be tough to present in public because of the language barrier - which affects communication. Even harder than communicating, is keeping an audience entertained. Making evident what's already obvious will release tension in the room and make people laugh. It also confirms you are present, and in the moment. If you're in a 30 person room delivering a presentation and someone sneezes very loudly and no one is paying attention anymore (because the sneeze was so loud it even scared some people), you've already lost everyone's attention in that moment.
Think about it, they're not listening. Instead, they're looking back to see if the person is okay and needs a tissue. A great public speaker will recognize that lack of attention and point out the elephant in the room by simply saying "Are you okay? That was loud." Everyone will laugh. The person gets acknowledged. Now we can move on and everyone will pay attention.

Know Your Audience

If you're delivering a speech or presentation, research your audience. You can't go to battle unless you know who's on the other side. You can't deliver a great speech unless you know who's going to be listening. When possible, things like their degree of previous knowledge on the topic, preferences, interests, ethnic background and cultural beliefs, and other specifics will help you deliver your speech more effectively. Always ask the organizer, "who's going to be there?" If the organizer doesn't know (maybe it's a drop-in event), then arrive early to the venue and start analyzing the attendees. If you can't arrive early or see who's there, once you're ready to speak to the audience don't be shy to ask the room questions. For example, if you're doing a financial presentation you might say, "Raise your hand if you are from the finance department." "Raise your hand if you know what quantitative easing stands for." And to break the ice you might say" Make some noise if you love the Toronto Raptors!" These specific questions give you great insight in terms of who's there and will allow you to better connect with them on a more meaningful level. Always comment on their participation and poke fun at yourself/the situation if no one raises their hand.

Declaration

I_____promise to be confident at all times, from this moment on.

NOTES

_____

_____

_____

_____

_____

_____

_____

SELF ACCEPTANCE

So, I have thighs, I have bums, I am little thick and I am tall. So, I have a little bit of meat? I thought African girls should have a bit of meat, but my friends make fun of me, they call me a giraffe. My boobs are bigger than other girls', and these pimples on my face make feel ugly. I have tried everything to get rid of them, but they won't go away. I am mocked because of the shape of my body. When I see the group of girls I change direction, because they laugh at me. They ridicule my body. I hear them laugh and it hurts. I used to be confident but now I am so insecure. I hate myself. I hate my body. God, why did you make me this way?

 Solution

Beautiful Child, you are okay, just as you are. Get comfortable with who you are, inside and out. Accept your size and your shape. Accept your feelings, and accept yourself, unconditionally. Honour your character traits, your talents, your achievements. Instead of trying to meet society's impossible standards of female beauty, affirm yourself on how special you really are.

Practice the below behaviour toward self-acceptance:

Recognize that beauty, health, and strength come in all sizes.
It's about being friendly, generous, and loving. Having strength and courage and respecting yourself just as you are -goals that we all can achieve.

Realize that your body size is okay.
You can change how you feel about your body by changing your self-talk. Recognize how destructive the obsession to be thin is and how much it harms the

people you love, especially teens and adolescents. Your weight is not a measure of your self-worth.

Be Size Positive.
Set an example of respect for size diversity. Be a role model who radiates confidence, self-respect and friendliness for other adults and teens who may fear going out in public. Our society is currently obsessed with thinness, which hurts us all.

Dress for success.
Dress in ways that make you feel good, that make your own statement and, most of all, in clothes that fit now. Rid your closet of outfits that don't fit. This makes room for clothes you will enjoy wearing.

Want what you already have.
The secret to happiness is not to get what you want, but to want what you have. Though much underrated today, contentment has long been valued in world religions and philosophy.

Keep a gratitude journal.
Have you inventoried the richness of your life assets? Write down three things you are grateful for in your journal. The everyday joys of family, friends, home, community, country, health, work, and the wonder of nature are all around us.

Learn and practice relaxation techniques.
Stress overload is linked to many health problems, such as exhaustion, insomnia, headache, diarrhea, anxiety, restlessness, depression, substance abuse, increased risk of heart attack and a weakened immune system. Relaxing is like re-booting a stressed-out computer.

Choose self-care.
Set aside time every day for yourself. Invest in small things that enrich your life: listening to music, reading a novel, napping after lunch, laughing with your spouse or best friend, eating a nourishing meal, telephoning a friend, taking a stretch break at your desk, or enjoying a sunset.

Strengthen your social support groups.
Maintain nurturing relationships with family and friends. Encourage positive self-talk, praise, and support for each other. Getting involved in volunteer work is an excellent way to increase your social network.

Live a balanced life.
Normalize your life by being regularly active and keeping yourself well-nourished without dieting. Take care of your health, but don't obsess over it or struggle for perfection.

RELATIONSHIPS

I really like him, but he doesn't feel the same way. He doesn't even look at me. All the boys seem to like my friend. They like all the cute girls, but it's like I don't exist, and nobody sees me. I want to be seen too; I also want to be loved. It appears everyone is in love, except me.

- Can nobody love me?
- Am I unlovable?
- Is something wrong with me?

Solution

Getting into relationships and dating at a young age has a negative impact and adverse effects on young children and teenagers. Dating during the high school years has many disadvantages including poor academic performance, social disobedience and increased levels of delinquency, depression, pregnancy, and drug use. Physiologists and educational professionals suggest that teenagers involved in romantic relationships are more likely to have behavioral problems because the majority of them are unable to cope with the emotional stress.

One of the negative effects of dating at a young age includes poor academic performance and low achievements. Teenagers from 13-16 years old who choose to have romantic relationships have poor academic outcomes in contrast to their peers who spend more time on home assignments and receive higher grades (Runhare et al 5). Many teens who become sexually active are more likely to drop out of school. Another negative outcome of dating at a young age is pregnancy and negative health effects. Early abortion leads to increased rates of depression, feeling of misery, serious and social or emotional difficulties. Dating increases the risk of drug abuse and alcohol as a result of depression and emotional problems. Intoxication may lead to sexual violence, sexual abuse and rape (Fernández-González et al 25).

The negative effects mentioned above take time away from studying and lead to psychological problems and emotional distress. Dating has a great impact on the emotional and psychological well-being of a person and may lead to distress and serious psychological problems as well as to pose threats to students' health and academic achievements. As the most negative consequences are the unplanned pregnancy, abortion, early childbearing, sexually transmitted diseases, drug and alcohol abuse, and dropping out of school. Parents and educators should provide teenagers with relevant information about sexual and romantic relations as well as sex and sexuality.

15 Sad Side Effects of People Who Start Dating Too Young

1. Growing up too soon

Forced to grow up prematurely, and missing out on childhood experience

2. Affect academic performance

Having a boyfriend or girlfriend when you're too young can be a distraction to your education. There is high chance to neglect your priorities, especially your studies. Texting and video calls take time from your studies and homework. disagreements can mean you don't get to study for your big exams the next day and as a result, your grades can suffer.

3. Early and unsafe sex

Being in a relationship usually inevitably means that you will be sleeping with your partner at a certain point. But whether you do the deed early in the relationship or later, it's still not advisable taking that big step when you're in a relationship as an adolescent. Can lead to risk of contracting STIs and unwanted teenage pregnancies.

here's having unsafe nookie because you're ill-informed on the forms of abstinence and contraception.

4. Serious problem with substances

When you start dating at such a young age, you usually have it in your mind that you're cooler and more mature than the rest of your peers who aren't dating yet. Being in a relationship becomes a status symbol of sorts and sets you above the rest. And because you think you're so mature, you also result to experimenting on things that you're too young to deal with or have control of

5. Strain in your relationship with parents

Parents usually disapprove of early relationships which in turn strains the relationship with your parents because you will be rebelling.

6. Dating violence

You're not emotionally capable yet of handling rough situations, which is why it's not recommended to date at that age. With dating comes great, mushy times—but with it also comes issues, no matter how small the scale. Physical fights are a very real possibility as well. And this kind of behavior can carry on until adulthood.

7. Emotional trauma

Because break-ups, at whatever age can be painful, but most especially the first time you experience heartbreak. And it's almost inevitable that dating at such a young age means that it won't really last since you're both so young. Whether you're the one who ends things or if you were the one who was dumped, it will still hurt. When you're so attached to that person, a break-up can cause heartbreak so intense that it's something you carry with you as you grow older. As a result, you suffer from emotional trauma, which can affect how you deal with situations and people as an adult.

8. Self-harm and dark thoughts

Emotional trauma can lead to many kinds of behavior, the most dangerous of which is probably depression. How many times have we heard cases of people falling into depression and doing things like harming themselves or even attempting suicide? And these are adults. Young people are even more susceptible to taking their depression out in harmful ways towards themselves, simply because they feel they weren't worthy of someone they thought loved them.

9. You avoid serious relationships as an adult

When someone breaks up with you, you can sometimes feel blind-sided because you thought you guys were so happy. Then you find out he so carelessly broke up with you just to get with another girl.

So, what do you do? You build walls around your heart and close yourself off to love because you're afraid of getting hurt again. You refuse to be vulnerable again, to give anyone the power to break your heart again. And as you grow up, you settle for casual dating or even the occasional one-night stand to scratch that proverbial itch. Anyone who tries to get close to you, you push away in favor of meaningless flings. In other words, having your heart broken at such a young age can really do a number on you and your future relationships.

10. You lose your friends

No matter what age you're at, when you're in a relationship, your tendency is to spend every waking hour with your partner, so much so that you forget about other people in your life.

11. Developing a negative body image

Being broken up with can do a number on anybody and girls who are on the receiving end of a break-up tend to be severely affected, especially when they're mere adolescents or teenagers. You tend to wrack your brain over and over and wonder what was so wrong with you that your partner preferred another person over you. You start thinking, "was I not pretty enough? Or smart enough? Or nice enough?"

12. Becoming too dependent and clingy

One of the many downsides of dating at such a young age is that you may not know what it's like anymore to be single. That's because you're so used to being with your partner every day at school and on weekends too. So when you stop dating that person, you feel empty. You feel the need to fill that void and what do you do? You jump right into another relationship. Then another and another, until you realize that you can't live without a partner. You've become so co-dependent on a significant other that you feel lost without one. This is dangerous territory especially once you reach adulthood. It means you will settle for just anyone, just for the sake of being in a relationship. Just so you never wind up alone. And that can take its toll on your partner, who may feel so stifled by your constant presence and constant texts and calls. That's guaranteed to drive any decent partner away.

13. May not be able to hold a job

If you were the type of person who let relationship problems affect you when you were younger, then this most likely can carry on to your adult life. As mentioned earlier, dating when you're too young can severely affect your studies since you get so distracted by your partner, that your grades take a nosedive. This experience can come back to haunt you when you're an adult and in the working world. Someone who's emotionally mature can compartmentalize her life and not let one aspect affect the other. But if you weren't taught to compartmentalize at a young age, it'll be a real struggle to do it as an adult. Your work gets affected and you end up underperforming or having to leave your job. And if you're not careful, it's a pattern that can repeat over and over.

14. Difficulty establishing an adult identity

You have to know and love yourself first before you decide to share your life with someone else. And when you're just a kid, your personality is still evolving, meaning you haven't found your true identity yet. So when you start dating as a kid, it may not be the healthiest of relationships because you're both still trying to get to know yourself. Being constantly with someone prevents you from getting to know who you really are and as a result, you can still be at a loss by the time you reach adulthood. What are your passions? Have you had the opportunity to pursue them? Are you independent and brave enough to be able to go on a long-haul trip on your own? These are questions you may not be able to answer if you're always saddled down with someone. It's best to learn to be alone and single first before letting someone into your life.

SOCIAL MEDIA EFFECTS ON TEENAGERS

They wrote terrible messages about him on Facebook- hurtful, mean words that cut so deep. What was worse, was that it was put on display for the whole world to see. They deprived him of his privacy.

Inevitably, everyone at school now knew, and everyone was laughing at him. They wrote sick notes on his media page. He cannot escape it. Even when he is at home, they follow him. They follow into the bathroom, in the kitchen; everywhere. He has no peace. At night he doesn't sleep, he just cries. He just needs someone to listen to him, someone to hug him; someone to tell him everything will be okay.
His parents had no clue that he was even going through this.

Everyone thinks he is gay, and they have made a fool of him on the internet. They have posted pictures of him, and He has no way of fighting back. He doesn't want to go to school anymore, because everyone stares at and ridicules him. He hates his life; he hates his body. His grades have dropped, he has stopped playing sports. All they do is poke at him. The more he interacts physically the more they post bad things about him. If they knew how much they hurt him, they would stop. But no one knew, they just posted and wrote and laughed until he couldn't take it anymore.

One Saturday he wrote a note saying, "I won't be a laughingstock anymore" and he hung himself. That was the end of his life. At 14 years old, he committed suicide. The instigators and the entire school felt so bad, but it was too late. He was gone.

Negative impact of Social Media o Youth and Teenagers:

- Copying super heroes in real life
- Increased cases of crimes
- Women harassment
- Superiority & inferiority complex
- Influence of wrong personalities
- Fearless attitude
- Rude attitude with parents
- Lack of interest in family gathering
- Following of unknown friendships
- Lack of interest in studies

IS FAILING THE END OF THE WORLD?

I have the lowest grade in my class. I got 20% for mathematics and accounting. Even Andiswa got 50%.
I must be stupid. My teacher did say that I am not smart. I am starting to believe her. I will probably end up selling potatoes on the streets. Stupid Amanda! Failure! Good for Nothing!
I feel like a loser. My classmates are smarter than I am. Even though I study hard, I can't seem to score high enough to get a passing mark. Will I even pass this grade? I am afraid and feeling demotivated.

One way to cope with failure is to talk to people. Talk to your family, talk to your friends, discuss the options you can take now that you have your exam results back. One thing you must remember is that failing is not the end of the world. Failure is one of the many hurdles you will have to overcome in your life, and there are always possibilities to learn and rise above it. After all, I'm sure most of you have heard the saying 'failure makes you stronger'. Funny enough, it really does. It gives you an understanding of what it means to fail, to lose, to receive a negative outcome that you may not have expected to get.

A common worry amongst students who have failed some of their tests, is that they will now fail the entire grade. Wrong. You should never let failing on a test or exam, force you into believing that you now cannot achieve any of your dreams. Sure, some things will be harder to reach, but that does not make them unreachable. Failing a test or an exam does not make you any less of a person, any less intelligent, or any less able to achieve what you want to, than those who may have gotten better results than you.

How to deal with your Test/Exam Results:
- Assess priorities, assets and difficulties
- Follow a normalized routine.
- Should not imagine extreme consequences and worst situations.
- Should not magnify failure or demean themselves.
- Contact the teachers or counselors on feeling low or anxious or disinterested.
- Develop alternative coping strategies and de-focus from the pain.
- Learn to be positive.
- Learn to relax.
- Talk to family and friends.
- Stop worrying.
- Result is not the ultimate decisive factor.
- It is more important to choose the next options

It doesn't matter how bad you did; it's going to be okay. You won't have to drop out. Your mom won't hate you. You'll be fine. Now, we are not saying it won't suck. It might suck a lot. Your heart may feel like it's suddenly in your stomach and in your throat at the same time. You might want to cry. You might cry a lot! You just have to pick yourself up, dust yourself off, and maybe tune up your study skills. Don't beat yourself up. Know that you tried your best and that it isn't that your best wasn't good enough, it's that sometimes our best isn't what we thought it was. Speaking of dusting yourself off, make sure that after your post-test slump, you take care of yourself. Don't allow yourself to fall into a deeper slump because of a test. That test isn't worth it. If you happen to not do too hot in the class as a result, you can take it again. That sucks, I know, but it's an option. A valid option. It isn't the end of the world, just the end of a semester, don't beat yourself over a test. It's going to be okay. I promise.

Declaration:

A failed experience delivers a lesson which teaches us to stand up to each problem. We learn more from our failures than from our triumphs. Don't let success blind you from the fact that failure was always your greatest teacher and inspiration. Failure is an experience or lesson which drives a person to their success if they will not give up.

> "I failed in some subjects in exam, but my friend passed in all. Now he is an engineer in Microsoft and I am the owner of Microsoft." - *Bill Gates*

Signature: _____

Signed by: _____ on the _____

CYBER BULLYING

According to recent statistics, from ages 14-to-24-years of age, 50% have experienced some form of digital abuse, including spreading lies, violation of trust, and digital disrespect. Another astounding finding of that survey is that 76% say digital abuse is a serious problem for people their age.
So cyberbullying is not some insignificant problem experienced by few. Cyberbullying is widespread and teens are aware of it, they understand how it happens and yet they are not aware of or concerned with the consequences of such actions.

Here are some more facts and findings:
- Half (52%) of young people say they have thought about the idea that things they post online could come back to hurt them later
- 1 in 4 have given some thought to the idea that things they post online could get them into trouble with the police and only 29% have considered that they could get in trouble at school for those things.

Studies show children/tweens/teens that were exposed to cyberbullying felt:
- Hurt feelings
- Sadness
- Anxiety
- Depression or other more serious mental health problems
- Anger
- Shame
- Fear
- Frustration
- Low self esteem
- Inability to trust in others

When these negative emotions aren't dealt with properly, victims may resort to the following behaviors:
- Withdrawal, seclusion, avoidance of social relationships
- Poor academic performance
- Bullying others – to feel in control
- In extreme cases – Suicide. Ryan Patrick Halligan was an American student who died by suicide at the age of 13 after being bullied by his classmates in person and cyber-bullying online. Other similar cases have been documented. It is widely known that face-to-face bullying can result in long-term psychological harm to victims, including low self-esteem, depression, anger, school failure and avoidance and in some cases, school violence or suicide.

In fact, in a study of over 3,000 students, one researcher found that 38% of bully victims felt vengeful, 37% were angry, and 24% felt helpless. According to a 2001 fact sheet on juvenile bullying produced by the the U.S. Department of Justice's Office of Juvenile Justice and delinquency Prevention, victims of schoolyard bullying fear going to school and experience loneliness, humiliation, and insecurity. Moreover, they tend to struggle with poor relationships and have difficulty making emotional and social adjustments.

Task: How about you? Do you understand the dangers of cyberbullying?

Cyberbullying is even more harmful to young people than face-to-face bullying for a number of reasons:
- Permanence: The insults, comments or images can be preserved by the person who was bullied or by others so that the victim may read or view them over and over again and the harm is re-inflicted with each reading or viewing.
- Audience size: The size of the audience that is able to view or access the damaging material increases the victim's humiliation.

- Familiarity: Many young people are friends with or know their cyber bully either through school or other personal connections, increasing the potential for embarrassment and humiliation.
- Social Networking: Social networking sites such as Facebook and Instagram allow cyber bullies to engage in campaigns against a particular person which may involve many others.
- Speed: The speed at which harmful messages can reach large audiences also plays a major part in making cyberbullying so damaging to the targets.

What to do when you are cyber being bullied
Note that most times than often we're bullies to our own friends and don't even realize it.

- Do Not Fight Back! When responding on social media it creates an even bigger problem than it needs to be.
- Stay off Social Media for a while, delete accounts and start afresh
- Speak to an adult or a counsellor about your anxiety and stress
- Report the matter to your school office or your parent
- Know It's Not Your Fault

📝 NOTES

_____

_____

_____

_____

_____

APPLYING IN TIME FOR UNIVERSITY

I waited up until the last minute to start applying for university. When I finally did apply, it was already January, and I was told there was no available space for me and that I should try again the following year. I passed well, but universities have a limited number of students they can enroll in a year. When I was told that I needed to wait another year before I could apply, I was crushed because I was looking forward to studying that year.

I didn't want to sit at home, in my township doing nothing with my life. I knew how the lives of those who stayed here turned out. They would end up drinking every day, running after girls and becoming fathers at a young age. I didn't want that for myself but was now forced to wait a year because I didn't apply in time.
I could not blame the university or my parents. This was my fault. I was too relaxed and thought things will happen on their own. I regret not applying in time. I wish I had taken things seriously.

I had been at home, idle for six months. I was becoming lazy and even beginning to enjoy this boring life of lazing around the house and drinking every weekend. I had nothing to look forward to. It was then that my girlfriend announced her pregnancy. I now needed to find a job. How could I go back to school, when I had a child to support?

I was now a father, and I needed to take care of my child.
I guess that degree was never meant for me. Maybe I could try again someday in the future, but for now, I need to hustle like a man. I work at a construction company as a brick layer to make ends meet. I knew better but didn't act in time.

"By failing to prepare, you are preparing to fail." - *Benjamin Franklin*

"Proper planning is fundamental to success. Most people fail, not because they lack talent, money, or opportunity; they fail because they never really planned to succeed. Plan your future because you have to live there!" - **Robert H. Schuller**

6 steps you need to take to apply to university:

1. Choose where you want to go and what you want to study

University is a big investment, so you'll want to make sure you choose the right place and course. When you're deciding which course to take, there are a few things you can consider to make your decision a bit easier. These include: the type of subject you want to study; how the course will be taught; how the course will be assessed; and whether the course has any particular grade requirements.

2. Make sure you know all the deadlines and key dates

Get those key dates down in your diary, so you can make sure you're not missing any deadlines. Everyone who applies on time is considered equally, whether they send their application in early or wait until the last minute.

3. Check the entry requirements

Entry requirements are the criteria set by the individual universities that students need to meet to be considered for a place on the course. These will vary depending on the university and course you're applying to, with some having much tougher entry requirements than others

4. Get your application started

Once you've chosen your dream course and university, it's time to get started on your application.

5. Write your personal statement

Your personal statement is a really important part of your application – it's your opportunity to show what makes you a great applicant and could end up being the deciding factor between you and someone else with similar qualifications. It should include things like why you want to take that particular course, any extra-curricular activities you've been involved in that are relevant to your application and the skills or qualities you have that would make you good at the subject.

6. Wait to start getting your offers!

There's no set date that you'll hear back from the universities by, although if you submit in time, you are likely to get a response in time.

LEARNING MONEY SKILLS

When I have money all I do is buy expensive clothes. I love shoes. I love brand labels. I don't like fake Chinese brands. my friends know that I am a "label guy". I look fancy all the time. From a young age my parents would buy expensive brands for me. My mom worked hard as a maid and made sure that my siblings and I wore nice clothes. Even though we didn't have a lot of money, we got fancy clothes. Now that I am older, I cannot stop myself from buying expensive brands.

What will people think if I show up with a fake brand? They will think less of me. I must 'represent' and look the part. I remember once I put my mom under such pressure, that she used the money needed for groceries, to buy me an Adidas sneaker which cost R1500. We struggled with food that month because she used half of her income to make me look good. Monthly, she had to pay a lot of expensive accounts so that my brother and I could look good. She used to go the mashonisa (loan shark) every month, just so we could survive. Her life consisted of paying clothing accounts and feeding us. It was tough, but we had to look good and show that we come from a stable home, that could afford these things, even though we could not.

I am now 30 years old. I have no pots of my own. I rent a backroom. I have a bed and a TV. I have degree and I earn pretty good money, in fact I earn more than my friends, but they seem more prosperous than me. They all have cars; they have bought homes and are living well. I often struggle just to take a taxi sometimes because when I get paid, I use all my money to impress my friends and I buy expensive clothing. I don't know how to stop this life of expenditure. I live from hand to mouth. I look good when I am walking on the streets and when I am out with my friends. Girls think I am well off, but once they see how broke I really am, they leave me. My mom's home had no fancy furniture. We had old furniture that was falling apart. To this day, she still has that same furniture. I wanted to buy her new furniture, but my money is gone as soon as it comes in. I failed my mom. I have failed myself. I have lost my job because I am always late and have been found drunk at work a few times. Where did I go wrong? Where do I start to fix my life?

In groups, discuss what went wrong in Nathi's story:
Give methods/strategies on how Nathi could have handled his money better.

_____

_____

_____

What age is the right age to start learning about money skills?

_____

What is your relationship with money?

_____

When you get money do you immediately want to spend it?

_____

When you have money does your head spin and your legs carry you to the mall?

_____

Do you see money as a friend or enemy?

_____

Do you know about a budget and savings?

_____

Do you think your parents know how to handle money? If you were in your parent's shoes how will you spend the family money?

_____

_____

_____

_____

_____

 Solution

One of the best things about having your own money is that you get to choose how to use it. Whether you get a weekly allowance or get paid for walking your neighbor's dog, your first step in handling your money well is to think about short-term and long-term goals. Then make a plan to reach them.

It takes a bit of practice to master your money, just like it takes time to learn to ride a bike. But once you get the hang of it, you'll be ready to tackle all sorts of money twists and turns. In this money guide, you'll learn to earn, save, budget, spend, borrow, protect and give.

Earn: Learn to Earn
HONE YOUR SKILLS

Earning is the first step in your journey to managing money wisely so that you can build a successful future.

We all have different talents and abilities. It's important to take the time to recognize your strengths and develop your skills so that you can excel at what you do. By investing in your education and interests, you will set yourself up for a path to success.

Get started by asking yourself these questions to help you think about what career path you might want to pursue.

What is your Passion?

What topic Interest You?

_____

What are you good at?

_____

What are your Hobbies?

_____

Save: Get Savvy at saving
MAKE IT A HABIT

Making smart choices with your money is the first step toward becoming financially fit. The easiest way to save is to pay yourself first. That means setting aside a certain amount of money you earn and keeping it in a savings account. The key to saving successfully is by making it a regular habit. By saving early and often, you'll set yourself up for a brighter financial future.

It's important to save money for a rainy day, just in case you need it for any unexpected expenses like a broken laptop. Another portion of the money you receive should be set aside for your various goals. These goals can be categorized as short-term, medium-term or long-term. You can reach your goals by saving your money over time

What is your Short-Term savings?

_____, _____, _____, _____

What us your Medium-term savings?

_____, _____, _____, _____

What is your long-term savings?

_____, _____, _____, _____

 Task: If you save R5 each week, you will have R260 by the end of the year.

SHARPEN YOUR SAVING SKILLS

It's tempting to spend all of your money as soon as you earn it, but you'll be better off in the long run if you save a portion of it.

Think about a short-, medium- and long-term savings goal and determine how much you can save each month toward each goal. Remember, the amount that you contribute per month toward your goals can't be more than you earn that month. Then calculate the cost of your goal divided by your weekly contribution to find out how long it will take you to reach each goal.

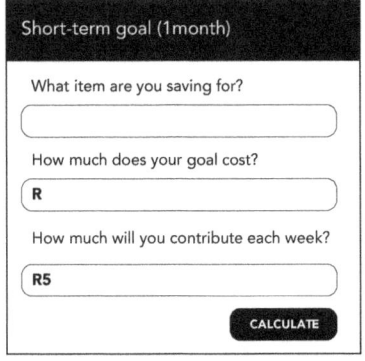
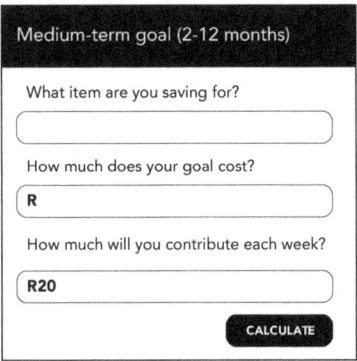
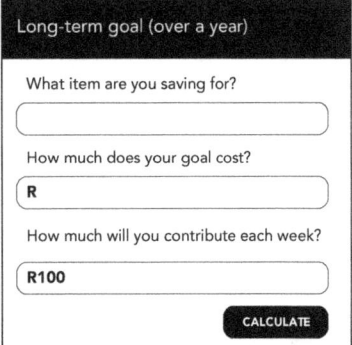

Watch your Money Grow

Savings is all about Interest. Compound interest in action!

Let's say you deposit R50 into your savings account each month at a 1% interest rate. Each year, the interest you earn will help your savings grow. See how 1% interest will increase your savings over the course of three years when it is compounded monthly:

Year	Balance	Balance + Interest
1	R600	R603.26
2	R1,200	R1,212.58
3	R1,800	R1,828.02

Compound interest can have a dramatic effect on the growth of your money over time. Determine how your savings will grow with this interest calculator.

 **Quiz:** TRUE OR FALSE?

The longer your money is in a savings account, the more money you will earn.
In a savings account, your money accumulates interest, so you will have more the longer it stays in that account?

The easiest way to save your money is to pay yourself first.

Compound interest is when you earn interest on both the money you've saved and the interest you earn, he interest rate on savings accounts decreases as you deposit more money.

Budget: Budget Builder
Needs vs. Wants

IT'S A BALANCING ACT

You need to buy a jacket, but you also want to buy a new phone. How do you choose?
To make good decisions about how to spend your money, start by setting your money goals and work toward achieving them with a plan in mind. A personal budget is a plan that helps you put the money you've earned toward savings, expenses (lunch, bus or entertainment money) or paying off debt (money you may have borrowed).

When you're creating a budget, it is important to understand the difference between something you need to have and something you want to have.

Remember to take care of your needs first, so you can think about saving for what you want. A budget can not only help you consider your immediate needs and wants but prepare you to achieve your long-term financial goals. You may have some short-term goals that you can achieve in a matter of weeks, or long-term goals that will take years to attain.

Needs: Food, Clothing, Shelter
Wants: Gaming Station, Bike, Skateboard, Earrings

IT ALL ADDS UP

Start creating a budget by setting goals for how you would like to spend and save your money over a specific time period.

Be sure to consider everything you may want or need to purchase and separate those into categories. A ride on the bus would go under transportation, and a slice of pizza would fall under food.

Complete the budget below by filling out how much money you would like to spend in different categories each month.

The goal of a budget is to have money left over for saving, so you should start by thinking

Build a Budget

Monthly Income

Money Earned	/ month
Allowance	/ month
Gifts	/ month
Other	/ month

Monthly Expenses

Movies, Music & Entertainment	/ month
Clothes & Accessories	/ month
Games	/ month
Snacks	/ month
Transportation	/ month
School Supplies	/ month
Charity	/ month
Other	/ month

CALCULATE

Spend
Smart Shopping

HOW TO SPEND YOUR MONEY WISELY

Spending may seem like the easy part of managing your money, but there are many tips and tricks that can help you save. As you make smarter decisions with your money and think carefully about your purchases, you will notice that saving a little with every purchase adds up over time. Using a budget and learning to plan your purchases can make it easier to save money.

The key to spending is to stay within your means. Don't spend more money than you have. As you plan to shop, make sure you keep your goals and your budget in mind.

THINK BEFORE YOU SHOP

When you make a decision, you are often weighing a lot of factors — not just how much money you're going to spend. Before you make a purchase, look at lots of different options to make sure you're getting the best deal. Rather than buying the first expensive pair of gym shoes you see, plan ahead to make sure you are getting the best value by researching quality and comparing pricing at multiple retailers — this is called comparison shopping. The exact same pair may be cheaper at another store.

BACKSTAGE VIP

GENERAL ADMISSION

If you want to go to a concert, there will be ticket features you want and features you need. When all you need is a basic ticket, you may sacrifice the features you want in order to save money, while still enjoying the concert.

SO MANY WAYS TO SAVE

When you do finally decide what to buy, you'll notice that you usually have a few options, such as name brands or generic items.

A name brand is recognizable; if you see one of its products you are likely to know the manufacturer. A generic brand item is one that typically isn't advertised. Many grocery and multi-purpose stores have their own generic versions of products. Most of the time, there's no significant difference between the two items besides price. Generic items are usually less expensive — making them a great savings opportunity.

What might you take into consideration when you buy something new?

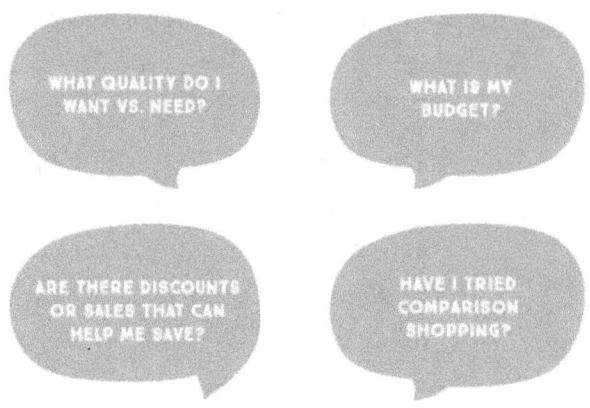

Sometimes, spending can also pay off in the long run. If you have your own business, you may need to spend money to be able to better serve your customers. For example, if you start a lawn mowing business in your neighborhood, you'll need a lawn mower, gas, and potentially other landscaping tools down the road.

 Quiz: TRUE OR FALSE?

When you do comparison shop, you go to one store and buy the first item you see?

_____

Comparison shopping requires looking at multiple stores for the best deal?

_____

Generic brand items are usually more expensive?

_____

When you consider what you want to buy, you shouldn't consider quality?

_____

Quality is one of many factors you should think about when you buy a product.?

_____

There are no steps that should be taken before you make a purchase?

_____

Careful planning before you make a purchase can help you save money?

_____

When you're choosing between two items, you should prioritize features you need over features you want? Needs are a higher priority than wants because they are absolute necessities?

_____

Borrow
Paying it back

DO YOU WANT TO GO TO COLLEGE OR BUY A CAR SOMEDAY?

You can reach your long-term goals by borrowing money and paying it back later. You may have borrowed money from a friend for an after-school snack or from your parents to see a baseball game, but in the future, you might need to borrow more than a few bucks. The cost of going to college or buying a car is usually more than you have saved in your bank account. Luckily, investing in your future or purchasing an expensive item is still possible with a loan. When you borrow money from a bank, it's not free money — you have to pay IT'S PAYBACK TIME!

Everyone borrows money at one time or another in life. If you make a plan to pay the owed money back on time and stay within your budget, your debt won't be out of control.

Have you watched car commercials where they're talking about car financing deals? In a few years, you might be driving. You may not be able to buy a car today, but for this exercise, let's look at how a car loan works. A typical length of a car loan is five years at about a 4% interest rate. If you are under 18 and want to take out a car loan, you will need your parent or guardian to be a cosigner.

Car loan	
Total amount borrowed	R5,000
Interest rate	4%
Length of loan	60 months
Monthly payment	R92
Total cost of loan plus interest	**R5,524.96**

What does that look like in real life? Use the calculator below to find out how much to back, plus interest. This means you have to pay back all the money you borrowed plus extra for the service.

What might you need to borrow money for in your future?

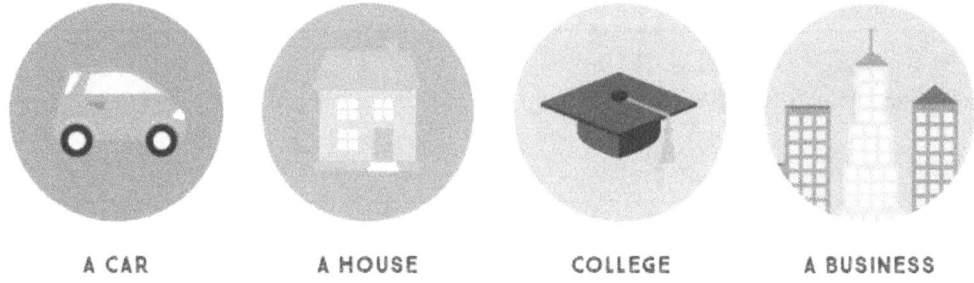

A CAR   A HOUSE   COLLEGE   A BUSINESS

WHY CREDIT MATTERS

Take control of your credit score by managing your debt.

The amount of debt you're in may impact how easily you can qualify for future loans after you turn 18. There is a written record, or credit history, that tracks how you've repaid previous loans, any outstanding debt and other financial history. Your credit history determines your credit score, which helps lenders decide the credit risk associated with loaning you money. Credit scores range from 300 to 850. Generally, the lower your credit score, the higher the interest rate you will have to pay on future loans because it's assumed there's a higher risk you might not pay it back on time.

Quiz: True or false?

If you pay back your loans late, you will pay more in interest and late fees than if you payed them back on time?

_____

Borrowed money is free money?

_____

You have to pay interest on money you borrow from a bank?

_____

If you owe money that you can't pay back, you will have a lower credit score?

_____

Debt doesn't cost you anything?

_____

The faster you pay back the money you borrowed, the lower the amount of interest you will pay?

_____

CREATING GENERATIONAL WEALTH

He came. He lived. He created. He left. What he left was a legacy for his children and grandchildren. From a young age Sifiso was different from his peers, he sold sweets and peanuts at school to help his family. At the age of 17, he had a small tuck-shop at his parents' house. He was always wise with his money. He spent less than he made. His dream was to stop the cycle of poverty in his family line. He didn't wear fancy clothing, and at a glance he looked like a beggar, but he was the most humble and richest man in his community. He didn't go to university after matriculating, instead he opened 4 more tuck-shops in his community. At the age of 35 he owned 15 taxis. He was a well-known and respected businessman, who always wanted to learn more and expand his knowledge base. He hired a financial advisor who showed him better ways to invest his money, so that it could make more money for him. He had stocks, offshore investments, shares, property, and gold. At the age of 70, when he passed away, his net worth was R18 million, which was inherited by his children, his grandchildren and his great grandchildren. Today his business still thrives. His children learnt a lot from him and are ensuring that the business continues in his memory.

His legacy continues in the orphanage he built for children needing shelter, where his statue proudly stands outside. And a street was named after him. His name lives on even after his death, and most importantly, his family line will never experience poverty because of the wise decisions he made in his lifetime.

Solution

Generational wealth means working hard now so that the generations after you do not experience the hardship and poverty lived now. Buying fancy cars and houses without building businesses or making investments is a disservice to our future grandkids. It's important, that as black people we stop the cycle of poverty. Our parents were poor, we are no better, and we leave nothing for our children and our future blood line. Creating wealth that will live on even after death means, starting at an early age and making the decision, to not only empower yourself financially, but also ensuring that your blood line lives in the legacy you have created.

Generation wealth is passed down from one generation to the next. You may also hear this called family wealth or legacy wealth. If you are able to leave something behind for your children or grandchildren, then you are contributing to the growth of generational wealth in your family.

How to build generational wealth

- Invest in the stock market

The stock market can be a great way to build wealth over the long-term. If you are aiming to build generational wealth, then it is a great option because it has the potential to continue growing for decades.

- Invest in real estate

Real estate is another major way to build wealth for the long-term. With the potential for steady cash flows in addition to increasing values over time, real estate can be a reliable path to wealth.

- Build a business to pass down

Family businesses have the potential for great success. More than 30% of family-owned businesses transition to the second generation. Imagine being able to hand over the keys of a successful business to your children.

- Take advantage of life insurance

Life insurance provides the opportunity to protect your family in the event of your untimely death. Without your income, your children might be forced into less than ideal financial circumstances.

- Invest in your child's education

In many cases, education can provide a way for your children to support themselves. With a college degree, many frequently have the opportunity to pursue high paying jobs that can help them navigate their own finances.

- Write a will

A will may be included in your estate plan, but it is important to create one even if you don't have an estate plan. The will should include your exact wishes. The more specific you can be about your plans for any assets you have accumulated, the better.

You simply have to acquire assets or save cash that you don't intend to spend in retirement. Then you pass those assets along to your children when you pass away.

What generational wealth are you leaving behind for your family?

_____

_____

_____

_____

_____

How will you ensure that you create generational wealth? Name 5 things that you will implement to realize this dream:

1. _____

2. _____

3. _____

4. _____

5. _____

Declaration: I _____ promise to leave a legacy and create generational wealth for my family. I promise to work hard to implement strategies and business that will ensure that my future family line never experiences poverty. It stop with me. I will work hard to ensure that I succeed so that they succeed too.

LETTER OF PROMISE TO SELF

Commitment letter to future self with promises of what you want to achieve in life

I promise to graduate high school with excellent marks. I promise to obtain a university degree. I promise to change my life, and the lives of my family members. I promise to be an inspiration to those around me. I promise to obtain a driver's license and own my own house and car. I promise to live in a safe, upmarket suburb. I promise to help those less fortunate than myself. I promise to have a successful business. I promise to make a success of my career. I promise to make my first million by the age of 21. I promise to travel the world and explore life. I promise to stop and smell the roses and to enjoy life as it comes. I promise to wait for my husband, and not I lose my virginity to someone not worthy of me. I promise to get married, have 2 children -a boy and a girl. I promise to take care of them and give them a better life than what I had. I promise to be a change in my community and in SA. I promise myself an easy, money-filled, healthy and peaceful life, filled with God. I promise that I am going to make it. I promise to leave a legacy. I promise to be creative and resourceful. I promise to be wise and kind. I promise to be kind to myself and love me first. I promise my cup will overflow with joy, peace, love, and prosperity. I promise you, that you will be financially independent; you will not know poverty in your life. I promise you a better tomorrow. I promise to work hard and give all I can to achieve this dream.

Promise to self.

Dear **Self**,

I promise to:

_____

_____

_____

_____

_____

_____

_____

_____

_____

_____

_____

_____

Letter written by: _____ on the _____

Signature: _____ Witness: _____

LETTER TO THE QUEEN

Dear black child, beautiful brown skinned daughter of Lizzy and Abel. You are important. You are enough. You matter. Life is going to be harsh, but you are resilient enough to win those battles. Rise up. Don't be ashamed of who you are. You are here for a purpose. You are not a mistake. God has chosen you out of a billion. He knows you; He knows every hair on your head. You are a conqueror. You are a lioness and an enabler, a helper, a sister and a pillar to others. Hold your head up, walk tall, smile and don't stop shaking the ground for a better life. Strive to be the best in all you do. Love, give, laugh, be kind to all. You are a queen. You are special, wonderfully created there is no one like you in all the world. Stay in your lane and don't get distracted. Trials and tribulation will come but don't lose sight of your goals and dreams. When life knocks you down, fall on your back so you can stand up straight. You matter. Don't be afraid to express your views, because they matter. Use that voice to change the world. The world needs you; It waits you to be the change. Miss "Change agent", don't stop running; crawl if you need to, cry if you need to, walk if you need to, but don't stop. The finish line is nearer than you think. Just keep at it. Soon you will be victorious!

Now write your own letter to the Queen / King in you!

Dear King / Queen: _____

_____

_____

_____

_____

IMPORTANCE OF ABSTINENCE

Amanda was known to be a church girl. She grew up in a good Christian home. Her father was a pastor. She was taught values of how a godly Christian girl should behave. She respected her elders and did well in school. She did not keep company with ill-behaved friends. Her future looked good. She finished her matric and went to university.

It was here that she was greatly tested. She didn't know how to handle the freedom she suddenly had. She met girls from all walks of life. She made friends with non-Christian people, who had their own beliefs and encouraged her to start partying and exploring. She didn't know this kind of life. She got a boyfriend who convinced her to sleep with him. Even though she knew that sex before marriage is a sin, she still did it. She was in love for the first time. Eight months into her first year at CPUT she found out she was pregnant. She was afraid to go back home She was ashamed of what she had done. She had embarrassed the family. Her once bright future now looked so bleak.

When she had finally gotten the strength to face her parents, they were disappointed, but they took her in and helped her raise her child. She went back to school, a year later, but she fell pregnant again. She could not stop herself from sleeping with this man. Sex was new to her, and she enjoyed it. She eventually dropped out of school with her new baby daddy and moved into a flat to raise the child. Her life was tough. She started drinking to escape the pain of poverty. When the child was only two years old, her boyfriend left her, and she moved into a shack where she met a new man. From this relationship, she had two more children. At age 35, she found herself single with five kids she could not take care of. She regrets the decisions she made. She wished she waited for her husband and abstained. She wished she could turn back the hands of time, but she can't.

Solution:
Once you cross that line, it's impossible to come back. Virginity is sacred and should be kept only for that special person God has chosen to be your husband of wife. Having sexual relations at a young age only bears negative results and can ruin your life. Decisions made when you are young cannot be undone. It's better to abstain and wait for marriage so you can commit to your spouse. Walk away from situations that will lead to sexual promiscuity. Stay away from friends who are dating at a young age. Do not put yourself in a position where you are alone with a boy/girl, without adult supervision. This often leads to sexual activities.

Declaration: I_____ promise to keep my virginity until I am married. I promise to abstain from sexual activities which will not benefit me but destroy my life. Prevention is better than cure, so I choose to keep myself intact until I am old enough and wise enough to make an informed decision.

Signature: _____

Signed by: _____ on the_____

NOTES

_____

_____

_____

_____

_____

_____

UZOYIZOTHOLA KANJANI UHLELE EKHONENI

She is shy. That is how she has been labelled. It has been that way since she was a young girl - everyone always saying how quiet and shy she ways. When she'd walk into a room, she would rush past everyone, so as not to be noticed. She never made conversation, and she never made any friends. This young, lovely but withdrawn girl had a beautifully melodic voice. She could sing like an angel. When she sang, it was like a supernatural experience, and her voice could make every hair on your body stand on end. But nobody knew. She had hidden this amazing talent from everyone and had shied away from every opportunity to display it.

One day, a well-known singer came to her school on a talent-search roadshow. They were looking for new and undiscovered talent among the youth. Her friend knew that she could sing, but when they asked for people to come up on stage, she didn't raise her hand or go to the front. She didn't like the attention or the crowds. All the students who went forward had a chance to sing, but the artist was not impressed.

When the roadshow team saw the shy girl being dragged and coerced by her friend, the famous singer, took the microphone, went to her and asked if she would like please sing for her. The sound that came from her lips, was so enchanting, and her voice was so mesmerizing that it gave everyone chills. She was signed to the record label, and today she is a renowned gospel singer. If it was not for the insistence of her friend, the keen observation of the artist and the appointment of time and chance, her talent would have never been discovered. She now uses her own story, going from school to school, to encourage young girls to grab every opportunity presented to them, and to not let anything stand in the way of their greatness.

Solution

In life you to stand up and grab opportunities as they come, they will not chase after you, waiting until you feel you are ready. Preparation meets opportunity. Being curious and ambitious are good attributes to have because they will propel you into the opportunities that you seek. Life will not give you anything on a silver platter. When you act first, the universe will respond. You get out of life, only what you put into it. If you sit and not do nothing, your life you will remain stagnant, and your peers will run overtake you. Stop feeling sorry for yourself. Take action and make moves toward the life you want.

If you want to be in business start selling something, even if it's just sweets as a beginning.

The important thing is to start. Talking and dreaming about what you want, will bear no fruit, it's in the action that results start showing - doors will begin to open and opportunities will come.

Hard work always pays off. Laziness gets you nowhere.

If you want to pass with good grades, its's simple- Just study hard, ask questions and ask for help. The results will show. After all uzoyithola kanjani uhleli ekhoneni.

Task: What are you going to do, to take action towards your dreams.
Name 5 things you will start doing daily towards achieving your goal

1._____

2._____

3._____

4._____

5._____

Declaration: I_____promise not to be lazy. I promise to the necessary action steps toward my goals. I will do all that is within my power to manifest my vision within me.

Signature: _____

Signed by: _____on the_____

NOTES

_____

_____

_____

_____

_____

_____

_____

NOBODY OWES YOU ANYTHING

He blamed his dad for not being part of his life. He so longed to have father that was present.

The father he had, had married another women and had other children. He took care of his new family but did not care about him or his siblings. He was angry, very angry. He thought of ways of getting his fathers attention. He started smoking dagga, skipping classes and even joined a gang in the neighborhood. Within a year, he had been to rehab three times and dropped out of school. His mother tried all she could to help him, but he was just too angry. Angry at life, angry at God but mostly angry at his absent father. Today he washes cars at the neighbourhood car wash. He gets paid R50 a day.

He wishes his life could have turned out differently, and he has many regrets. His anger toward his father blinded him so much, that he made so many wrong choices. Yes, his life might have been different had his father been around, and loved him, but he realized that providence owed him nothing, and the choices he made were his. It's too late now. His only wish is that he could go back and make different choices.

Solution
Remember life is not always going to be easy, we don't choose our families. We don't choose the home we are born into. Blaming others only makes it harder for you. Owning your environment helps you think outside of the box; helps you see the ways you can change things and change your future. Your parents are doing all they can to raise you, and they are not perfect, but that doesn't mean that their failures and shortcomings should define you. Having a positive fighting spirit makes

a big difference. Do not make rash decisions, trying to hurt others. You only end hurting yourself.

**Task:**

Make a list of all the hurt and hardship you have experienced in your life. Write down every grudge you still hold against any person, whether friend, family member or enemy.

Once you have done this, burn the paper. By doing this you are releasing and letting go of all that hurt and allowing yourself to now take charge of your own life.

Declaration: I_____promise to take charge of my life. My life may not be perfect but I will not blame anyone. It's not parents' fault, or my teachers fault. I am in full control of my life. I have the steering wheel. I choose where this bus goes, and I choose the road of bliss and success. I choose to let go of all hurt and grudges in my life. I choose to forgive all those who have wronged me. I choose a better life. I choose happiness.

NOTES

_____

_____

_____

_____

_____

FORGIVENESS

It was no secret that her mom preferred her younger sister over her. Her sister got more pocket money, and better clothes. She was bitter because of this. Bitter because her mom loved her sister more than her. She felt like an outsider in her own home. She worked harder than her sister but somehow, she could not get her mom's approval. Nothing she did was ever good enough.

She would ask herself "Am I even really her daughter?" "Why can't she love me the way she loves her?" Her mom would always shout at her and call her names. She didn't know what it was to have the love of her mother. She felt isolated.

She found solace in the fact that she would soon leave for university and would no longer have to be in that home. She would watch them laughing together, and her only thought would be "they are laughing at me."

She would hear her mother tell her younger sister that she loved her. Was it because her sister was light skinned? Or because she excelled in school?

She was darker skinned, and thicker than her younger sister. She struggled to excel in school. Looking back at into her childhood, she couldn't recall one instance, where her mom declared any form of love to her.

Did she even love her at all? She cannot help but be bitter toward her sister as well. She can see the love they have for each other, with nothing to spare for her. If she could choose her family, she would choose a different mother.

They didn't see how they were hurting her. Or they didn't care. They just carried on.

Solution

We don't choose what happens to us in life. Sometimes we are handed miserable circumstances, and we become angry and bitter. Sometimes the people who hurt us don't even know they are hurting us.

But we will miss out in enjoying life if we choose to live in anger. Anger generates turmoil which eventually overwhelms your life.

You can become lethargic, depressed and even suicidal because of it. It is important therefore, to forgive those who have hurt you, and to release all the offence. All that negative energy, unforgiveness and resentment only creates toxins psychologically and in your physical body, having an adverse effect on your life. It's like drinking poison and hoping the person who hurt you will die.

The reality is, that the people you are angry with, usually just go on with their lives as normal. So, you need to heal your heart, but you can't do so while holding onto your anger.

Forgiving those who hurt you, releases you from them, clears your mind and brings peace to your soul. Your life will start flourishing once the anger is gone, and you can fly higher and reach the sky.

So as of today, we are choosing to forgive and let go of all our past hurts. Forgiveness frees you! Choose to live a happy and joyful life by letting go.

Task:
Write the names of the people that have hurt you, and next to their name write the words: I forgive you.

Group exercise:

Write a list of past hurts. Share the list with your mates, and once you are done, tear the list up, burn it and shout out aloud: I FORGIVE YOU! I AM FREE!

Declaration:

Today, I_____ choose to forgive_____ and _____ for hurting me.

I choose to release my anger and move forward with my life. I choose to be free from this pain. I choose a joyful life. I let go. I am free

NOTES

_____

_____

_____

_____

_____

_____

_____

_____

BUSINESS

South Africa has a shortage of jobs. Many school leavers and college graduates are not finding employment. It is therefore imperative, that cultivate a business minded culture. We need to start creating jobs, instead of looking for job opportunities. We need to start businesses, be business owners, and help boost the economy. After all, we can't all be employees, some of us need to be employers. There is no guarantee that having a university degree will land you a job. In order to break the cycle of poverty, we need to start teaching business skills at young age.

Young people need to be innovative and think of owning a business as the norm, not some far off idea for the select few. These businesses will support their dreams, and the dreams of those around them.

Sbu completed his degree in 2015 but has since been looking for employment. He lives with his grandmother, and they are both supported by her pension money- which is barely enough to get by. The first year after university, Sbu tried hard to find a job in his field or an internship program, but to no avail. The next year, he lost his vigor, because he grew tired of unsuccessful interviews, tired of being told "no", tired of going out and coming back with nothing to show for it. It's been five years since he graduated, and his degree is just collecting dust. He gets odd jobs here and there to help out the family, but nothing that will sustain them long-term. On the other hand, Sbu has a skill. When his dad was alive, he taught Sbu everything he knew about plumbing. But Sbu does not like hard labour. So instead of using the skill his hand, he chooses to hold onto his engineering degree in the hope that he will one day find employment in that field. In the meantime, he sits unemplyed and unable to contribute to his family's needs. Sbu could have started a small plumbing business in the community and grown it to hire more people like him. The skill in his hand could help him stop the cycle of poverty. But we can't really blame Sbu, because society has taught him that a degree means more than a "menial skill: and no one has ever taught him the value or beginnings of business. So how do we break this pattern of helplessness? How do we instill a mind for business in young people?

We start now.

Task: Look around your community, what gap can you see, that you can fill by starting your business?

Remember, business is about solving a problem, what problem can you solve? Once you identify the need, write it below and discover the kind of business you can start, that will generate money for you.

Give your business a name, draw a picture of the product or service and give it a price, how will you promote and market it?

Business name

_____

Logo/picture of the business *(draw or paste your image here)*

Where will it operate:

_____

Brief description of the business

_____

_____

_____

_____

_____

Who is your target audience?

_____

_____

Price of the service or product:

_____

_____

_____

How will you market the product?

_____

_____

_____

_____

Did you know you can turn your hobby, skill, or talent into a business?

List all your hobbies below and describe how you can turn them into a business
Skill/talent/hobby:

_____

_____

_____

_____

How will you turn that into a business?

_____

_____

_____

Research Task: Find a businesswoman/man in your community and interview them on how they started their business. Share those tips and information with the class.

There are so many business ideas in the world, jot down a few business ideas that you find attractive and stipulate why:

1._____

_____

_____

2._____

_____

_____

3._____

_____

_____

Think of the craziest, wildest, most innovative business idea and share it with your peers.

Crazy business idea:

_____

_____

_____

_____

_____

_____

_____

_____

_____

_____

_____

_____

_____

FACING RESPONSIBILITY AT A YOUNG AGE

I did not ask for this life. It wasn't my choice for my parents to die at such a young age. This is hard. I can't not do this. My siblings are so young, and we need an adult to care for us. I must go to school, but when I get back, I need to prepare food, clean the house, help them with schoolwork and homework, prepare uniforms for the next day. We don't have enough money, and the grant we receive is not much help either. We are out of food before the month ends. This is a lot of responsibility. I am too young for this. I didn't ask for this.

We are at a loss. It feels as though is God not hearing our prayers. Our extended family does not care, they just watch us suffer. Sometimes I feel like running away, but I can't. My sister and my brother need me. They only have me.

I can't wait to be an adult so I can give them a better life. It's unbearably hard, but every day I pray for the strength to keep going. Next year I will be in grade 11. Thereafter I will matriculate, study further, and give them everything they need. It's hard, but I refuse to give up. I take it one day at a time. I will conquer.

 Solution:
Life is unpredictable.
It can hand us challenging circumstances at a young age, without warning and without permission.

But how we approach these challenges, will determine whether we win or lose.
The situation maybe hard but your attitude will determine your altitude.
Your attitude is like an inner architect building resilience in your mindset.

Your outlook involves your perception of success (or failure) and has a big impact on how your life turns out.

The great thing is, that although there are many things in your life that you did not choose, you can still choose your attitude.

Declaration:
I will focus my mind on my vision, not my circumstances or condition.
Even though life is hard right now, I promise to work even harder to make my future better. I will not wallow in self-pity, I will push forward, and I will win.

NOTES

_____
_____
_____
_____
_____
_____
_____

Signature: _____

Signed by: _____ on the _____

GOSSIP, HATE & JEALOUSY

Queens, fix each other's crowns!

She was such an unhappy girl, who never had anything good to say about other kids. She was always blaming and shaming and making fun of others. Her heart was full of envy and hate, but before you judge her, consider that she did not get the love of her parents at home.

She channeled all her resentment into gossiping and speaking ill of others. She was jealous of her peers' successes. She was always in competition, vying with others over everything and she never accepted defeat. She was bitter and angry, and it showed in how she spoke, how she lived, and how she treated others. She was a broken girl, seeking love and acceptance. Her brokenness made her mean, and this is who she was all throughout high school and well into her adult life.

 Solution

Queens, fix each other's crowns!

We live in a very competitive world, but the simple truth is, women are more powerful when they work together. So instead of rivalry, we should be embracing collaboration. And it's something worth reminding yourself of on a regular basis. Instead of beating one another down, lets lift one another up. When a sister is bitter or hurt, lets look for way to straighten her crown, to help her love, to usher her out of that toxic space.

✏️ **Declaration:** I choose not to be jealous of others, instead I will help them win and succeed by doing the following:

_____

_____

_____

_____

_____

_____

_____

_____

_____

_____

_____

_____

Signature: _____

Signed by: _____ on the _____

WHAT STORY DO YOU TELL YOURSELF?

"The single most important factor in determining your attitude toward a situation and influencing the outcome is the story you tell yourself about that situation. The problem is most likely not the situation itself but how you choose to explain the situation to yourself. Notice the use of the word "choose" — because it really is a choice.

This is something to celebrate: We all have complete control over our view of life's challenges, which gives us a great measure of influence over outcomes. I am an eternal control freak so this was one of the most liberating discoveries of my life. No longer was I hostage to my circumstances.

With this new mindset, I could refuse to play victim for being born in a poor family. The word "victim" accurately illustrates how many people feel about a situation: Victims succumb to circumstance. Victims are helpless.

They have no control or power. Victims, quite frankly, are losers.
I initially fell prey to that line of thinking myself because it's a natural human response.

Emotion can overcome anyone facing a hardship, loss of a loved one, or any condition that materially alters our lifestyle.

That reaction is natural. In fact, not having that reaction would be very unnatural. However, over the next few years I realized that living in negativity was creating a toxicity and bitterness that consumed me. I had to find a way out of the prison that was my life, and I soon realized a great escape was to hatch my mind.

While I could not control the physical world around to make correct my vision, I could control the way I chose to see the world. Instead of choosing to see what I did not have, I opted to see what I did have. I still had my cognitive faculties, superb hearing, a tremendous family, and very good health."

Create Personal Mission Statement

1. What is important? What/whom do you value? How is your life connected to those things?

2. Where do you want to go?

You can answer this many ways.
Your answer may involve a spiritual, mental, or physical destination. It might describe your career arc.

3. What does "the best" look like for me? Describe your best possible result. This isn't the time to be realistic. This is the time to dream.

4. How do I want to act? How do you want people to describe you? Think of a few words you would want to come to mind when people think about you.

5. What kind of legacy do I want to leave behind? Imagine you're 100 years in the future. What does the impact you've left look like?

"To inspire positive change through teaching and coaching."
"To create opportunities for today's youth."
"To encourage, engage, and equip others to believe in the possibilities."
"To positively impact the life of every person I meet."
"To encourage everyone, I interact with on a daily basis."
And, of course, my personal mission statement… "To help others live the lives they would if they only knew how."

Write your new Personal Mission Statement:

GREAT THINGS RESULT WHEN YOU REFUSE TO ACCEPT EXCUSES

She complained about everything. "Life is not fair; I am unhappy; I am lonely; I am fat; I am poor; I am unlovable; I don't have friends; the weather is too hot; it's too cold, etc." She was never happy about anything in her life. She was a bitter young lady. Nothing was ever good enough, or right enough, or suitable enough. She made excuse after excuse as to why she was not able to succeed.

 Solution

"You could have found a thousand great reasons to give up, but "reasons" is just another word for "excuses." Excuses are for losers. How many people have you seen atop the Olympic podium receiving the gold medal and making excuses? None! The people unwilling to make excuses are those who make it to the top. Who would you rather be: someone who found a way to break through barriers to achieve your goals, or someone who found good, and even possibly legitimate, reasons to fail? For me the decision is clear.

What is your decision? Again, it comes down to the story you're told about your circumstances. But remember — you are the narrator! You choose how to frame your story. Will your story help you find legitimate reasons to fail, or will it set you up to bulldoze your barriers?"

"Excuses prevent growth, the laziness that is leading you to not challenge yourself can also prevent you from growing or changing. Your excuses help you live with the failed expectations that you already had for yourself."

"Excuses lead to a failure in reaching your full potential, when you make an excuse, you aren't even giving yourself a shot to succeed, which can limit you in every area of your life. You may never even know what you're capable of if you have an excuse for everything that comes your way. Excuses can hold you back from a lot of things, including getting further in your career or even getting healthier."

12 Steps to Stop Making Excuses

1. Stop Comparing Yourself to Others
When you compare yourself to other people, especially those who have already achieved what you want to achieve, you're focusing on your weaknesses rather than your strengths. This probably makes you feel defeated and hopeless if you see a big gap between where you are today and where they are.

2. Stop Fearing the Unknown
People tend to be wary of taking risks that could disrupt their current reality, and are often opposed to making even the smallest change to the comfort of their daily behaviors, even if their current actions aren't in their best interest.

3. Stop Blaming Others
One of the most destructive things you can do in life is to play the blame game. It is the basis for a considerable amount of frustration and unhappiness in people's lives.

4. Take Responsibility for ALL Your Actions
Being responsible requires acting on your ability to respond to things that happen. It involves using your power to change and to offer the most practical responses to life's everyday problems.

5. Act Every Day

Part of taking action is taking risks. You may have big plans that sound great in theory, but you never plan on actually following through with them. Stop making excuses and take the action that is needed to achieve the goals you want in life and create success for yourself. One of the first things you must do to eliminate your excuses is to take that first step.

6. Set Small, Attainable Goals

Setting large goals may seem so overwhelming that you don't even know where to start. Further, you may start working towards your long-term goal and find that you're not getting anywhere fast and give up.

7. Learn from Your Mistakes

Not only can you learn what not to do when you make a mistake, but you can also analyze what went wrong and figure out how you can do better in the future. All mistakes are learning opportunities, no matter how big or small the mistake may be. Often, trial and error are the best way to work something out.

8. Don't Focus on Your Weaknesses

Be aware of your weaknesses, but don't focus on them. Rather, focus on your strengths and the things that you have to offer that other people do not. Ask questions that make you think more deeply about your life.

9. Change your Attitude

Realize that you have the power to change. You just have to be motivated to do so. You can't feel defeated or complacent with your life just being "okay." Without making excuses, you have the power to change anything in your life.

10. Believe in Yourself

Believing in yourself plays an important role in whether or not you are able to achieve the results you want in life. You have to be able to envision yourself reaching your final goal in order for you to believe it will actually happen.

11. Visualize Your Success

Literally visualize what it would look like and feel like to achieve your goal and have success. Close your eyes and think about who will be waiting for you at the finish line and the amount of pride you will be feeling as you're running your final few meters.

12. Remember: It's Okay to Not Be Perfect

Accept your mistakes and know that other people are willing to accept your mistakes as well, especially if you own up to them and learn from them. This is something that happens to everyone, even the most successful people.

Declaration: I_____ make this promise, on_____(date) that no excuse will be uttered by my mouth. I promise to speak positive words even when days are dark. I promise to give life to all I can so I can succeed. I refuse to sit and complain and make excuses. I am not disabled in anyway, I am capable. I have a brain that functions properly. I am always on my toes, always thinking outside of the box. Excuses are for the weak. I am ready to tackle my challenges head on.

MY STORY

Change your perspective, change your story.

Write the story you want to tell – the story you want to see; the story of how you want your life to turn out.

I grew up under tough circumstances and surroundings, but when I was 14 years old, I was selected to represent my province in table tennis. I was so excited to be selected.

The tournament was to be held in Cape Town, and I was extremely excited that I would fly for the first time, sleep in a hotel for the first time, and be the first in my school to represent my entire province on a national level. My hometown is very small so visiting The Mother City was huge for me, and obviously meant a great deal. My parents- especially my dad- were so excited for me. But this wonderful opportunity, came with a great financial burden.

My parents were already struggling to take of their seven children, in their 2-bedroom home, and the costs involved with this trip, would only be adding to that burden. I had two choices: I could forgo the trip, or I could think outside the box and find the means to fund the trip. The thought of not going was too unbearable. I was too hungry and too excited not to go, so I had to think of creative ways to make it happen. My coach knew of my family's financial situation, still when I shared the news that I might not go he was not happy. We then decided to put our heads together and think of ways around this mountain. He came up with an idea to ask for donations in town.

As a teenager, it was embarrassing to go door-to-door asking for money. My peers would make fun of me and see me as desperate and poor. But I didn't care. My dream was much bigger than a few laughs and *ukuhletshwa (gossip)*, so I headed out to businesses on my hometown, to ask for donations.

To my surprise, people were excited to fund a young girl going to represent their province. They were happy to donate a R2 here and a R5 there. Soon, all those little amounts added up to everything I needed to make the trip happen.

We did not win the tournament, but the trip taught me a lot. I slept in a hotel for the first time in my life. I ate fancy food for the first time in my life. I experienced things and places I would have never seen had I chosen to allow my circumstances to get the better of me. That experience shaped me into the person I am today. From that day on, I was made aware of the life that awaits outside my small town of Ermelo. I knew I had to study hard and make money so I could experience this fancy, beautiful life I had gotten a glimpse of over the week we stayed in Cape Town. I went back to school with a different mindset. I worked harder than I ever did. I studied harder. I wanted to get out of my hometown so I can go to university and make things happen. It is not by mistake that now, 20 years later I now live in Cape Town. I get to live the life I briefly experienced, so many years ago, in that one week that I was able to represent my province. I am happy. I love the life I have built for myself here, and it all started with one decision.

What is Your Story:

_____
_____
_____
_____
_____
_____

VISION BOARD

"A dream board or vision board is a collage of images, pictures, and affirmations of one's dreams and desires, designed to serve as a source of inspiration and motivation, and to use the law of attraction to attain goals." - *Wikipedia*

I am on 37 years old and on my third vision board. My first vision board was back in high school when I wanted to graduate matric. This vision board had basic pictures on it. One of those pictures was a girl in a gown graduating with a degree. Another one, was a picture of a big double-story house, and a fancy car. Fast forward to 2020- I have achieved all that was in that vision board and more. After university when I landed my first job I, did my second vision board, because all the dreams that were in my first vision board had come true.

My third vision board was done in 2019, with even bigger dreams. I have no doubt that they will come true. Because I command the universe to bring me my heart desires. A vision Board is powerful tool to manifest your life desires. Ask me I am proof that it works.

 **Solution:**

1. The power of choice

Visions boards force you to examine your desires and focus on those that truly matter to you. Whether creating one or several boards, the limited space forces you and empowers you to focus in on your most treasured desires.

2. The power of visualization

Without a doubt, it is the visual aspect of a dream board that really drives home your desires and sends a very loud, clear message. It's easy to think that choosing and focusing on a desire helps achieve it that specific desire, but visualization isn't as straightforward as we think it is. To understand why visualizing your desires is so powerful, we need to look at the brain. Our brain is an incredible machine that is geared toward making us successful with every action we take. Our brain trains our bodies to prepare for action — when we imagine ourselves preparing for an activity, our brains run through the process and send signals to the rest of our body to complete the action.

Visualization is nearly as powerful as performing the action. When you visualize yourself living in your dream home, your brain trains your body for that reality.

3. The power of consistency

It's no secret that consistency is important. Whether attempting to learn a new skill or create a new habit, consistency is the key. We're wired for repetition, and every time we repeat an action, we become stronger with that action. By creating a vision board and placing it in a spot you see every day, you create the opportunity for consistent visualization to train your mind, body, and spirit to manifest your desires. The wonderful thing about a dream board is that it only requires time and energy for the initial creation. After that, the consistency in the visualization happens every time you look at it.

 **Task:**
Create your own Vision Board

Before you begin, ask yourself the following questions and commit to the suggested action (your shopping list) to follow through with.

What true wishes and desires do you want to reflect on your dream board?
Think about:

- ✓ Your values, Career goals, family life, Love life, Health & Wellness, how you spend your free time
- ✓ What you want to learn or grow into

Keep in mind that you'll need to place this board in a visible area that you see every day

You can source these images from:

- ✓ Newspaper cutouts
- ✓ Magazine cutouts
- ✓ Images/Quotes printed from the internet
- ✓ Your Pinterest boards
- ✓ Photographs
- ✓ Pages from a book
- ✓ Brochures/pamphlets/flyer

Images are a major component of vision boards. For photographs printed from the internet and cut out from magazines, use stick glue, tape, or hot glue. For precious items or photographs, buy acid-free, removable *adhesive that is safe for photos.*

Take time to cut your images out.
Sit with your images for a moment before you attach them to your board.
Hold them in your hand and stare at them.
Feel the desire running through your body.
Notice what emotions arise when you think of that image and the desires that it conjures. See yourself getting what you want and feel the happiness radiating from it. Whatever you're feeling in this moment is exactly what you want to experience every time you look at your vision board.

Once you've created your vision board, place it in an area that you see every day. Many people like to notice their vision board near their nightstand or other place that they look at first thing in the morning.
After a time, and to avoid "not really seeing" your vision board, make a positive habit out of sitting with your board at least once a week.
Simply take 10 minutes to look at your board, reflect on why you specifically chose those images, and revisit the feelings of happiness and gratitude of eventually having those desires in your life.
Not only is a vision board a wonderful reminder of what you truly want in life, it's a powerful motivator to enact on achieving your goals.
Treat your vision board like it's sacred — it's a special gift you've given to yourself, and a powerful tool to attract all your desires into your life.

My Vision Board   Date:_____

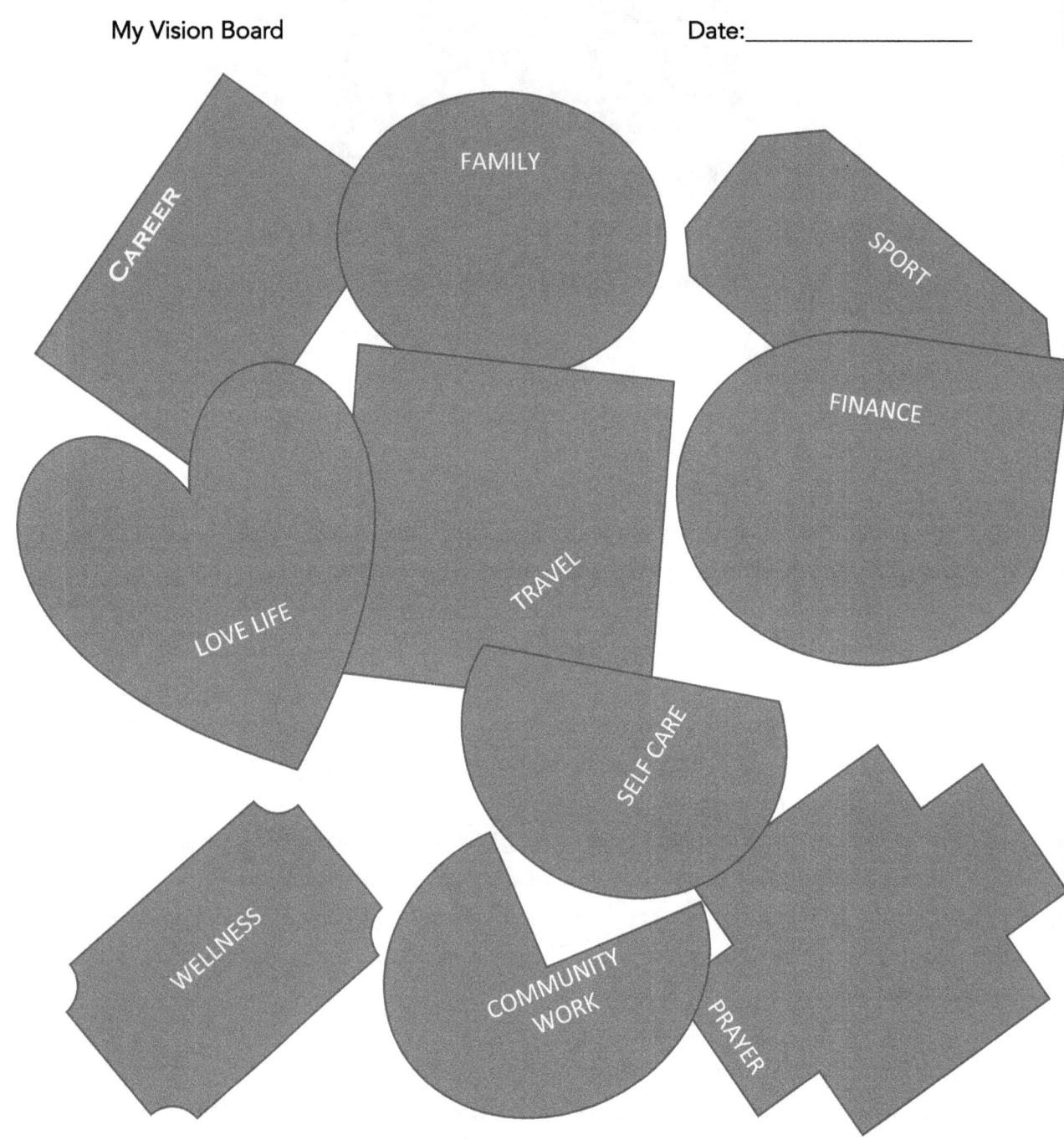

DEVELOP HUNGER FOR SUCCESS

I had to act as though I couldn't care for the opportunities that presented themselves. I wanted to fit in with the boys. If I acted too hungry, too driven, I would be cast out like Vuyo. Vuyo was shunned because he was too eager to take advantage of opportunities that came his way. We used to laugh at him and ridicule him, calling him "cheeseboy" or "nerd-boy". He eventually quit the group and has since been awarded a scholarship which pays for his school fees and sport activities, in a good school in the suburbs. I envy his life but I'm still in the township and I need my friends so I cannot act all eager like him and lose my chance to be part of their scheme. These boys are my brothers and I need them. So, I play low-key and act like them just so they don't shut me out. I act like a fool, I know. I act like I don't care, even when I do care. I don't agree with half of the things they do or say but I cast risk being alone or being an outcast. I want to belong, so I act like I have it all figured out. The truth is. I know we are just fools; the blind leading the blind. But I am too proud and afraid to walk away.

 Solution

"Be hungry for success. That way a natural eagerness will permeate your attitude. It will seem that you cannot wait to get to work and put that hunger into motion. This energy serves as the driving force behind your attaining your goals when you have 100 percent commitment to what you are doing. Total commitment cuts through doubt."

> *Be hungry for success, hungry to make your mark, hungry to be seen and to be heard and to have an effect. And as you move up and become successful, make sure also to be hungry for helping others.* **– Arnold Schwarzenegger**

When we are this hungry, you can bet we will do anything that's necessary to get what we desire. So why is it then that when we desire success in any area of life, be it money, health, wellness, or in our relationships, we settle?

Hunger leads to action, action leads to success, Hunger is the greatest motivator of action, and action is the key to success. When you are dying of hunger, you will do whatever it takes to get yourself a meal. And if you don't succeed, you will die trying. If we truly want to be great, to do great things, to find success in life however it might look to each of us, we need to stop snacking and let those hunger pains push us a little harder. We can't keep munching on the little things while our biggest dreams draw further away.

What does "hangry" for success look like?

Being hangry for success is when you sit on the toilet with a pen and notepad writing new ideas instead of scrolling on your phone. It's reading books instead of watching TV shows. It's following thought leaders instead of celebrities and meeting like-minded people instead of party people.

If we want to succeed, we can't be killing our appetites. We must stay hungry. We must not settle for the little victories of life which only temporarily subdue our search for greatness.

We must want it bad enough that everything else becomes a distraction, and the lack of success becomes life-threatening. We have to get hungry for success. There is a better way to live!"

Declaration:

If I spend my time with incredible people, I have no choice but to step up my game. I will continuously monitor whom I spend my time with. If I surround myself with people who have achieved incredible things, not only can I soak up their habits, but I will also inherit their hunger.

NOTES

DIVA

Powerful women value financial independence. Get your education game on. Start investing, develop a mind for business. Do not rely on a man to take care of you, or they may disappoint you. Never stop growing.

Concentrating on expensive weaves, nails, and fancy clothes will leave you poor. Life is full of surprises. You just never know what tomorrow will bring. We've seen CEOs here today, gone tomorrow. Civilizations rise and decline, let alone our small little human existence. Change is truly the only thing constant in the universe.

When roughly 50% of marriages dissolve in this country, you really don't want to count on your spouse to provide for all your expenses. Even if the loving relationship lasts forever, the sole breadwinner might lose the job, become disabled, or simply decide to stop working altogether.

Then what do you do?

You don't want to be at the mercy of someone else. You want to be in control of your financial well-being, regardless of what anyone else around you is doing.

Solution
Women are different from men, and how they choose to manage their financial lives is going to be different.

To have a more enjoyable lifestyle
Who doesn't want the financial freedom to buy whatever you want and go wherever you desire?

Without an extra source of income and with a relatively tight budget, it's just more difficult to live life to the fullest.

Why not put in some work now so that you can have that vacation you've always dreamed of?

To have peace of mind
Based on statistics, fights over finances are oftentimes one of the leading causes of marital breakdowns. Regardless of your relationship status, having more money in the bank and being financially independent does provide more peace of mind in times of distress.

After all, you shouldn't worry about not having a roof over your head if, for whatever reason, you're on your own suddenly.

How to Achieve Financial Independence
- Get necessary education and training
- budget wisely and save every month
- reduce and eliminate debt
- maintain a good credit score
- start saving for retirement
- give to charities
- Get your resume in shape
- Apply through various job search engines

I declare that I will unleash the **DIVA** in me by committing to do the following:

_____

_____

_____

_____

_____

_____

_____

_____

_____

_____

_____

Signature: _____

Signed by: _____ on the _____

CAREERS

Below is a list of every possible career.
Feel free to research the ones that appeal to you.

1) Able Seamen	26) Agricultural Workers, All Other
2) Accountants	27) Air Crew Members
3) Accountants and Auditors	28) Air Crew Officers
4) Actors	29) Air Traffic Controllers
5) Actuaries	30) Aircraft Body and Bonded Structure Repairers
6) Acupuncturists *** New ***	31) Aircraft Cargo Handling Supervisors
7) Acute Care Nurses *** New ***	32) Aircraft Engine Specialists
8) Adapted Physical Education Specialists *** New ***	33) Aircraft Launch and Recovery Officers
9) Adjustment Clerks	34) Aircraft Launch and Recovery Specialists
10) Administrative Law Judges, Adjudicators, and Hearing Officers	35) Aircraft Mechanics and Service Technicians
11) Administrative Services Managers	36) Aircraft Rigging Assemblers
12) Adult Literacy, Remedial Education, and GED Teachers and Instructors	37) Aircraft Structure Assemblers, Precision
13) Advanced Practice Psychiatric Nurses *** New ***	38) Aircraft Structure, Surfaces, Rigging, and Systems Assemblers
14) Advertising and Promotions Managers	39) Aircraft Systems Assemblers, Precision
15) Advertising Sales Agents	40) Airfield Operations Specialists

16) Aerospace Engineering and Operations Technicians	41) Airframe-and-Power-Plant Mechanics
17) Aerospace Engineers	42) Airline Pilots, Copilots, and Flight Engineers
18) Agents and Business Managers of Artists, Performers, and Athletes	43) Allergists and Immunologists *** New ***
19) Agricultural and Food Science Technicians	44) Ambulance Drivers and Attendants, Except Emergency Medical Technicians
20) Agricultural Crop Farm Managers	45) Amusement and Recreation Attendants
21) Agricultural Engineers	46) Anesthesiologist Assistants *** New ***
22) Agricultural Equipment Operators	47) Anesthesiologists
23) Agricultural Inspectors	48) Animal Breeders
24) Agricultural Sciences Teachers, Postsecondary	49) Animal Control Workers
25) Agricultural Technicians	50) Animal Scientists

51) Animal Trainers	76) Astronomers
52) Anthropologists	77) Athletes and Sports Competitors
53) Anthropologists and Archeologists	78) Athletic Trainers
54) Anthropology and Archeology Teachers, Postsecondary	79) Atmospheric and Space Scientists
55) Appraisers and Assessors of Real Estate	80) Atmospheric, Earth, Marine, and Space Sciences Teachers, Postsecondary
56) Appraisers, Real Estate	81) Audio and Video Equipment Technicians
57) Aquacultural Managers *** New ***	82) Audiologist *** New ***

58) Arbitrators, Mediators, and Conciliators	83) Audiologists
59) Archeologists	84) Audio-Visual Collections Specialists
60) Architects, Except Landscape and Naval	85) Auditors
61) Architectural and Civil Drafters	86) Automatic Teller Machine Servicers
62) Architectural Drafters	87) Automotive Body and Related Repairers
63) Architecture Teachers, Postsecondary	88) Automotive Engineering Technicians *** New ***
64) Archivists	89) Automotive Engineers *** New ***
65) Area, Ethnic, and Cultural Studies Teachers, Postsecondary	90) Automotive Glass Installers and Repairers
66) Armored Assault Vehicle Crew Members	91) Automotive Master Mechanics
67) Armored Assault Vehicle Officers	92) Automotive Service Technicians and Mechanics
68) Art Directors	93) Automotive Specialty Technicians
69) Art Therapists *** New ***	94) Auxiliary Equipment Operators, Power
70) Art, Drama, and Music Teachers, Postsecondary	95) Aviation Inspectors
71) Artillery and Missile Crew Members	96) Avionics Technicians
72) Artillery and Missile Officers	97) Baggage Porters and Bellhops
73) Artists and Related Workers, All Other	98) Bailiffs
74) Assemblers and Fabricators, All Other	99) Bakers
75) Assessors	100) Bakers, Bread and Pastry

101) Bakers, Manufacturing	170) Cashiers
102) Barbers	171) Casting Machine Set-Up Operators
103) Baristas *** New ***	172) Ceiling Tile Installers
104) Bartenders	173) Cement Masons and Concrete Finishers
105) Battery Repairers	174) Cementing and Gluing Machine Operators and Tenders
106) Bench Workers, Jewelry	175) Central Office and PBX Installers and Repairers
107) Bicycle Repairers	176) Central Office Operators
108) Bill and Account Collectors	177) Chefs and Head Cooks
109) Billing and Posting Clerks and Machine Operators	178) Chemical Engineers
110) Billing, Cost, and Rate Clerks	179) Chemical Equipment Controllers and Operators
111) Billing, Posting, and Calculating Machine Operators	180) Chemical Equipment Operators and Tenders
112) Bindery Machine Operators and Tenders	181) Chemical Equipment Tenders
113) Bindery Machine Setters and Set-Up Operators	182) Chemical Plant and System Operators
114) Bindery Workers	183) Chemical Technicians
115) Biochemical Engineers *** New ***	184) Chemistry Teachers, Postsecondary
116) Biochemists	185) Chemists
117) Biochemists and Biophysicists	186) Chief Executives
118) Biofuels Processing Technicians *** New ***	187) Chief Sustainability Officers *** New ***
119) Biofuels Production Managers *** New ***	188) Child Care Workers

164) Cargo and Freight Agents	189) Child Support, Missing Persons, and Unemployment Insurance Fraud Investigators
165) Carpenter Assemblers and Repairers	190) Child, Family, and School Social Workers
166) Carpenters	191) Chiropractors
167) Carpet Installers	192) Choreographers
168) Cartographers and Photogrammetrists	193) City Planning Aides
169) Cartoonists	194) Civil Drafters

101) Bakers, Manufacturing	127) Biomass Plant Technicians *** New ***
102) Barbers	128) Biomass Power Plant Managers *** New ***
103) Baristas *** New ***	129) Biomedical Engineers
104) Bartenders	130) Biophysicists
105) Battery Repairers	131) Biostatisticians *** New ***
106) Bench Workers, Jewelry	132) Boat Builders and Shipwrights
107) Bicycle Repairers	133) Boiler Operators and Tenders, Low Pressure
108) Bill and Account Collectors	134) Boilermakers
109) Billing and Posting Clerks and Machine Operators	135) Bookbinders
110) Billing, Cost, and Rate Clerks	136) Bookkeeping, Accounting, and Auditing Clerks
111) Billing, Posting, and Calculating Machine Operators	137) Brattice Builders
112) Bindery Machine Operators and Tenders	138) Brazers

113) Bindery Machine Setters and Set-Up Operators	139) Brickmasons and Blockmasons
114) Bindery Workers	140) Bridge and Lock Tenders
115) Biochemical Engineers *** New ***	141) Broadcast News Analysts
116) Biochemists	142) Broadcast Technicians
117) Biochemists and Biophysicists	143) Brokerage Clerks
118) Biofuels Processing Technicians *** New ***	144) Brownfield Redevelopment Specialists and Site Managers *** New ***
119) Biofuels Production Managers *** New ***	145) Budget Analysts
120) Biofuels/Biodiesel Technology and Product Development Managers *** New ***	146) Buffing and Polishing Set-Up Operators
121) Bioinformatics Scientists *** New ***	147) Building Cleaning Workers, All Other
122) Bioinformatics Technicians *** New ***	148) Bus and Truck Mechanics and Diesel Engine Specialists
123) Biological Science Teachers, Postsecondary	149) Bus Drivers, School
124) Biological Scientists, All Other	150) Bus Drivers, Transit and Intercity
125) Biological Technicians	151) Business Continuity Planners *** New ***
126) Biologists	152) Business Intelligence Analysts *** New ***

153) Business Operations Specialists, All Other	180) Chemical Equipment Operators and Tenders
154) Business Teachers, Postsecondary	181) Chemical Equipment Tenders
155) Butchers and Meat Cutters	182) Chemical Plant and System Operators

156) Cabinetmakers and Bench Carpenters	183) Chemical Technicians
157) Calibration and Instrumentation Technicians	184) Chemistry Teachers, Postsecondary
158) Camera and Photographic Equipment Repairers	185) Chemists
159) Camera Operators	186) Chief Executives
160) Camera Operators, Television, Video, and Motion Picture	187) Chief Sustainability Officers *** New ***
161) Captains, Mates, and Pilots of Water Vessels	188) Child Care Workers
162) Caption Writers	189) Child Support, Missing Persons, and Unemployment Insurance Fraud Investigators
163) Cardiovascular Technologists and Technicians	190) Child, Family, and School Social Workers
164) Cargo and Freight Agents	191) Chiropractors
165) Carpenter Assemblers and Repairers	192) Choreographers
166) Carpenters	193) City Planning Aides
167) Carpet Installers	194) Civil Drafters
168) Cartographers and Photogrammetrists	195) Civil Engineering Technicians
169) Cartoonists	196) Civil Engineers
170) Cashiers	197) Claims Adjusters, Examiners, and Investigators
171) Casting Machine Set-Up Operators	198) Claims Examiners, Property and Casualty Insurance
172) Ceiling Tile Installers	199) Claims Takers, Unemployment Benefits

173) Cement Masons and Concrete Finishers	200) Cleaners of Vehicles and Equipment
174) Cementing and Gluing Machine Operators and Tenders	201) Cleaning, Washing, and Metal Pickling Equipment Operators and Tenders
175) Central Office and PBX Installers and Repairers	202) Clergy
176) Central Office Operators	203) Climate Change Analysts *** New ***
177) Chefs and Head Cooks	204) Clinical Data Managers *** New ***
178) Chemical Engineers	205) Clinical Nurse Specialists *** New ***
179) Chemical Equipment Controllers and Operators	206) Clinical Psychologists

207) Clinical Research Coordinators *** New ***	235) Computer and Information Research Scientists *** New ***
208) Clinical, Counseling, and School Psychologists	236) Computer and Information Scientists, Research
209) Coaches and Scouts	237) Computer and Information Systems Managers
210) Coating, Painting, and Spraying Machine Operators and Tenders	238) Computer Hardware Engineers
211) Coating, Painting, and Spraying Machine Setters and Set-Up Operators	239) Computer Network Architects *** New ***
212) Coating, Painting, and Spraying Machine Setters, Operators, and Tenders	240) Computer Network Support Specialists *** New ***
213) Coil Winders, Tapers, and Finishers	241) Computer Operators

214) Coin, Vending, and Amusement Machine Servicers and Repairers	242) Computer Programmer *** New ***
215) Combination Machine Tool Operators and Tenders, Metal and Plastic	243) Computer Programmers
216) Combination Machine Tool Setters and Set-Up Operators, Metal and Plastic	244) Computer Science Teachers, Postsecondary
217) Combined Food Preparation and Serving Workers, Including Fast Food	245) Computer Security Specialists
218) Command and Control Center Officers	246) Computer Software Engineers, Applications
219) Command and Control Center Specialists	247) Computer Software Engineers, Systems Software
220) Commercial and Industrial Designers	248) Computer Specialists, All Other
221) Commercial Divers	249) Computer Support Specialists
222) Commercial Pilots	250) Computer Systems Analyst *** New ***
223) Communication Equipment Mechanics, Installers, and Repairers	251) Computer Systems Analysts
224) Communications Equipment Operators, All Other	252) Computer Systems Engineers/Architects *** New ***
225) Communications Teachers, Postsecondary	253) Computer User Support Specialists *** New ***
226) Community and Social Service Specialists, All Other	254) Computer, Automated Teller, and Office Machine Repairers
227) Community Health Workers *** New ***	255) Computer-Controlled Machine Tool Operators, Metal and Plastic
228) Compensation and Benefits Managers *** New ***	256) Concierges

229) Compensation and Benefits Managers	257) Conservation Scientists
230) Compensation, Benefits, and Job Analysis Specialist *** New ***	258) Construction and Building Inspectors
231) Compensation, Benefits, and Job Analysis Specialists	259) Construction and Related Workers, All Other
232) Compliance Managers *** New ***	260) Construction Carpenters
233) Compliance Officers, Except Agriculture, Construction, Health and Safety, and Transportation	261) Construction Drillers
234) Composers	262) Construction Laborers
325) Derrick Operators, Oil and Gas	350) Duplicating Machine Operators
326) Design Printing Machine Setters and Set-Up Operators	351) Earth Drillers, Except Oil and Gas
327) Designers, All Other	352) Economics Teachers, Postsecondary
328) Desktop Publishers	353) Economists
329) Detectives and Criminal Investigators	354) Editors
330) Diagnostic Medical Sonographers	355) Education Administrators, All Other
331) Dietetic Technicians	356) Education Administrators, Elementary and Secondary School
332) Dietitians and Nutritionists	357) Education Administrators, Postsecondary
333) Dining Room and Cafeteria Attendants and Bartender Helpers	358) Education Administrators, Preschool and Child Care Center--Program
334) Directors- Stage, Motion Pictures, Television, and Radio	359) Education Teachers, Postsecondary

335) Directors, Religious Activities and Education	360) Education, Training, and Library Workers, All Other
336) Directory Assistance Operators	361) Educational Psychologists
337) Dishwashers	362) Educational, Vocational, and School Counselors
338) Dispatchers, Except Police, Fire, and Ambulance	363) Electric Home Appliance and Power Tool Repairers
339) Distance Learning Coordinators *** New ***	364) Electric Meter Installers and Repairers
340) Document Management Specialists *** New ***	365) Electric Motor and Switch Assemblers and Repairers
341) Door-To-Door Sales Workers, News and Street Vendors, and Related Workers	366) Electric Motor, Power Tool, and Related Repairers
342) Dot Etchers	367) Electrical and Electronic Engineering Technicians
343) Drafters, All Other	368) Electrical and Electronic Equipment Assemblers
344) Dragline Operators	369) Electrical and Electronic Inspectors and Testers
345) Dredge Operators	370) Electrical and Electronics Drafters
346) Drilling and Boring Machine Tool Setters, Operators, and Tenders, Metal and Plastic	371) Electrical and Electronics Installers and Repairers, Transportation Equipment
347) Driver-Sales Workers	372) Electrical and Electronics Repairers, Commercial and Industrial Equipment
348) Drywall and Ceiling Tile Installers	373) Electrical and Electronics Repairers, Powerhouse, Substation, and Relay
349) Drywall Installers	374) Electrical Drafters

375) Electrical Engineering Technicians	400) Emergency Management Specialists
376) Electrical Engineering Technologists *** New ***	401) Emergency Medical Technicians and Paramedics
377) Electrical Engineers	402) Employment Interviewers, Private or Public Employment Service
378) Electrical Parts Reconditioners	403) Employment, Recruitment, and Placement Specialists
379) Electrical Power-Line Installers and Repairers	404) Endoscopy Technicians *** New ***
380) Electricians	405) Energy Auditors *** New ***
381) Electrolytic Plating and Coating Machine Operators and Tenders, Metal and Plastic	406) Energy Brokers *** New ***
382) Electrolytic Plating and Coating Machine Setters and Set-Up Operators, Metal and Plastic	407) Energy Engineers *** New ***
383) Electromechanical Engineering Technologists *** New ***	408) Engine and Other Machine Assemblers
384) Electromechanical Equipment Assemblers	409) Engineering Managers
385) Electro-Mechanical Technicians	410) Engineering Teachers, Postsecondary
386) Electronic Drafters	411) Engineering Technicians, Except Drafters, All Other
387) Electronic Equipment Installers and Repairers, Motor Vehicles	412) Engineers, All Other
388) Electronic Home Entertainment Equipment Installers and Repairers	413) English Language and Literature Teachers, Postsecondary

389) Electronic Masking System Operators	414) Engraver Set-Up Operators
390) Electronics Engineering Technicians	415) Engravers, Hand
391) Electronics Engineering Technologists *** New ***	416) Engravers--Carvers
392) Electronics Engineers, Except Computer	417) Entertainers and Performers, Sports and Related Workers, All Other
393) Electrotypers and Stereotypers	418) Entertainment Attendants and Related Workers, All Other
394) Elementary School Teachers, Except Special Education	419) Environmental Compliance Inspectors
395) Elevator Installers and Repairers	420) Environmental Economists *** New ***
396) Eligibility Interviewers, Government Programs	421) Environmental Engineering Technicians
397) Embalmers	422) Environmental Engineers
398) Embossing Machine Set-Up Operators	423) Environmental Restoration Planners *** New ***
399) Emergency Management Directors *** New ***	424) Environmental Science and Protection Technicians, Including Health

425) Environmental Science Teachers, Postsecondary	448) Family and General Practitioners
426) Environmental Scientists and Specialists, Including Health	449) Farm and Home Management Advisors
427) Epidemiologists	450) Farm and Ranch Managers *** New ***
428) Equal Opportunity Representatives and Officers	451) Farm Equipment Mechanics

429) Etchers	452) Farm Labor Contractor *** New ***
430) Etchers and Engravers	453) Farm Labor Contractors
431) Etchers, Hand	454) Farm, Ranch, and Other Agricultural Managers
432) Excavating and Loading Machine and Dragline Operators	455) Farmers and Ranchers
433) Excavating and Loading Machine Operators	456) Farmworkers and Laborers, Crop, Nursery, and Greenhouse
434) Executive Secretaries and Administrative Assistants	457) Farmworkers, Farm and Ranch Animals
435) Exercise Physiologists *** New ***	458) Fashion Designers
436) Exhibit Designers	459) Fence Erectors
437) Explosives Workers, Ordnance Handling Experts, and Blasters	460) Fiber Product Cutting Machine Setters and Set-Up Operators
438) Extraction Workers, All Other	461) Fiberglass Laminators and Fabricators
439) Extruding and Drawing Machine Setters, Operators, and Tenders, Metal and Plastic	462) File Clerks
440) Extruding and Forming Machine Operators and Tenders, Synthetic or Glass Fibers	463) Film and Video Editors
441) Extruding and Forming Machine Setters, Operators, and Tenders, Synthetic and Glass Fibers	464) Film Laboratory Technicians
442) Extruding, Forming, Pressing, and Compacting Machine Operators and Tenders	465) Financial Analysts

443) Extruding, Forming, Pressing, and Compacting Machine Setters and Set-Up Operators	466) Financial Examiners
444) Extruding, Forming, Pressing, and Compacting Machine Setters, Operators, and Tenders	467) Financial Managers
445) Fabric and Apparel Patternmakers	468) Financial Managers, Branch or Department
446) Fabric Menders, Except Garment	469) Financial Quantitative Analysts *** New ***
447) Fallers	470) Financial Specialists, All Other

471) Fine Artists, Including Painters, Sculptors, and Illustrators	496) First-Line Supervisors-Managers of Food Preparation and Serving Workers
473) Fire Inspectors	497) First-Line Supervisors-Managers of Helpers, Laborers, and Material Movers, Hand
474) Fire Inspectors and Investigators	498) First-Line Supervisors-Managers of Housekeeping and Janitorial Workers
475) Fire Investigators	499) First-Line Supervisors-Managers of Landscaping, Lawn Service, and Groundskeeping Workers
476) Fire-Prevention and Protection Engineers	500) First-Line Supervisors-Managers of Mechanics, Installers, and Repairers
477) First-Line Supervisors and Manager-Supervisors - Agricultural Crop Workers	501) First-Line Supervisors-Managers of Non-Retail Sales Workers
478) First-Line Supervisors and Manager-Supervisors - Animal Care Workers, Except Livestock	502) First-Line Supervisors-Managers of Office and Administrative Support Workers

479) First-Line Supervisors and Manager-Supervisors - Animal Husbandry Workers	503) First-Line Supervisors-Managers of Personal Service Workers
480) First-Line Supervisors and Manager-Supervisors - Fishery Workers	504) First-Line Supervisors-Managers of Police and Detectives
481) First-Line Supervisors and Manager-Supervisors - Horticultural Workers	505) First-Line Supervisors-Managers of Production and Operating Workers
482) First-Line Supervisors and Manager-Supervisors - Landscaping Workers	506) First-Line Supervisors-Managers of Retail Sales Workers
483) First-Line Supervisors and Manager-Supervisors - Logging Workers	507) First-Line Supervisors-Managers of Transportation and Material-Moving Machine and Vehicle Operators
484) First-Line Supervisors and Manager-Supervisors- Construction Trades Workers	508) First-Line Supervisors-Managers of Weapons Specialists--Crew Members
485) First-Line Supervisors and Manager-Supervisors- Extractive Workers	509) First-Line Supervisors-Managers, Protective Service Workers, All Other
486) First-Line Supervisors of Agricultural Crop and Horticultural Workers *** New ***	510) Fish and Game Wardens
487) First-Line Supervisors of Animal Husbandry and Animal Care Workers *** New ***	511) Fish Hatchery Managers
488) First-Line Supervisors, Administrative Support	512) Fishers and Related Fishing Workers
489) First-Line Supervisors, Customer Service	513) Fitness and Wellness Coordinators *** New ***
490) First-Line Supervisors-Managers of Air Crew Members	514) Fitness Trainers and Aerobics Instructors

491) First-Line Supervisors-Managers of All Other Tactical Operations Specialists	515) Fitters, Structural Metal- Precision
492) First-Line Supervisors-Managers of Construction Trades and Extraction Workers	516) Flight Attendant *** New ***
493) First-Line Supervisors-Managers of Correctional Officers	517) Flight Attendants
494) First-Line Supervisors-Managers of Farming, Fishing, and Forestry Workers	518) Floor Layers, Except Carpet, Wood, and Hard Tiles
495) First-Line Supervisors-Managers of Fire Fighting and Prevention Workers	519) Floor Sanders and Finishers
520) Floral Designers	551) Funeral Directors
521) Food and Tobacco Roasting, Baking, and Drying Machine Operators and Tenders	552) Furnace, Kiln, Oven, Drier, and Kettle Operators and Tenders
522) Food Batchmakers	553) Furniture Finishers
523) Food Cooking Machine Operators and Tenders	554) Gaming and Sports Book Writers and Runners
524) Food Preparation and Serving Related Workers, All Other	555) Gaming Cage Workers
525) Food Preparation Workers	556) Gaming Change Persons and Booth Cashiers
526) Food Science Technicians	557) Gaming Dealers
527) Food Scientists and Technologists	558) Gaming Managers
528) Food Servers, Nonrestaurant	559) Gaming Service Workers, All Other
529) Food Service Managers	560) Gaming Supervisors
530) Foreign Language and Literature Teachers, Postsecondary	561) Gaming Surveillance Officers and Gaming Investigators
531) Forensic Science Technicians	562) Gas Appliance Repairers

532) Forest and Conservation Technicians	563) Gas Compressor and Gas Pumping Station Operators
533) Forest and Conservation Workers	564) Gas Compressor Operators
534) Forest Fire Fighters	565) Gas Distribution Plant Operators
535) Forest Fire Fighting and Prevention Supervisors	566) Gas Plant Operators
536) Forest Fire Inspectors and Prevention Specialists	567) Gas Processing Plant Operators
537) Foresters	568) Gas Pumping Station Operators
538) Forestry and Conservation Science Teachers, Postsecondary	569) Gaugers
539) Forging Machine Setters, Operators, and Tenders, Metal and Plastic	570) Gem and Diamond Workers
540) Foundry Mold and Coremakers	571) General and Operations Managers
541) Frame Wirers, Central Office	572) General Farmworkers
542) Fraud Examiners, Investigators and Analysts *** New ***	573) Genetic Counselors *** New ***
543) Freight and Cargo Inspectors *** New ***	574) Geneticists *** New ***
544) Freight Forwarders *** New ***	575) Geodetic Surveyors *** New ***
545) Freight Inspectors	576) Geographers
546) Freight, Stock, and Material Movers, Hand	577) Geographic Information Systems Technicians *** New ***
547) Fuel Cell Engineers *** New ***	578) Geography Teachers, Postsecondary
548) Fuel Cell Technicians *** New ***	579) Geological and Petroleum Technicians
549) Fundraisers *** New ***	580) Geological Data Technicians
550) Funeral Attendants	581) Geological Sample Test Technicians

582) Geologists	607) Health Diagnosing and Treating Practitioners, All Other
583) Geoscientists, Except Hydrologists and Geographers	608) Health Educators
584) Geospatial Information Scientists and Technologists *** New ***	609) Health Specialties Teachers, Postsecondary
585) Geothermal Production Managers *** New ***	610) Health Technologists and Technicians, All Other
586) Geothermal Technicians *** New ***	611) Healthcare Practitioners and Technical Workers, All Other
587) Glass Blowers, Molders, Benders, and Finishers	612) Healthcare Support Workers, All Other
588) Glass Cutting Machine Setters and Set-Up Operators	613) Hearing Aid Specialists *** New ***
589) Glaziers	614) Heat Treating Equipment Setters, Operators, and Tenders, Metal and Plastic
590) Government Property Inspectors and Investigators	615) Heat Treating, Annealing, and Tempering Machine Operators and Tenders, Metal and Plastic
591) Government Service Executives	616) Heaters, Metal and Plastic
592) Grader, Bulldozer, and Scraper Operators	617) Heating and Air Conditioning Mechanics
593) Graders and Sorters, Agricultural Products	618) Heating Equipment Setters and Set-Up Operators, Metal and Plastic
594) Graduate Teaching Assistants	619) Heating, Air Conditioning, and Refrigeration Mechanics and Installers
595) Graphic Designers	620) Helpers, Construction Trades, All Other

596) Green Marketers *** New ***	621) Helpers--Brickmasons, Blockmasons, Stonemasons, and Tile and Marble Setters
597) Grinding and Polishing Workers, Hand	622) Helpers--Carpenters
598) Grinding, Honing, Lapping, and Deburring Machine Set-Up Operators	623) Helpers--Electricians
599) Grinding, Lapping, Polishing, and Buffing Machine Tool Setters, Operators, and Tenders, Metal and Plastic	624) Helpers--Extraction Workers
600) Grips and Set-Up Workers, Motion Picture Sets, Studios, and Stages	625) Helpers--Installation, Maintenance, and Repair Workers
601) Grounds Maintenance Workers, All Other	626) Helpers--Painters, Paperhangers, Plasterers, and Stucco Masons
602) Hairdressers, Hairstylists, and Cosmetologists	627) Helpers--Pipelayers, Plumbers, Pipefitters, and Steamfitters
603) Hand and Portable Power Tool Repairers	628) Helpers--Production Workers
604) Hand Compositors and Typesetters	629) Helpers--Roofers
605) Hazardous Materials Removal Workers	629) Helpers--Roofers
606) Health and Safety Engineers, Except Mining Safety Engineers and Inspectors	630) Highway Maintenance Workers

631) Highway Patrol Pilots	656) Industrial Engineering Technicians
632) Historians	657) Industrial Engineering Technologists *** New ***
633) History Teachers, Postsecondary	658) Industrial Engineers

634) Histotechnologists and Histologic Technicians *** New ***	659) Industrial Machinery Mechanics
635) Hoist and Winch Operators	660) Industrial Production Managers
636) Home Appliance Installers	661) Industrial Safety and Health Engineers
637) Home Appliance Repairers	662) Industrial Truck and Tractor Operators
638) Home Economics Teachers, Postsecondary	663) Industrial-Organizational Psychologists
639) Home Health Aides	664) Infantry
640) Hospitalists *** New ***	665) Infantry Officers
641) Hosts and Hostesses, Restaurant, Lounge, and Coffee Shop	666) Informatics Nurse Specialists *** New ***
642) Hotel, Motel, and Resort Desk Clerks	667) Information and Record Clerks, All Other
643) Housekeeping Supervisors	668) Information Security Analysts *** New ***
644) Human Factors Engineers and Ergonomists *** New ***	669) Information Technology Project Managers *** New ***
645) Human Resources Assistants, Except Payroll and Timekeeping	670) Inspectors, Testers, Sorters, Samplers, and Weighers
646) Human Resources Manager *** New ***	671) Installation, Maintenance, and Repair Workers, All Other
647) Human Resources Managers	672) Instructional Coordinators
648) Human Resources Managers, All Other	673) Instructional Designers and Technologists *** New ***
649) Human Resources, Training, and Labor Relations Specialists, All Other	674) Insulation Workers, Floor, Ceiling, and Wall
650) Hunters and Trappers	675) Insulation Workers, Mechanical

651) Hydroelectric Plant Technicians *** New ***	676) Insurance Adjusters, Examiners, and Investigators
652) Hydroelectric Production Managers *** New ***	677) Insurance Appraisers, Auto Damage
653) Hydrologists	678) Insurance Claims and Policy Processing Clerks
654) Immigration and Customs Inspectors	679) Insurance Claims Clerks
655) Industrial Ecologists *** New ***	680) Insurance Policy Processing Clerks

681) Insurance Sales Agents	703) Landscaping and Groundskeeping Workers
682) Insurance Underwriters	704) Lathe and Turning Machine Tool Setters, Operators, and Tenders, Metal and Plastic
683) Intelligence Analysts *** New ***	705) Laundry and Drycleaning Machine Operators and Tenders, Except Pressing
684) Interior Designers	706) Laundry and Dry-Cleaning Workers
685) Internists, General	707) Law Clerks
686) Interpreters and Translators	708) Law Teachers, Postsecondary
687) Interviewers, Except Eligibility and Loan	709) Lawn Service Managers
688) Investment Fund Managers *** New ***	710) Lawyers
689) Investment Underwriters *** New ***	711) Lay-Out Workers, Metal and Plastic
690) Irradiated-Fuel Handlers	712) Legal Secretaries
691) Janitorial Supervisors	713) Legal Support Workers, All Other

692) Janitors and Cleaners, Except Maids and Housekeeping Cleaners	714) Legislators
693) Jewelers	715) Letterpress Setters and Set-Up Operators
694) Jewelers and Precious Stone and Metal Workers	716) Librarians
695) Job Printers	717) Library Assistants, Clerical
696) Judges, Magistrate Judges, and Magistrates	718) Library Science Teachers, Postsecondary
697) Judicial Law Clerks *** New ***	719) Library Technicians
698) Keyboard Instrument Repairers and Tuners	720) License Clerks
699) Kindergarten Teachers, Except Special Education	721) Licensed Practical and Licensed Vocational Nurses
700) Labor Relations Specialists *** New ***	722) Licensing Examiners and Inspectors
701) Laborers and Freight, Stock, and Material Movers, Hand	723) Life Scientists, All Other
702) Landscape Architects	724) Life, Physical, and Social Science Technicians, All Other

725) Lifeguards, Ski Patrol, and Other Recreational Protective Service Workers	749) Maids and Housekeeping Cleaners
726) Loading Machine Operators, Underground Mining	750) Mail Clerks and Mail Machine Operators, Except Postal Service
727) Loan Counselor *** New ***	751) Mail Clerks, Except Mail Machine Operators and Postal Service
728) Loan Counselors	752) Mail Machine Operators, Preparation and Handling

729) Loan Interviewers and Clerks	753) Maintenance and Repair Worker *** New ***
730) Loan Officers	754) Maintenance and Repair Workers, General
731) Locker Room, Coatroom, and Dressing Room Attendants	755) Maintenance Workers, Machinery
732) Locksmiths and Safe Repairers	756) Makeup Artists, Theatrical and Performance
733) Locomotive Engineers	757) Management Analysts
734) Locomotive Firers	758) Managers, All Other
735) Lodging Managers	759) Manicurists and Pedicurists
736) Log Graders and Scalers	760) Manufactured Building and Mobile Home Installers
737) Logging Equipment Operators	761) Manufacturing Engineering Technologists *** New ***
738) Logging Tractor Operators	762) Manufacturing Engineers *** New ***
739) Logging Workers, All Other	763) Manufacturing Production Technicians *** New ***
740) Logisticians	764) Mapping Technicians
741) Logistics Analysts *** New ***	765) Marine Architects
742) Logistics Engineers *** New ***	766) Marine Cargo Inspectors
743) Logistics Managers *** New ***	767) Marine Engineers
744) Loss Prevention Managers *** New ***	768) Marine Engineers and Naval Architects
745) Low Vision Therapists, Orientation and Mobility Specialists, and Vision Rehabilitation Therapists *** New ***	769) Market Research Analysts
746) Machine Feeders and Offbearers	770) Market Research Analysts and Marketing Specialists *** New ***

747) Machinists	771) Marketing Managers
748) Magnetic Resonance Imaging Technologists *** New ***	772) Marking and Identification Printing Machine Setters and Set-Up Operators

773) Marking Clerks	800) Medical Assistants
774) Marriage and Family Therapists	801) Medical Equipment Preparers
775) Massage Therapists	802) Medical Equipment Repairers
776) Material Moving Workers, All Other	803) Medical Records and Health Information Technicians
777) Materials Engineers	804) Medical Scientists, Except Epidemiologists
778) Materials Inspectors	805) Medical Secretaries
779) Materials Scientists	806) Medical Transcriptionists
780) Mates- Ship, Boat, and Barge	807) Meeting and Convention Planners
781) Mathematical Science Occupations, All Other	808) Mental Health and Substance Abuse Social Workers
782) Mathematical Science Teachers, Postsecondary	809) Mental Health Counselors
783) Mathematical Technicians	810) Merchandise Displayers and Window Trimmers
784) Mathematicians	811) Metal Fabricators, Structural Metal Products
785) Meat, Poultry, and Fish Cutters and Trimmers	812) Metal Molding, Coremaking, and Casting Machine Operators and Tenders
786) Mechanical Door Repairers	813) Metal Molding, Coremaking, and Casting Machine Setters and Set-Up Operators
787) Mechanical Drafters	814) Metal Workers and Plastic Workers, All Other

788) Mechanical Engineering Technicians	815) Metal-Refining Furnace Operators and Tenders
789) Mechanical Engineering Technologists *** New ***	816) Meter Mechanics
790) Mechanical Engineers	817) Meter Readers, Utilities
791) Mechanical Inspectors	818) Methane Landfill Gas Generation System Technicians *** New ***
792) Mechatronics Engineers *** New ***	819) Methane/Landfill Gas Collection System Operators *** New ***
793) Media and Communication Equipment Workers, All Other	820) Microbiologists
794) Media and Communication Workers, All Other	821) Microsystems Engineers *** New ***
795) Medical and Clinical Laboratory Technicians	822) Middle School Teachers, Except Special and Vocational Education
796) Medical and Clinical Laboratory Technologists	823) Midwives *** New ***
797) Medical and Health Services Managers	824) Military Enlisted Tactical Operations and Air--Weapons Specialists and Crew Members, All Other
798) Medical and Public Health Social Workers	825) Military Officer Special and Tactical Operations Leaders--Managers, All Other
799) Medical Appliance Technicians	826) Milling and Planing Machine Setters, Operators, and Tenders, Metal and Plastic

827) Millwrights	850) Multiple Machine Tool Setters, Operators, and Tenders, Metal and Plastic

828) Mine Cutting and Channeling Machine Operators	851) Municipal Clerks
829) Mining and Geological Engineers, Including Mining Safety Engineers	852) Municipal Fire Fighters
830) Mining Machine Operators, All Other	853) Municipal Fire Fighting and Prevention Supervisors
831) Mixing and Blending Machine Setters, Operators, and Tenders	854) Museum Technicians and Conservators
832) Mobile Heavy Equipment Mechanics, Except Engines	855) Music Arrangers and Orchestrators
833) Model and Mold Makers, Jewelry	856) Music Composers and Arrangers *** New ***
834) Model Makers, Metal and Plastic	857) Music Directors
835) Model Makers, Wood	858) Music Directors and Composers
836) Models	859) Music Therapists *** New ***
837) Mold Makers, Hand	860) Musical Instrument Repairers and Tuners
838) Molders, Shapers, and Casters, Except Metal and Plastic	861) Musicians and Singers
839) Molding and Casting Workers	862) Musicians, Instrumental
840) Molding, Coremaking, and Casting Machine Setters, Operators, and Tenders, Metal and Plastic	863) Nannies *** New ***
841) Molecular and Cellular Biologists *** New ***	864) Nanosystems Engineers *** New ***
842) Morticians, Undertakers, and Funeral Directors *** New ***	865) Nanotechnology Engineering Technicians *** New ***
843) Motion Picture Projectionists	866) Nanotechnology Engineering Technologists *** New ***
844) Motor Vehicle Inspectors	867) Natural Sciences Managers

845) Motor Vehicle Operators, All Other	868) Naturopathic Physicians *** New ***
846) Motorboat Mechanics	869) Network and Computer Systems Administrator *** New ***
847) Motorboat Operators	870) Network and Computer Systems Administrators
848) Motorcycle Mechanics	871) Network Systems and Data Communications Analysts
849) Multi-Media Artists and Animators	872) Neurodiagnostic Technologists *** New ***

873) Neurologists *** New ***	900) Occupational Health and Safety Technicians
874) Neuropsychologists and Clinical Neuropsychologists *** New ***	901) Occupational Therapist Aides
875) New Accounts Clerks	902) Occupational Therapist Assistants
876) Non-Destructive Testing Specialists *** New ***	903) Occupational Therapists
877) Nonelectrolytic Plating and Coating Machine Operators and Tenders, Metal and Plastic	904) Office and Administrative Support Workers, All Other
878) Nonelectrolytic Plating and Coating Machine Setters and Set-Up Operators, Metal and Plastic	905) Office Clerks, General
879) Nonfarm Animal Caretakers	906) Office Machine and Cash Register Servicers
880) Nuclear Engineers	907) Office Machine Operators, Except Computer
881) Nuclear Equipment Operation Technicians	908) Offset Lithographic Press Setters and Set-Up Operators

882) Nuclear Medicine Physicians *** New ***	909) Online Merchants *** New ***
883) Nuclear Medicine Technologists	910) Operating Engineers
884) Nuclear Monitoring Technicians	911) Operating Engineers and Other Construction Equipment Operators
885) Nuclear Power Reactor Operators	912) Operations Research Analysts
886) Nuclear Technicians	913) Ophthalmic Laboratory Technicians
887) Numerical Control Machine Tool Operators and Tenders, Metal and Plastic	914) Ophthalmic Medical Technicians *** New ***
888) Numerical Tool and Process Control Programmers	915) Ophthalmic Medical Technologists *** New ***
889) Nurse Anesthetists *** New ***	916) Ophthalmologists *** New ***
890) Nurse Midwives *** New ***	917) Optical Instrument Assemblers
891) Nurse Practitioners *** New ***	918) Opticians, Dispensing
892) Nursery and Greenhouse Manager *** New ***	919) Optometrists
893) Nursery and Greenhouse Managers	920) Oral and Maxillofacial Surgeons
894) Nursery Workers	921) Order Clerks
895) Nursing Aides, Orderlies, and Attendants	922) Order Fillers, Wholesale and Retail Sales
896) Nursing Assistants *** New ***	923) Orderlies *** New ***
897) Nursing Instructors and Teachers, Postsecondary	924) Ordinary Seamen and Marine Oilers
898) Obstetricians and Gynecologists	925) Orthodontists
899) Occupational Health and Safety Specialists	926) Orthoptists *** New ***

927) Orthotists and Prosthetists	955) Personnel Recruiters
928) Outdoor Power Equipment and Other Small Engine Mechanics	956) Pest Control Workers
929) Packaging and Filling Machine Operators and Tenders	957) Pesticide Handlers, Sprayers, and Applicators, Vegetation
930) Packers and Packagers, Hand	958) Petroleum Engineers
931) Painters and Illustrators	959) Petroleum Pump System Operators
932) Painters, Construction and Maintenance	960) Petroleum Pump System Operators, Refinery Operators, and Gaugers
933) Painters, Transportation Equipment	961) Petroleum Refinery and Control Panel Operators
934) Painting, Coating, and Decorating Workers	962) Pewter Casters and Finishers
935) Pantograph Engravers	963) Pharmacists
936) Paper Goods Machine Setters, Operators, and Tenders	964) Pharmacy Aides
937) Paperhangers	965) Pharmacy Technicians
938) Paralegals and Legal Assistants	966) Philosophy and Religion Teachers, Postsecondary
939) Park Naturalists	967) Phlebotomists *** New ***
940) Parking Enforcement Workers	968) Photoengravers
941) Parking Lot Attendants	969) Photoengraving and Lithographing Machine Operators and Tenders
942) Parts Salespersons	970) Photographers
943) Paste-Up Workers	971) Photographers, Scientific
944) Pathologists *** New ***	972) Photographic Hand Developers
945) Patient Representatives *** New ***	973) Photographic Process Workers

946) Patternmakers, Metal and Plastic	974) Photographic Process Workers and Processing Machine Operators *** New ***
947) Patternmakers, Wood	975) Photographic Processing Machine Operators
948) Paving, Surfacing, and Tamping Equipment Operators	976) Photographic Reproduction Technicians
949) Payroll and Timekeeping Clerks	977) Photographic Retouchers and Restorers
950) Pediatricians, General	978) Photonics Engineers *** New ***
951) Percussion Instrument Repairers and Tuners	979) Photonics Technicians *** New ***
952) Personal and Home Care Aides	980) Physical Medicine and Rehabilitation Physicians *** New ***
953) Personal Care and Service Workers, All Other	981) Physical Scientists, All Other
954) Personal Financial Advisors	982) Physical Therapist Aides

983) Physical Therapist Assistants	1009) Police Identification and Records Officers
984) Physical Therapists	1010) Police Patrol Officers
985) Physician Assistants	1011) Police, Fire, and Ambulance Dispatchers
986) Physicians and Surgeons, All Other	1012) Political Science Teachers, Postsecondary
987) Physicists	1013) Political Scientists
988) Physics Teachers, Postsecondary	1014) Postal Service Clerks
989) Pile-Driver Operators	1015) Postal Service Mail Carriers

990) Pilots, Ship	1016) Postal Service Mail Sorters, Processors, and Processing Machine Operators
991) Pipe Fitters	1017) Postmasters and Mail Superintendents
992) Pipelayers	1018) Postsecondary Teachers, All Other
993) Pipelaying Fitters	1019) Potters
994) Plant and System Operators, All Other	1020) Pourers and Casters, Metal
995) Plant Scientists	1021) Power Distributors and Dispatchers
996) Plasterers and Stucco Masons	1022) Power Generating Plant Operators, Except Auxiliary Equipment Operators
997) Plastic Molding and Casting Machine Operators and Tenders	1023) Power Plant Operators
998) Plastic Molding and Casting Machine Setters and Set-Up Operators	1024) Precious Metal Workers *** New ***
999) Plate Finishers	1025) Precision Agriculture Technicians *** New ***
1000) Platemakers	1026) Precision Devices Inspectors and Testers
1001) Plating and Coating Machine Setters, Operators, and Tenders, Metal and Plastic	1027) Precision Dyers
1002) Plumbers	1028) Precision Etchers and Engravers, Hand or Machine
1003) Plumbers, Pipefitters, and Steamfitters	1029) Precision Instrument and Equipment Repairers, All Other

1004) Podiatrists	1030) Precision Lens Grinders and Polishers
1005) Poets and Lyricists	1031) Precision Mold and Pattern Casters, except Nonferrous Metals
1006) Poets, Lyricists and Creative Writers *** New ***	1032) Precision Pattern and Die Casters, Nonferrous Metals
1007) Police and Sheriffs Patrol Officers	1033) Precision Printing Workers
1008) Police Detectives	1034) Prepress Technician *** New ***

1035) Prepress Technicians and Workers	1067) Psychiatric Technicians
1036) Preschool Teachers, Except Special Education	1068) Psychiatrists
1037) Press and Press Brake Machine Setters and Set-Up Operators, Metal and Plastic	1069) Psychologists, All Other
1038) Pressers, Delicate Fabrics	1070) Psychology Teachers, Postsecondary
1039) Pressers, Hand	1071) Public Address System and Other Announcers
1040) Pressers, Textile, Garment, and Related Materials	1072) Public Relations Managers
1041) Pressing Machine Operators and Tenders- Textile, Garment, and Related Materials	1073) Public Relations Specialists
1042) Pressure Vessel Inspectors	1074) Public Transportation Inspectors
1043) Preventive Medicine Physicians *** New ***	1075) Pump Operators, Except Wellhead Pumpers
1044) Print Binding and Finishing Workers *** New ***	1076) Punching Machine Setters and Set-Up Operators, Metal and Plastic

1045) Printing Machine Operators	1077) Purchasing Agents and Buyers, Farm Products
1046) Printing Press Machine Operators and Tenders	1078) Purchasing Agents, Except Wholesale, Retail, and Farm Products
1047) Printing Press Operators *** New ***	1079) Purchasing Managers
1048) Private Detectives and Investigators	1080) Quality Control Analysts *** New ***
1049) Private Sector Executives	1081) Quality Control Systems Managers *** New ***
1050) Probation Officers and Correctional Treatment Specialists	1082) Radar and Sonar Technicians
1051) Procurement Clerks	1083) Radiation Therapists
1052) Producers	1084) Radio and Television Announcers
1053) Producers and Directors	1085) Radio Frequency Identification Device Specialists *** New ***
1054) Product Safety Engineers	1086) Radio Mechanic *** New ***
1055) Production Helpers	1087) Radio Mechanics
1056) Production Inspectors, Testers, Graders, Sorters, Samplers, Weighers	1088) Radio Operators
1057) Production Laborers	1089) Radiologic Technician *** New ***
1058) Production Workers, All Other	1090) Radiologic Technicians
1059) Production, Planning, and Expediting Clerks	1091) Radiologic Technologists
1060) Professional Photographers	1092) Radiologic Technologists and Technicians
1061) Program Directors	1093) Radiologists *** New ***
1062) Proofreaders and Copy Markers	1094) Rail Car Repairers

1063) Property, Real Estate, and Community Association Managers	1095) Rail Transportation Workers, All Other
1064) Prosthodontists	1096) Rail Yard Engineers, Dinkey Operators, and Hostlers
1065) Protective Service Workers, All Other	1097) Railroad Brake, Signal, and Switch Operators
1066) Psychiatric Aides	1098) Railroad Conductors and Yardmasters

1099) Railroad Inspectors	1130) Respiratory Therapy Technicians
1100) Railroad Yard Workers	1131) Retail Loss Prevention Specialists *** New ***
1101) Rail-Track Laying and Maintenance Equipment Operators	1132) Retail Salespersons
1102) Range Managers	1133) Riggers
1103) Real Estate Brokers	1134) Risk Management Specialists *** New ***
1104) Real Estate Sales Agents	1135) Robotics Engineers *** New ***
1105) Receptionists and Information Clerks	1136) Robotics Technicians *** New ***
1106) Recreation and Fitness Studies Teachers, Postsecondary	1137) Rock Splitters, Quarry
1107) Recreation Workers	1138) Rolling Machine Setters, Operators, and Tenders, Metal and Plastic
1108) Recreational Therapists	1139) Roof Bolters, Mining
1109) Recreational Vehicle Service Technicians	1140) Roofers
1110) Recycling and Reclamation Workers *** New ***	1141) Rotary Drill Operators, Oil and Gas

1111) Recycling Coordinators *** New ***	1142) Rough Carpenters
1112) Reed or Wind Instrument Repairers and Tuners	1143) Roustabouts, Oil and Gas
1113) Refractory Materials Repairers, Except Brickmasons	1144) Sailors and Marine Oilers
1114) Refrigeration Mechanics	1145) Sales Agents, Financial Services
1115) Refuse and Recyclable Material Collectors	1146) Sales Agents, Securities and Commodities
1116) Registered Nurses	1147) Sales and Related Workers, All Other
1117) Registered Nurses *** New ***	1148) Sales Engineers
1118) Regulatory Affairs Managers *** New ***	1149) Sales Managers
1119) Regulatory Affairs Specialists *** New ***	1150) Sales Representatives, Agricultural
1120) Rehabilitation Counselors	1151) Sales Representatives, Chemical and Pharmaceutical
1121) Reinforcing Iron and Rebar Workers	1152) Sales Representatives, Electrical--Electronic
1122) Religious Workers, All Other	1153) Sales Representatives, Instruments
1123) Remote Sensing Scientists and Technologists *** New ***	1154) Sales Representatives, Mechanical Equipment and Supplies
1124) Remote Sensing Technicians *** New ***	1155) Sales Representatives, Medical
1125) Reporters and Correspondents	1156) Sales Representatives, Services, All Other

1126) Reservation and Transportation Ticket Agents	1157) Sales Representatives, Wholesale and Manufacturing, Except Technical and Scientific Products
1127) Reservation and Transportation Ticket Agents and Travel Clerks	1158) Sales Representatives, Wholesale and Manufacturing, Technical and Scientific Products
1128) Residential Advisors	1159) Sawing Machine Operators and Tenders
1129) Respiratory Therapists	1160) Sawing Machine Setters and Set-Up Operators

1161) Sawing Machine Setters, Operators, and Tenders, Wood	1186) Sewing Machine Operators, Garment
1162) Sawing Machine Tool Setters and Set-Up Operators, Metal and Plastic	1187) Sewing Machine Operators, Non-Garment
1163) Scanner Operators	1188) Shampooers
1164) Screen Printing Machine Setters and Set-Up Operators	1189) Shear and Slitter Machine Setters and Set-Up Operators, Metal and Plastic
1165) Sculptors	1190) Sheet Metal Workers
1166) Search Marketing Strategists *** New ***	1191) Sheriffs and Deputy Sheriffs
1167) Secondary School Teachers, Except Special and Vocational Education	1192) Ship and Boat Captains
1168) Secretaries, Except Legal, Medical, and Executive	1193) Ship Carpenters and Joiners
1169) Securities and Commodities Traders *** New ***	1194) Ship Engineers
1170) Securities, Commodities, and Financial Services Sales Agents	1195) Shipping, Receiving, and Traffic Clerks

1171) Security and Fire Alarm Systems Installers	1196) Shoe and Leather Workers and Repairers
1172) Security Guards	1197) Shoe Machine Operators and Tenders
1173) Security Management Specialists *** New ***	1198) Shop and Alteration Tailors
1174) Security Managers *** New ***	1199) Shuttle Car Operators
1175) Segmental Pavers	1200) Signal and Track Switch Repairers
1176) Self-Enrichment Education Teachers	1201) Silversmiths
1177) Semiconductor Processors	1202) Singers
1178) Separating, Filtering, Clarifying, Precipitating, and Still Machine Setters, Operators, and Tenders	1203) Sketch Artists
1179) Septic Tank Servicers and Sewer Pipe Cleaners	1204) Skin Care Specialists
1180) Service Station Attendants	1205) Slaughterers and Meat Packers
1181) Service Unit Operators, Oil, Gas, and Mining	1206) Slot Key Persons
1182) Set and Exhibit Designers	1207) Social and Community Service Managers
1183) Set Designers	1208) Social and Human Service Assistants
1184) Sewers, Hand	1209) Social Science Research Assistants
1185) Sewing Machine Operators	1210) Social Sciences Teachers, Postsecondary, All Other

1337) Tree Trimmers and Pruners	1363) Web Administrators *** New ***
1338) Truck Drivers, Heavy	1364) Web Developers *** New ***

1339) Truck Drivers, Heavy and Tractor-Trailer	1365) Weighers, Measurers, Checkers, and Samplers, Recordkeeping
1340) Truck Drivers, Light or Delivery Services	1366) Welder-Fitters
1341) Tutors *** New ***	1367) Welders and Cutters
1342) Typesetting and Composing Machine Operators and Tenders	1368) Welders, Cutters, and Welder Fitters *** New ***
1343) Umpires, Referees, and Other Sports Officials	1369) Welders, Cutters, Solderers, and Brazers
1344) Upholsterers	1370) Welders, Production
1345) Urban and Regional Planners	1371) Welding Machine Operators and Tenders
1346) Urologists *** New ***	1372) Welding Machine Setters and Set-Up Operators
1347) Ushers, Lobby Attendants, and Ticket Takers	1373) Welding, Soldering, and Brazing Machine Setters, Operators, and Tenders
1348) Validation Engineers *** New ***	1374) Welfare Eligibility Workers and Interviewers
1349) Valve and Regulator Repairers	1375) Well and Core Drill Operators
1350) Veterinarians	1376) Wellhead Pumpers
1351) Veterinary Assistants and Laboratory Animal Caretakers	1377) Wholesale and Retail Buyers, Except Farm Products
1352) Veterinary Technologists and Technicians	1378) Wind Energy Engineers *** New ***
1353) Video Game Designers *** New ***	1379) Wind Energy Operations Managers *** New ***
1354) Vocational Education Teachers Postsecondary	1380) Wind Energy Project Managers *** New ***

1355) Vocational Education Teachers, Middle School	1381) Wind Turbine Service Technicians *** New ***
1356) Vocational Education Teachers, Secondary School	1382) Woodworkers, All Other
1357) Waiters and Waitresses	1383) Woodworking Machine Operators and Tenders, Except Sawing
1358) Watch Repairers	1384) Woodworking Machine Setters and Set-Up Operators, Except Sawing
1359) Water and Liquid Waste Treatment Plant and System Operators	1385) Woodworking Machine Setters, Operators, and Tenders, Except Sawing
1360) Water Resource Specialists *** New ***	1386) Word Processors and Typists
1361) Water/Wastewater Engineers *** New ***	1387) Writers and Authors
1362) Weatherization Installers and Technicians *** New ***	1388) Zoologists and Wildlife Biologists

I AM THE HERO OF MY OWN LIFE

Becoming the person you have always wanted and needed to be.

Everyone dreams of becoming the very best version of themselves. You may want to be a professional ball player, a world-renowned painter, or simply the very best parent you can be. Achieving your full potential can seem like a mighty task to undertake, but it's possible once you release all the unhelpful traits that are holding you back. Take inventory of your inner traits to start moving towards being the person you want to be.

1. Recognize that you are already the person you want to be.

The secret to becoming all you want to be lies in remembering that you already are! You already are the very best version of yourself. You just need to know how to be this person. Everything you desire is already inside of you, and all the resources you need to create it are inside of you, too.

What you are looking for is not out there in the world. If your level of self-love, confidence or abundance is dependent on circumstances that are external to you, then you will live in constant fear of them being taken away. True inner power comes from believing that the source of all that you desire to become is within you

2. Look for roadblocks in your path.

There's a quote that says, "the only thing holding you back is you." This is true. However, you must take stock of any attributes or habits you have that do not reflect the person you want to be. This may even require speaking to a few loved ones and asking them if they notice any unhelpful attributes that may be holding you back.

Two common attributes that may be holding you back are:

Self-doubt: This is one attribute that can leave you immobile, never changing and never reaching your true potential. If you are afflicted by a fear of failure or insecurities, you need to combat them now. A great way to combat self-doubt is to look for evidence of your successes. Identify all the wonderful achievements you have already obtained. Then, reach out to a few close friends and have them tell you a few things they admire about you.

Procrastination: This undesirable trait generally comes down to your self-talk. You tell yourself you work well under pressure, or that the task won't take that long, so you don't have to do it right now. Putting it off for an hour becomes days, and the next thing you know you're pulling an all-nighter to finish.
Overcome procrastination by attempting to figure out why you put off tasks in the first place. Then, change the way you look at large tasks. Instead of trying to cram a lot of work into one sitting, tell yourself if you complete a small chunk, you can have a break. Also, go to an environment that is conducive to working - and not filled with possible distractions.

If you are struggling with deeply buried and painful memories, fears, depression, or substance abuse, you may not be able to tackle these issues on your own. Reach out to a trained mental health professional who can guide you through the process of healing old wounds so that you can claim the healthy, vibrant future you desire.

   3. Find your truth.

Every person has something they were born to do. You have a unique purpose for being here, and you have to find it. As Pablo Picasso declare, "The meaning of life is to find your gift. The purpose of life is to give it away."

Do a self-assessment to get closer to your truth, and closer to becoming the person you were meant to be.

Ask yourself these questions:
- What do you wake up for every morning? What makes you feel truly alive?
- What classes did you enjoy while in school? What do you like to learn more about?
- What jobs have you held that made you feel purposeful?
- What activities do you participate in that make you lose track of time because you love doing them so much?
- What do people frequently tell you you're good at?
- What ideas are you most passionate about?
- What can you simply not go without in this life?

4. Release any thoughts that contradict your truth.

Any time you think a negative, critical, fearful, or harmful thought about yourself, you are disconnecting from your truth. Any time you tell yourself you cannot do something or have something; it becomes a self-fulfilling prophecy - you cannot reach your goals this way. Your truth is that you have the ability to become anything you wish to become. All you have to do is believe it, and you can achieve it.

To stop unhelpful thoughts, strive to first identify them, then challenge them. If you find yourself saying "I can't do that" when trying a new thing, demand evidence that shows you can't. Many people have negative self-talk that does not serve them. Aim to become aware of these thoughts and replace them with positive statements, such as "I am afraid of trying this. But I won't know if I'm good at it unless I try."

Sometimes, believing in yourself can be difficult, especially when you have negative self-talk. As you learn to challenge negative self-talk, also began to envision yourself achieving your goals. Visualization can be a powerful motivator and help you to feel more confident in your abilities.

To practice visualization, go into a quiet room and sit comfortably. Close your eyes. Take a deep breath. See yourself accomplishing a goal. Try this with smaller goals, such as losing 10 Kg's or completing a grade with A's, Imagine yourself at the finish line, but also go back and envision every small step you will have to take to get there example: eating right and working out or studying daily and getting tutoring.

5. Listen for the answers within you.

Too many of us ignore the soft inner calling of our intuition which loves and adores us. It reminds us to just relax and trust. You see, there is often a much louder voice which booms through our minds and tell us to get to action. It prevents us from trusting ourselves, and instead lures us in to looking to the material and superficial world for all that we seek.

Practice making the distinction between the harsh, critical voice that pushes you, and the soft, nurturing voice which loves and supports you. Then, make a conscious choice about which one you are going to listen to.

6. Identify what you don't want.

You cannot fully reach your potential unless you know what that is. Oftentimes in life, our goals change, and, occasionally, we may feel lost and have no idea what we're working towards. Knowing what you don't want, however, pushes you into the direction you should be moving and allows you to set clear boundaries.

7. Practice optimistic thinking.

Science reveals that optimistic people tend to live longer and enjoy greater physical and mental health than those who think pessimistically. Seeing the glass as half-full means smiling often, refraining from comparing yourself to others in a competitive way, and finding the silver lining in most situations.

One research-backed way to become more optimistic is to do the best possible future self-exercise. In this exercise, you will write expressively about your future self for 20 minutes. "Think about your life in the future. Imagine that everything has gone as well as it possibly could. You have worked hard and succeeded at accomplishing all your life goals. Think of this as the realization of all your life dreams.

Now, write about what you imagined." Complete the exercise three days in a row.

8. Take risks.

Have you been nervous up until now to put yourself out there for fear of failure? Learn to be courageous and take advantage of more opportunities that come your way. Successful people don't get that way by playing it safe all the time. Read situations and people to determine which opportunities are worth your time, then, bunker down to develop a winning strategy.

Risk-takers are constantly experimenting with their methods to refine them and develop the most efficient way of getting results.

Never stop experimenting.
Expect success, but readily embrace failure.
You should always envision yourself accomplishing your goals.
 However, failure is inevitable.

Take mistakes in stride and acknowledge them as teachable moments to refine your skills and come back stronger than before. Constantly living within your comfort zone can lead to boredom and disengagement.

Step outside your comfort zone by taking initiative and taking on a project beyond your regular duties. Volunteer, and when you do, work with a population that you have previously been biased towards example: substance abusers, homeless people, etc.). Another way to shake up your routine is to stop taking a backseat in your work. Step into a leadership position where you have more responsibilities and more people counting on you.

9. Learn to say "no" sometimes.

 Risk-takers may be classically known to say "yes" more than "no". This inclination is built on not letting fear or doubts cause them to miss incredible opportunities for growth. However, when you are striving to reach your full potential, you must learn to use your voice and say "no" on occasion. Respect yourself and uplift your core values by refusing to participate in activities that do not serve your goals.

Of course, there will be times when you are urged to say "yes" to preserve a relationship. In these situations, agreeing to do something might serve your goals, if having that person in your life provides a positive impact.

If you are confident that saying "no" is the best option for you, do so without providing an excuse or an apology.

10. Promoting Good Vibes

Surround yourself with positive people. The people you spend the most time with reflect you. As the old saying goes, "birds of a feather flock together."

Examine your social circle to see if the individuals you are around on a daily or weekly basis represent you well. These people should have characteristics and traits that you admire, traits that someday may rub off on you. Resist the urge to surround yourself with people who may be fun or exciting in the moment but pull you away from reaching your potential.

Hans F. Hansen said, "People inspire you or they drain you. Choose them wisely." Exercise this in your life by assessing those closest to you. Think about how you feel with these people. Do they lift you up and motivate you? Do they encourage you to have healthy, positive habits?

If you have people around you that are draining or bringing you down, you could be sacrificing reaching your potential by keeping them in your life. Decide if you need to cut off contact with people who are not representative of the life you want to lead.

Magnify your strengths. Discover your unique abilities and talents and be sure to make use of them every day. By doing this, you hone your abilities and make them even better. When you work to your strengths, you give the world the very best of you. Plus, you boost your self-confidence and feel more accomplished.

This is not to say it is unimportant to analyze your weaknesses - it is very important to know what areas you could use work. However, knowing and playing to your strengths enables you to realize your dreams and self-actualize.

Think about it: you were given these gifts for a reason. Use them!

    11. Treat yourself.

While you are on the journey of self-actualization, remember to take time off to be good to yourself. Pushing yourself further and further can be a good thing, but everyone requires breaks and self-care to jump back in the saddle at 100%. When you are feeling stressed or overwhelmed, turn to a few self-care practices that let you clear your mind and relieve negative energy so that it does not affect the work you are doing on yourself.

Self-care consists of any activities you can engage in that promote mental, physical, or emotional well-being.

This will look different for different people. It may include taking a bubble bath, writing in a journal, exercising, meditating, praying or virtually any activity you find relaxing.

Test out a few activities to see what works best for you and call on them when you're feeling stressed.
A daily or weekly ritual might be a great idea to implement to fend off stress before it becomes too much.

12. Build self-trust and relax.
Maintain a good relationship with yourself. Sometimes, we can get so caught up in life that we neglect ourselves.

Regularly get in touch with your inner self and run a diagnostic. Is there something that you need?
Do you need a break?
Spend time with yourself and frequently reassess where you're headed and if you like where you're going.

We are all works in progress, so don't fret when you have to change your plans or regroup. Be a champion for yourself!

NOTES

_____

_____

_____

_____

_____

_____

_____

LETTER TO THE KING

Open Letter to The Boy Becoming a Man (Matt Jacobson)

Dear Son,

It is a great honor and privilege to be able to write this letter to you. I'm blessed to be your dad. Son, you are becoming a man. What follows comes from a heart that truly wants the very best for you in this life and, more importantly, the next.

THE NEXT LIFE

The day of your death is already marked. Unknown to us, God has decided how long we will live. You may live a "natural" life of about 70 or 80 years, or you may be killed by a drunk driver moments after reading this letter. You simply don't know when you will be required to give an account of yourself to God. But you most certainly will. The Bible says, ". . . it is appointed for a man to die once and after that, the judgement:" - **Hebrews 9:27**

There is a man spoken of in the New Testament who went about his happy life, building bigger and bigger barns to hold all his possessions. Just when he was really enjoying his self-absorbed life, he heard the words (from God), "You fool! Tonight, your soul is required of you." - **Luke 12:20**

Long before you came to the threshold of manhood, the world was busy trying to press you into its mold – to conform you to its values – to make you think in a worldly manner. But we are Christian men, followers of Christ. The Bible says, "Be not conformed to the world." - **Romans 12:2**

That means we are not to think like, or act according to the values of, this world. As a man making his way in the world, you must wrestle with this if you are to walk worthy of the name 'Christian' and remember, your appointment with God is already set.

THIS LIFE

Whether you like it or not, you are in the process of establishing your reputation. Welcome to manhood. What kind of man will you be? That's something you choose every day. Anyone can have a "moment" when they seem to others to have good character only to have the next decision remove that good will. Consistency over time is the only way to reveal your true character to others. You are building who you are every day. You look after your character and God will look after your reputation.

CHOICES

As a young man your age, I had a poor understanding of how the choices I made would impact my future. It is as true today as it ever was – what you choose today will affect tomorrow. If you tune your ear carefully to the important things of life, you will have a growing sense that the substance of life is little more than a combination of two things: 1) Choices you make each day and, 2) Your response to events, both positive and negative) and circumstances in your life that you didn't cause.

I'll never forget an old poster of John Wayne, hanging on the wall of some office I had walked through many years ago. There's only one John Wayne. But the caption below his photograph is what really stuck in my mind: Life's Tough . . . but, It's Tougher if You're Stupid. Which is to say, if you make a habit of wrong choices, you are in for a tough life. The choices you make today are making your future.

FRIENDS

You have a winsome way about you, son. You can get along with just about anybody. That is a real gift. And, you are a real gift – a truly worthy person. While you, as Christian young man, are commanded by Christ to be kind to people, there are many who are not worthy of your friendship – not worthy of your trust.

The Bible makes it clear that, "Bad company corrupts good morals." 1 Corinthians 5:33. You will be known by the company you keep. People will make a judgment about the quality of your mettle (your worth as a person) by the quality of those you have chosen to count among your friends.

Test those with whom you would spend time by this standard:
- Are they the kind of people who will challenge me to be a better person?
- Will these guys challenge me to be more like Christ?

One of these days you are going to happen across a stream that is flowing crystal clear and then, downstream, it will be met by another muddy stream flowing into the channel.
The clean stream will never clean up the dirty stream – not far from where they join, both streams are muddy.
So, it is with life. Choose friends of clean character, friends worthy of you.
Be polite to everyone but give your friendship only to those of sound character.
Those of poor character, while needing your guidance, are not worthy of your friendship.

YOUR FUTURE WIFE
You are some woman's dream-come-true, Son.
Right now, your wife is somewhere in the world.
Don't you wonder how she's spending her time?
Do you think she's wondering how you are spending yours?
How would you feel right now if you could look through a window at your future wife and see her without her seeing you?
What kind of behavior do you expect from her?
What if her parents were away and she had a boyfriend over?
And they had their hands all over each other and he was kissing her?
Wait a minute, that's your wife! What's he doing with your future wife?
I hope you'd want to thrash him for what he is stealing from you.

Why was your wife giving herself, a little at a time, to other guys?
Does it make you crazy to think that some slob is even near her trying to put his slimy lips on her beautiful mouth?
If you want to marry a girl who hasn't given herself to every jerk that chased her; if you want a girl who has saved herself for the man of her dreams (you);
If you want a girl who has honored Christ with her life and body and mind –

YOU OWE HER THE SAME!
You will never be sorry for waiting for your wife.
The world's (and most of the Church's) thinking says, "Hey, date around, get to know people."
Not so for the follower of Christ. Could you marry various people and have a great marriage? Sure. But God knows exactly who you will marry. Don't give one bit of yourself to some person you won't marry; not physically or emotionally. Don't get entangled in a relationship, even if it isn't physical, with someone who isn't your future wife.
Only the girl of your dreams deserves to know you intimately and to know the secrets of your heart.
Start your romance long before you even meet her. Any fool can run from one relationship to the next but, it takes a real lover to keep one woman satisfied for life.
You will never regret being completely faithful to your wife before you meet and marry her.

ADVERSITY
Sooner or later, life deals everyone a tough hand. When this happens, you have a choice to make: Fold or press ahead knowing that "All things work together for good, to them that love God..." Romans 8:28

Many falls into the trap of thinking that their circumstances are so much worse than anyone else's.

This isn't true.

You can always find someone who has it worse.

Some people focus on the problem until they are completely consumed and destroyed by it.

This is not what a man does.

A man braces and steps into the wind of adversity, knowing that God has declared in the Bible that He will always, be with him. - *Hebrews 13:5*

Adversity is going to come – that I can guarantee you – but in one sense, it doesn't matter.

How you respond to it is what matters. Embrace your trials and purpose in your heart to honor God through them, regardless of what happens, and He will honor you for your faithfulness, in His way.

WORK

Purpose in your heart to be a diligent, hard worker. You know me well enough to know I can't abide the presence of a young man on the job site who doesn't know how to work hard – doesn't know how to sweat. Of course, when he's young, it's not his fault. He wasn't taught to work hard. But you were! A man of character works hard. A lazy man is a disgrace – to his God, his wife, his kids, and to himself. Tell yourself every morning when you get out of bed, I am a man who works diligently and works hard.

TRUTH

In every age, the Truth has been under assault. Our Times are no different. Truth is often a casualty in the battle of ideas – a battle that will rage until the End of Time. Good men cannot avoid this battle.

You, Son, cannot avoid this battle.

We must take our place in the public square, standing for what is good, right, and true.

What you are guaranteed in this battle are enemies.

I like what Winston Churchill said: You have enemies? Good! That means you stood for something. Son don't live your life trying to be everyone's friend.

Stand for the Truth.

There are many things I could share with you, but these are a few that will touch almost every area of your life.

Please know that I'm proud to call you my son and pray that you will fulfill the purposes for which God created you.

If you do, you will have found the best this life has to offer and an eternity that begins with the smile of God.

With much love and hope for your bright future, Dad

P.S. Only in the Scripture will you learn God's expectations for you . . . and yes, He does have them. Read your Bible every day. It will wash your mind. Sin will keep you from the Bible and the Bible, read and applied, will keep you from sin. Walk Tall, Son.

NOTES

_____

_____

_____

_____

_____

_____

MY DEAR SON, THIS IS HOW TO TREAT A WOMAN

"My dear Son"

You told me you were messaging a girl and you were planning to meet somewhere at school.
I wanted to ask if it was a date, but I didn't want to embarrass you.
I wanted to ask what she's like. Is she nice?
Is she smart?
What type of music does she listen to?
Is she like your mom?
It has been too long ago for me to remember. Was it like a switch? One minute you find girls annoying, and then suddenly, all you want to do is hang around them.
It seemed like only yesterday that the only girl you didn't find annoying was your mom.
When did that switch flip?
When did you start liking girls?
I guess it doesn't really matter how it happened. Or when. What's important now is that you know what to look for, and more importantly, how to behave when you've found her.

When you were little you told mom that you wanted to marry her when you grow up.
Well now you know that's not possible.
But at that time, you wanted to marry mom because she had all the qualities you want in a girl.
If that's true, then you should ask ME because I'm the only one that managed to marry her.

I'm the "expert," so to speak.
I know you're only 12. And you will likely have several girlfriends before marrying the right one.
But you might as well learn from the Expert so that you don't waste time making all the mistakes I made.

Do not get advice from your friends. Remember, "If a blind man leads a blind man, both will fall into a pit."
So here is a list that helped me when I met your mom.

What to look for:
Look for someone that's better than you. It's as simple as that. Look for someone that you admire, not only for her beauty, but also for her brains, her attitude, how she treats her family and friends.
When you find someone that is better than you, you will automatically want to be a better person around her. When you strive to be a better person for her, it will also uplift you.
Nothing else matters. Her race, ethnicity, how many friends she has or how many likes she can get on Instagram. Not her social status or even her religion.
None of that matters.
Ask yourself this; "Does she make me want to be a better person?" If the answer is YES – then you're with the right person at this time.

How to behave – List of DO'S:
This will sound corny but it's true because I'm the Expert. Chivalry is not dead. Be a gentleman. There's the easy stuff you hear all the time; hold doors, help her carry stuff, pull out the chair for her, give her your coat when she's cold. These are all good.

But then there are some details that seem to be lost to your generation.

Like:
1) Let her order first and wait for her food to arrive before you eat.
2) Compliment her on how beautiful she looks.
3) Be respectful in front of her parents. Don't say "Hey, how's it going". Say "Good morning Mr. ____."
4) Be respectful to her parents even when they're not around. Even if she's angry at them, stay respectful.
5) Surprise her with something for no reason. Like flowers, not like a snapchat. However, a snapchat story on how you got those flowers might be cool.
6) Watch to make sure she gets home safely before you leave.
7) Walk on the outside of the sidewalk when you're with her.
8) Don't kiss and tell (come talk to me if you do not get this.)
9) Make her laugh.
And then there is the really important stuff. Like:
10) Encourage her to aim higher (do better at school, run faster at track, play harder in sports.)
11) Challenge her to try new things, new experiences that will improve her as an individual.
12) Respect her opinions and decisions at all times.
If you can do 80% of these, she'll love you. Do 100%, she'll love and respect you.

How to behave – A list of DON'TS:

In no particular order – just don't do this stuff:
1) Hurtful pranks. I don't get how anyone can play a hurtful prank on their girlfriend for a laugh. I know it's all over YouTube and it gets a million likes. That just tells me there are at least a million people out there that won't have a worthwhile partner. You don't want to be one of them.
2) Bodily emissions on purpose. Just like how you wouldn't walk up to your teacher and fart or burp in her face, don't do that to your girl. It's not respectful. Save that for your buddies.

3) Profanity. Don't use any profanity directed at her, her family or friends. In front of her or behind her back. Respect.

4) Let her down. If you say you're going to be somewhere or do something, do it. Don't let her down intentionally. Girls like men, not little boys. And men stick to their word.

5) Stare at your phone. Don't text, talk. If you're with her, keep your eyes on her, not technology.

6) Lie and hide. If you make a mistake, own up to it. Change, improve, and move on. If you are practicing all these hacks, she will forgive you.

7) Shame or belittle. Similarly, she might make mistakes, forgive with sincerity. Never hold a grudge, shame, or belittle her.

Declaration: I_____ promise to abide by and practices being a better man every day of my life.

I Promise to:

_____

_____

_____

_____

_____

Signature: _____

Signed by: _____on the_____

BOOST YOUR BODY IMAGE WITH DAILY POSITIVE AFFIRMATIONS

Morning affirmations and bedtime affirmations are the most powerful to harness the power of positive thinking.

If you'd like to repeat your affirmations more often or want to say them to yourself at a time you need a self-esteem or positivity boost, please do!

1. I love my body and I love myself.
2. I am perfect and complete just the way I am.
3. I feed my body healthy nourishing food and give it healthy nourishing exercise because it deserves to be taken care of.
4. I know the answers and solutions. I listen to myself and trust my inner judgement.
5. My brain is my sexiest body part.
6. My life is what I make of it. I have all the power.
7. My body is a vessel for my awesomeness.
8. I eat a variety of foods for my health, wellness, and enjoyment.
9. There is more to life that worrying about my weight. I'm ready to experience it.
10. Food is not good or bad. It has no moral significance. I can choose to be good or bad and it has nothing to do with the number of calories or carbohydrates I eat.
11. Being grounded and whole makes me beautiful. I can get there just by being still, breathing, listening to my intuition, and doing what I can to be kind to myself and others.
12. I deserve to be treated with love and respect.

13. Even if I don't see how amazing I am, there is someone who does. I am loved and admired.
14. I look exactly the way I'm supposed to. I know because this is the way God (use whatever religious or spiritual higher power you believe in) made me!
15. It's not about working on myself; it's about being okay with who I already am.
16. Body, if you can love me for who I am, I promise to love you for who you are.
17. My body can do awesome things.
18. My body is a gift. I treat it with love and respect.
19. Life is too short and too precious to waste time obsessing about my body. I am going to take care of it to the best of my ability and get out of my head and into the world.
20. A goal weight is an arbitrary number; how I feel is what's important.
21. As long as I am good, kind, and hold myself with integrity, it doesn't matter what other people think of me.
22. I trust the wisdom of my body.
23. I use my energy to pay attention to myself, my inner wisdom, my virtues, my path, and my journey.
24. When I look to others to dictate who I should be or how I should look, I reject who I am.
25. Accepting myself as I am right now is the first step in growing and evolving.
26. All magazine photos are airbrushed, photoshopped, and distorted.
27. I love and respect myself.
28. I enjoy feeling good. I deserve to feel good.
29. Being skinny or fat is not my identity. I am identified by who I am on the inside, a loving, wonderful person.
30. My opinion of myself is the only one that counts.
31. I am compassionate and warm. My presence is delightful to people.
32. My very existence makes the world a better place.

33. My well-being is the most important thing to me. I am responsible for taking care of me.
34. No one has the power to make me feel bad about myself without my permission.
35. I eat for energy and nourishment.
36. My needs are just as important as anyone else's.
37. Chocolate (or fill in a food you have a challenging relationship with) is not the enemy. It's not my friend either. It's just chocolate, it has no power over me.
38. Life doesn't start 10 pounds from now (fill in a number that's meaningful for you), it's already started. I make the choice to include myself in it.
39. Thighs, thank you for carrying me to where I want to go.
40. Belly, thank you for helping me digest.
41. Skin, thank you for protecting me.
42. Other people don't dictate my choices for me, I know what's best for myself.
43. I feed my body life-affirming foods so I am healthy and vital.
44. Taking care of myself feels good.
45. I choose to do and say kind things for and about myself.

My personal affirmations:

_____

_____

_____

_____

_____

_____

FIGHTING AGAINST ALL ODDS

Frederick Douglass was born into slavery, separated from his mother at a young age, he taught himself to read in secrecy, and was beaten severely when his attempts at learning were found out. He rebelled and finally escaped after numerous attempts. He became the leader of the abolitionist movement gaining notoriety for his dazzling oratory and incisive antislavery writing.

Claudius, a Roman from a noble family, suffered from several health problems throughout his life, avoided assassination of his family because nobody thought he was a threat, later he became the emperor, conquered Britain which was considered impossible at that time, and became one of the greatest rulers of ancient Rome.

Franklin D. Roosevelt was elected US president four times even though he was paralyzed from the waist down after suffering from polio. To run for public office, he taught himself to walk a short distance using a cane while wearing iron braces and took great care to never appear in public in a wheelchair.

African-American track star, Wilma Rudolph, suffered scarlet fever, whooping cough, and measles, survived infantile paralysis, and required a leg brace until age nine. She went on to win three Olympic gold medals and was considered the "Fastest woman on Earth."

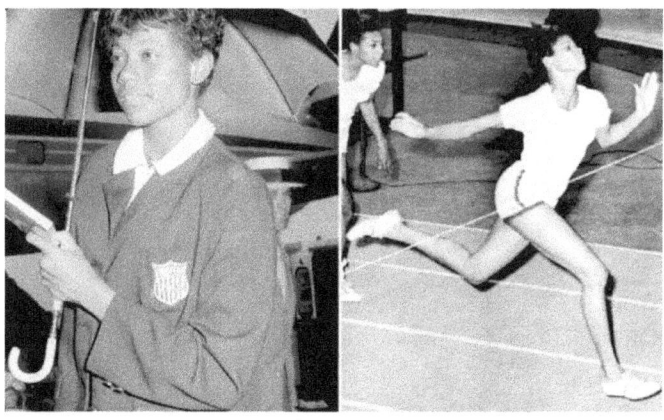

Helen Keller went blind and deaf as a toddler but still was able to learn sign language. She also learned to speak, read lips with her hands, go to school, earn a bachelor's degree (rare for any woman in her time), and became an author, political activist, and lecturer.

Orphaned at the age of four, Paul Revere Williams, a Black man, became one of the most important architects of the Los Angeles area during the time when it was becoming a megacity and when racial exclusion was the norm across the entire country.

After suffering from a massive stroke at the age of 43, Jean-Dominique Baby became entirely speechless. His mouth, arms, and legs were paralyzed, and he could only blink, yet he wrote the number-one best-selling book The Diving Bell and the Butterfly which was later adapted to produce a multiple award-winning movie.

Abraham Lincoln faced many hardships during his childhood and a number of failures during his later years. These included losing jobs, failed businesses, demotion in the army, and losing elections eight times before he became the President of the United States.

What are the odds against you?

_____

_____

_____

How do you plan to change them?

I_____ choose to change the odds against me by:

_____

_____

_____

_____

Signature:_____

Signed at_____ on the_____

13 THINGS TO TEACH YOUR SON ABOUT HOW TO TREAT WOMEN

We have the power to help populate the world with more awesome men!

While it might be too late to change a grown man, here are some lessons to impart to boys so they can grow into great men.

1. Model the Behavior
Rule number one: Raising boys means making sure that the adult men in your life treat you right. You ultimately want your son to see what you consider to be the standard for how a man should treat women. the kind of men that treat women like queens.

2.Teach Him to Listen
Do this by being present when he's communicating with you and validating his feelings. Allow him to express them and show him that you're always there to hear him out. With your guidance he will learn to do the same for others.

3. Teach Him to Open Doors
Let him know that he really wants to be a stellar gentleman, he can even open the car door for ladies. Teach him to hold the door so women can enter first. If you are raising a son in today's uber-feminist world, it's especially crucial to teach them the (lost) art and value of being chivalrous.

4. Teach Him to be Sensitive
Show him how important it is to always be a friend to women and listen to their problems. Even if it's about a fight she had with a girlfriend and he doesn't really get it, teach him to listen, ask questions, and always take her side.

5. Teach Him to be a Companion

Make sure he understands how important it is to be a team player—which means it's not always about what he wants to do. Show him the fun in preparing for an afternoon baseball game by going to the farmer's market first to get ingredients for a nice lunch.

6. Teach Him to Be Comforting

When raising boys, it's crucial to make sure they know how to make the women in their lives feel better. From PMS to general moodiness, we women can be all over the place with our emotions. Sometimes she just needs to vent, get a hug and maybe a cup of tea.

7. Teach Him to Engage

Boys need to learn the basics like how to run the dishwasher, washing machine and the vacuum. Helping around the house is a great way to show affection to someone who might be feeling sick or overwhelmed. No one likes a helpless dude.

8. Teach Him to Love the Kitchen

Your boy doesn't need to get a culinary degree, but it would be nice if he mastered the basics such as a simple egg or pasta dish. Cooking a delicious meal is a great way to wow a lady.

9. Teach Him to Make Her Laugh

Appealing to a woman's sense of humor is often the way to her heart. After physical chemistry fizzles—and it does fizzle—humor is often the best thing left to share. Being light and playful in a way that takes into account her participation is a great way to interact with a lady.

10. Teach Him to Surprise Her
Some of the best catches out there are the guys who know the value of keeping a woman on her toes. Teach your son to do something unexpected that shows her he's thinking about her when they are not together.

11. Teach Him to Always Have her Back
If you are raising a son, show him how important it is to always respect her and make your friends and family respect her, too. Teach him that if he mistreats her, others will pick up on that and think she is less deserving of respect.

12. Teach Him to Be Transparent
Make sure he knows that lying is the ultimate deal breaker. Women are good at picking up on lies, and while the truth may sometimes have negative repercussions, a lie always will.

13. Teach Him to be Her Rock
Show your boy how much it means to be supportive. If she has an idea, teach him to troubleshoot it with her. If she's running ragged, teach him to help her out. If she needs a hand, make sure he knows he should offer it before she even asks.

NOTES

_____

_____

_____

_____

BOYS ARE ALLOWED TO CRY TOO

Growing up, being a Black man consisted of three things: strength, endurance, and fortitude. You were supposed to be able to perform physical tasks, address any danger that may come to you and your loved ones, and provide for your family. Anything else was not allowed; manhood was a very rigid role. This thought pattern was shared by my family and friends.

The men that I knew were raised around fit this mold.

My grandfather, the greatest man I will ever know, is a pure Alpha male: a take charge and solve any problem kind of guy. I would see him laugh, joke, and occasionally get angry, but emotional? Never.

The first time I witnessed him cry was when his mother died. I was 15, and that was all of 5 seconds.
Possibly sensing me watching him, he stopped immediately, wiped off the little tears that he had and walked away.
Whenever my brother, friends, or I would even start to cry or show any emotion, we were met with "Toughen up!" "Come on man, stop acting soft" and of course the classic "Boys don't cry" by adult male family and friends.
To this day, this is drilled into little boys' heads every day, to the point that many grow to be emotionally stunted men.
Praise and congratulations in my family were given in forms of handshakes, daps, and half hugs.

Growing up, there was never any real deep affection shown by male friends or family.

We got that from our mothers, grandmothers, sisters, and girlfriends. A clear message was sent – only women were allowed show any feelings. This affected me in so many ways. I didn't want to cry in front of people, and I kept a lot of my emotions bottled up. Whenever folks would call me "sensitive", I would immediately switch up my attitude or become angry. I didn't want to be labeled as weak or a "punk", I had to be a man. Looking back on this, I can see how this might have affected some of my romantic relationships at the time. I didn't know how to balance my feelings. Either I was too emotional or too aloof and detached. The first time I heard a man tell another man he loved him, I was blown away. Here were two men in a platonic relationship, having no problem expressing their feelings to each other.

When I witnessed it, I had no words?
This was something new. I was 23.
The men were so grounded and secure in themselves.
They didn't have to prove anything to no one, the men were just "still."
I looked at them said to myself, "I want to be like that."
from that day on, I knew something was wrong in how most boys are raised into men.

If I show emotion or become sensitive, why am I immediately labeled weak, soft, or effeminate?
Why do we as men have to be locked into this tight box of masculinity?
Why is it that a man cannot be in touch with who he is?
Calling somebody a "punk" because they are expressing their feelings is terrible. As I became older, I started to let go of these restrictions. I became more comfortable with expressing myself and becoming vulnerable to not only the women I dated, but to my male friends. It started by me telling my brother I love him.

From there, it was easier to let myself be vulnerable, to just let myself "be." I was done with all of these bullshit restrictions on what a man was. I wasn't worried about someone calling me gay because I am not.

I wasn't worried about someone calling me soft and a wussy, because I didn't care what they thought. From that moment, I became a better son, a better brother, a better boyfriend, a better friend, and a better man. I realized that in relationships, one of the most important factors is communication and expressing oneself. I cannot tell you how many times I have cried in front of my brother or my best friends. Heck, I cried in front of my brother Chris recently over the murder of San Francisco native Alex Nieto. That doesn't make me less of a man because I can show my emotions. Believing that I can't or shouldn't express how I feel is a weakness.

When I look at the picture of Jordan and Cooglar, I get a sense of pride and love. They are posing exactly how I would with my brother or close friends. That picture screams the love that one friend has for another. Every time I talk with my brother Brent, Chris, or any of my close male friends, I tell them I love them.

Rapper Tony Yayo once said, "I tell my guys I love them all the time because I may not talk with them again." We as men need to shake these asinine and outdated shackles of gender norms. There is nothing wrong with showing emotion, expressing to your homeboy how much you mean to him, and even crying in front of him. It is healthy, mature, and normal.

In 2015 over 307,000 men died due to heart failure, and keeping emotions bottled up inside is a big part of that. We should not be passing this poisonous behavior on to the next generation. Emotionally healthy men express themselves in a constructive way. They don't grow up to be physically and verbally abusive to their partners. They do not look at being in touch with their feelings as being effeminate nor gay bash other men that are.

They do not participate in self-harming behavior such as mutilation or abuse drugs and alcohol. Our responsibility as fathers, older brothers, mentors, and role models is to show our youth a better way of doing things.

We can teach them that there is nothing wrong with displaying vulnerability and sadness. Doing so does not equate into weakness, but strength. Today, men and masculinity is changing and it needs to be. We as men need to evolve to a higher plane, to higher beings. Part of that evolution is being able to express our feelings openly without shaming ourselves, others and being attacked for it. I have three beautiful nephews and I want them to know that they can come to me about anything.

I am not going to judge who they are or how they act in front of me.
I want them to be still and secure in themselves.
I want my nephews to know that sometimes the only thing a man can do is cry.
Heck, I may cry with them!
To all my brothers of all colors and around the world, let's leave this behavior in the past and let 2016 be the year of the emotionally healthy man! (LeRon Barton)

Declaration

I _____ I promise to cry when I need to.
I will not bottle up my feelings.

I am allowed to cry, and I will allow myself to cry and heal so that I can be a healthy man.

Signature: _____

Signed at _____ on the _____

RESPONSIBILITY

Here are 12 major concepts related to responsibility that teaches their teens to be responsible individuals.

- Being accountable
- Exercising self-control
- Planning and setting goals
- Choosing positive attitudes
- Doing one's duty
- Being self-reliant
- Pursuing excellence
- Being proactive
- Being persistent
- Being reflective
- Setting a good example
- Being morally autonomous

Being Morally Autonomous
Responsible people think for themselves and do not let other people's opinions and attitudes control them. They are free moral agents, with strong reasoning skills and the freedom to choose between right and wrong. Teens tend to lean toward conformity. They find comfort and identity in being part of a group.

The reality of peer pressure makes your child's choice of friends one of the most important choices he or she can make. Parents can counteract the effects of peer pressure by teaching their teens to make their own choices and not blindly follow the pack.

While parents should instill in their children the ability to think for themselves, they should not give up their right to govern their family.

Families are not democracies. Children have a right to be respectfully heard, but their "vote" does not carry the same weight as their parents' votes.

Responsibility = Power

Teens want more freedom and more control over their lives. Parents must show their teens that they do have real power - the ability to choose. They can choose their attitudes, words, and actions. Teens also want to be treated like adults.

Parents can do this, first by teaching their teens they are responsible for the consequences of their choices, and second by holding them accountable for these choices. Consequences can be both positive and negative.

When your teen brings you an M-rated video game he borrowed from a friend to approve before he plays it, he has shown respect for house rules and your authority. He has made a good choice and earned your praise and trust. When your daughter lies about going to a movie with her friend so she can attend a party where alcohol is being served, she has chosen to violate your rules and has lost your trust.

You should always know what your kids are doing and with whom. You are your child's parent, not his or her friend. Ask who, what, where, when, why, and how, all the time. Tell your teens you will be checking up on them and DO IT. Give your teens an "escape clause" by telling them they can use you as an excuse for passing on an activity that makes them uncomfortable.

Enforce consequences when necessary, using the following concepts as a guide:

Establish clear expectations for behavior and set clear consequences for not meeting those expectations.

Be sure to give positive consequences for good behavior, as well as negative consequences for inappropriate behavior.
Be consistent when enforcing consequences.
If you give a consequence (either positive or negative), follow through.
Connect your consequences to the behavior; they're more likely to have the desired results (e.g., taking away driving privileges for not putting gas in the car).
Use short-term consequences, like assigning chores, for minor infractions and long-term consequences, like losing cell phone privileges, for larger infractions.

Keep in mind the SANE acronym regarding consequences:

Small consequences are better.
Avoid punishing yourself with the restrictions you place on your child.
Never abuse your child with a consequence.
Effective consequences are consistent consequences.

Consequences are important because they reinforce the cause-effect relationship between what your teen does choices and what happens as a result.
Consequences help teach teens to make better choices in the future, which subsequently helps them become responsible adults who know the difference between right and wrong and try to do the right thing.

✏️ Declaration

I_____ choose to be responsible by_____

_____

_____

_____

_____

_____

_____

Signature:_____

Signed at_____on the_____

📝 NOTES

_____

_____

_____

_____

_____

_____

_____

_____

ACCOUNTABILITY

Accountability is about learning how to build a self-value system and affirm individual value as part of the community.

This includes being responsible for the world and being part of the global citizenship by becoming involved and responsible. Teen responsibility requires using words and communication based on reasoning, love, and affirmation.

The goal of parents teaching teens responsibility is to understand the point of view of the young person and at the same time, help the teen to understand why the responsibility is important.

The meaning of accountability is simply a willingness to be answerable for an outcome. Accountability isn't something that you can just flip the switch on and be done with it; consider doing one thing a week for an entire quarter to keep accountability top of mind.

1. Review your current goals, objectives and focus areas with your manager and/or team members. Are measures of success and failure explicit and measurable? Discuss suggestions for modifications of processes, benchmarks, timelines, and roles. Collaborate to obtain full buy-in and official commitment on all.

2. Review and clarify departmental and company-wide key performance indicators (KPIs). How does your work contribute to those KPIs? Which personal KPIs must you hit in order to be successful?

3. Break large goals into quarterly, monthly and even weekly enabling goals. Smaller objectives will help you to stay focused on timely progress.

4. Monitor your speech—the words that you use. In conversations, do you hear yourself blaming others when processes or plans don't turn out exactly as you intended?

5. Spend a few hours reading articles you can find on the internet. Search on terms like ownership mindset, accountability and commitment, accountability and responsibility, employee accountability.

6. Approach someone you know who readily accepts responsibility for small and large failures. Practice emulating their behavior of accepting accountability. Consider inviting them for coffee to discuss their views on accountability.

7. Speak up, early, if you have concerns. If you believe that expectations are unrealistic, you may not speak up but instead may go through the motions of attempting to meet them, knowing it will fail in the end. In these cases, lean on your professional encourage to "push back", question, and share your concerns in a professional way.

8. Develop the habit of daily or weekly reviews on all your important projects. It's better to identify problems or "failures" early before they turn into a bigger failure.
9.Ask a trusted colleague to become an "accountability partner" who can check on your results and call you out if you are using blaming language.

10. Develop the habit of always giving a balanced "after-action review." Even successful outcomes come at the end of some challenges, problems, or lessons learned.

11. Discuss with your team or peers the challenge of accepting full accountability and the rewards of trust gained and the reputation for integrity earned by admitting responsibility for errors or failure.

The biggest impact you can make is to become an accountability role model yourself. You can create an accountability culture by influencing others with your own actions.

<u>Three ways to improve self-accountability.</u>

CREATE WEEKLY AND PRIORITY LISTS
While you still should have a catch-all list so you don't forget things, the weekly and daily priority list addresses the key areas that will make your week or day a success.

Where should you be spending your time to reach your goals? Plan your priorities so you can actually get there.

Then, for your Greatest Impact Activities, put them on your calendar in advance.

At the end of the week or beginning of the next, review your list with someone else (see next point), and reflect on how you did.

Did you achieve all that you had hoped to?
If not, what got in your way and why? Do you need to adjust your expectations for the time required to complete activities? Are you truly committed to your priority list? If you are, what will you do differently next week to ensure that you're able to achieve all that you set out to? By defining your goals and planning your actions each week, writing them down, reviewing how you did, and debriefing on what happened, you will improve your self-accountability.

MEET WITH AN ACCOUNTABILITY PARTNER

You can take the above idea a step farther by sharing your to-do list with an accountability partner and connecting with them on a weekly basis to review your list together.

When you share your priorities with someone else, you're much more likely to follow through. After all, none of us like to admit to someone else that we failed to do what we said we would. This is a very powerful self-accountability strategy.

Your accountability partner doesn't need to be your direct manager. It can be a colleague, a friend, a family member, or anyone who's willing to check in with you on a weekly basis.

Choose someone as your accountability partner who will push you. It's easy to make excuses for why you didn't accomplish certain things. An accountability partner can keep you on target, ask good questions, offer time management tips, and keep you focused.

The simple habit of writing your to-do list, sharing it with a partner, and reviewing what you accomplished will help you achieve more.

SIGN A COMMITMENT CONTRACT

If you're serious about improving accountability, sign a commitment contract. A commitment contract is a signed agreement with yourself outlining what you'll do by when.

You can even attach a monetary amount to your contract. The company has found that financial stakes increase chances of keeping to your commitments by up to 3X. If you don't meet your commitments, you pay it to either a friend, a charity, or even an anti-charity of your choosing.

Commitment to Life Contract

Make a contract with a friend or a trusted partner, person

For today and the next……days, I commit to

Example:	Positive changes I will make
☐ Decrease negative self-talk ☐ Build positive experiences ☐ Use my coping skills ☐ I will take action to remove harmful substances or objects ☐ I will set some personal goals ☐ I commit to LIFE	
What are my personal GOALS? Break them down into smaller, achievable steps Example: Goal 1: Be with others more 2. Join reading group (phone library) 3. Join walking group 4. Contact an old friend 5. Go to a coffee morning 6. Plan an event with friend	Positive changes I will make

Positive self-talk What can I say to myself that will encourage me and help me cope? **Example**: • This will pass • I've coped before - I will cope now • It will get better • There are things I can do to help myself feel better	Positive changes I will make
Positive aspects of my life Example: • People • Possessions • Positive aspects of self-e.g. character trait or personal skill	Positive changes I will make
My safety plan What can I do that will help reduce the pain? What can I do that will help me cope better? Who or where can I go? **Example:** Who can I telephone? • Self-soothe, be with others • STOPP, Opposite Action, writing, distract • Family or friend, Health professional, Samaritans or Befrienders, Accident & Emergency Department, Emergency services	Positive changes I will make

I commit to life for .... days with the option of renewing for another ...... days.

☐ I commit to making the positive changes as detailed in this Commitment to Life contact.

☐ I will give a copy of this Commitment to Life to an important person in my life to help me through this difficult time.

Signature:_____

Signed at_____on the_____

📝 NOTES

_____

_____

_____

_____

_____

_____

_____

_____

_____

_____

_____

RESPECT & GOOD MANNERS

Respect is fundamental to the development of various other character traits. Respect for elders, respect for other people, respect for authority, respect for oneself is crucial for becoming a good human being. Being respectful helps generate the feeling of self-worth and empathy for others. It may teach children to peacefully co-exist and accept people as they are irrespective of their caste, creed, and religion. Important qualities like cleanliness, obedience, self-control, kindness, determination may follow if there is basic human respect.

Parents may like to instill good manners in their child as early as they can start. Good manners may help you to shape your child into a pleasant and loving person and boost his social IQ. You may like to commonly use phrases like 'please' and 'thank you' while dealing with your child. Be sure to conduct yourself rightfully as kids learn more by observing an adult's actions. Constant and consistent modelling of good manners may assist your child in adopting them so that they become an integral part of his life.

In spite of these influences, if you, while you are young, can come to realize the power of practicing good manners and treating others in respectful ways, you can gain an important social advantage over many of your peers and friends. Contrary to the often-quoted phrase… "good guys almost always finish at the top or very near to it."

Understanding the Basics

A few important questions for you:
- Does it really matter if you remember to always say "please" and "thank you?"

- Will saying "please" and "thank you" actually help in getting you what you may want?
- Do you think saying "'please" and "thank you" may be one of the marks of having good manners?
- And is it possible that saying "please" and "thank you" can help your peers as well as yourself?

The unequivocal answer to all the above questions is YES. Using these small but important words can be beneficial to you in countless ways. Even if others around you do not use these terms, I assure you that almost everyone around you – adults and peers alike – will notice and admire you for your use of these simple words.

People determine your value to them, in great part, by the way you make them feel when they are in contact with you. Showing good manners in your speech reveals that you have respect for others as well as for yourself – and makes you much more enjoyable to be around.

The Manners Test
Let's explore the state of good manners. Ask yourself the following questions as they relate to people with whom you regularly interact. Each of these can be answered by a simple yes or no…be honest with yourself and tally your score at the end.

- Do you smile at friends and family members when you come in contact with them?
- Do you look people in the eye when you are talking with them?
- Do you let your parents know that you appreciate them and all that they do for you?

- Do you offer to help with chores around the house instead of waiting to be asked?
- Do you show respect by consistently saying "please" and "thank you" to those around you?
- Do you show your respect for your teachers and school staff and thank them for their efforts to teach you important things that you need to know?
- Do you speak to teachers by respectively addressing them as Mr., Ms., or Dr.?
- Do you show your appreciation to your friends' parents/guardians when they have you in their home or help you in some special way?
- Do have a firm and welcoming handshake that you readily share when meeting someone new for the first time?
- Would most of your friends characterize you as a really nice person?

Take your time and go back over your answers to this little test, recording your yes and no responses…be honest, no one is looking, and an honest score can tell you if you need to make some improvements or not. No one makes a 100 on this, but a 70 to 90 is a good score and indicates that, with just a little practice here and there, you could become a well-mannered young person. A score of 50 or 60 means you need to do some work and pay a lot more attention to how you are treating the people around you. Below 50…well, there may still be hope for you, but you better get on it quickly or you are not likely to have many friends left before too long.

This scoring system cannot be used without an adequate understanding as to how we are coming up with the numbers? The little things really do count, probably much more than you have been thinking. Saying "please" and "thank you" and looking folks in the eye during conversation are all parts of the basics of good manners. Most of these are simply the application of the "Golden Rule" – treating others as you would want them to treat you.

It is impossible to overstate the importance of having and practicing good manners. Saying "please" and "thank you" is just a start, but a very good one. They are literally magic words. If you have not been using them consistently, just try it out. I can guarantee you that you will gain an abundance of respect from people of all ages. And by seeing the power of these basics now, you will learn to appreciate the power of practicing good manners throughout your life. The human being who lives only for himself reaps nothing but unhappiness.

Don't put off the joy derived from doing helpful, kindly things for others. B. C. Forbes

What are Good Manners?

A person with good manners shows respects towards feelings and sentiments of others living in the surroundings. He/she never differentiates people and shows equal regard to everyone. Modesty, humbleness, kindness, and courtesy are the essential traits of a well-behaving person. Hence, a well-behaved person never feels proud or arrogant and always take care of the feelings of others. Practicing good manners and following them all through the day will definitely bring sunshine and add qualities to life.

Must have Good Manners
Though traits within good manners are uncountable, some traits are a must. These good manners are necessary for all. Some of such good manners which we can practice in our daily life are like:

- o We must learn the habit of sharing things to others.
- o We should be helpful, polite, and humble to others in every possible way.
- o We must use the words 'sorry', 'please', 'thank you', 'excuse me' and 'time wish' as and when required.

- We must respect the other's property and always take permission before using.
- We must be responsible as well as self-dependent for everything at every place.
- We must behave in a good way with humble respect to our teachers, parents, other elders, and senior citizens.
- We should always maintain cleanliness at home, school, and all other public places.
- We should not use any offensive or abusive language to others at home or any other place.
- We must give the seat for senior citizens while using public transport.

Importance of Good Manners in our Life

Good manners are very important in our daily life.
Importance of these in life is the well-known facts.

Good manner creates an effective interaction with friends as well as make a good impression on a public platform.
It helps us to be positive throughout the day.
Therefore, parents must help their kids to inculcate all possible good manners in their habit.
Good manners always give the opportunity for a new conversation with people and hence the ultimate success in life.

If someone talks to you badly, then still don't talk him in the same way.
Always talk him in your own positive way of behaving to give him the chance to change.

Good manners are vital to each and everyone in the society.

These will definitely help us for getting popularity and success in life because nobody likes mischief and misbehaved person.

Good manners are like a tonic to the people living in society.
People with polite and pleasant nature are always popular and respectable by a large number of people.

Obviously, such people are having magnetic influence over others. Thus, we must practice and follow good manners in our life always.

✎ Declaration:
I_____ commit to always respect others and practice good manners by
_____
_____
_____
_____

Signature:_____

Signed at_____on the_____

TIME MANAGEMENT

Time Management can improve productivity and competence. Good time management can also help to increase focus and enhance decision-making abilities.

Whether we assign a dollar value to it or not, time is valuable to us.

Think about it: How much of your typical work week do you spend stressed about not having enough time to complete a task or reach a goal? There are lots of different ways to tackle the issue of time management — you can download apps, adjust your sleep time, create lists, etc.

But if you don't fully understand why it's important for you to better manage your time, those apps and lists aren't going to help you. If you don't have the motivation to use them, you won't.

You have to first look at the big picture. Get a handle on why managing your time effectively is important, and what you stand to gain from it. You can get started by reviewing these 8 reasons time management is crucial: Time is limited.
No matter how you slice it, there are only 24 hours in a day. That applies to you, and to your coworker who only seems able to do half the amount of work you do. But it also applies to the former coworker who consistently accomplishes more than you and was promoted as a result. If you want to rise through the ranks, you have to acknowledge the importance of finding a way to manage this limited resource. You can accomplish more with less effort. When you learn to take control of your time, you improve your ability to focus. And with increased focus comes enhanced efficiency because you don't lose momentum.

You'll start to breeze through tasks more quickly (the workday will also seem to fly by.

Improved decision-making ability.
Whether you rely on a time-chunking technique or discover the power of list-making, you'll soon find that a nice side benefit of good time management skills is the ability to make better decisions. When you feel pressed for time and have to make a decision, you're more likely to jump to conclusions without fully considering every option. That leads to poor decision making. Through effective time management, you can eliminate the pressure that comes from feeling like you don't have enough time. You'll start to feel calmer and in control. When the time comes to examine options and decide, instead of rushing through the process, you can take time to carefully consider each option. And when you're able to do that, you diminish your chances of making a bad decision.

Become more successful in your career.
Time management is the key to success. It allows you to take control of your life rather than following the flow of others. As you accomplish more each day, make more sound decisions, and feel more in control, people notice. Leaders in your business will come to you when they need to get things done. And that increased exposure helps put you in line for advancement opportunities.

Learning opportunities are everywhere.
Obviously, the more you learn, the more valuable you are to your employer. And great learning opportunities are around you if you've got time to stop and take advantage them. When you work more efficiently, you have that time. You can help with that new product launch your development team's been working on. Volunteer to help host your company's open house. Even just enjoying a nice lunch with teammates in other departments can prove eye-opening. The more you learn about your company and your industry, the better your chances of making a positive impression on the C-suite.

Reduce stress.
When you don't have control of your time, it's easy to end up feeling rushed and overwhelmed. And when that happens, it can be hard to figure out how long it's going to take to complete a task. (Think of a time when you were about to miss a deadline and were frantically trying to finish the project. If someone dumped a surprise on your desk at that moment and asked you how long it would take to finish the surprise task, how could you even begin to answer their question?)

Once you learn how to manage your time, you no longer subject yourself to that level of stress. Besides it being better for your health, you have a clearer picture of the demands on your time. You're better able to estimate how long a given task will take you to complete, and you know you can meet the deadline.

Free time is necessary.
Everyone needs time to relax and unwind. Unfortunately, though, many of us don't get enough of it.
Between jobs, family responsibilities, errands, and upkeep on the house and the yard, most of us are hard-pressed to find even 10 minutes to sit and do nothing.
Having good time management skills helps you find that time.
When you're busy, you're getting more done.
You accumulate extra time throughout your day that you can use later to relax, unwind, and prepare for a good night's sleep.

Self-discipline is valuable.
When you practice good time management, you leave no room for procrastination. The better you get at it, the more self-discipline you learn. This is a valuable skill that will begin to impact other areas of your life where a lack of discipline has kept you from achieving a goal.

EFFECTS OF POOR TIME MANAGEMENT

Time. It's the one thing you really can't get back. And when we hear the term "time management", we often think of it in relation to the schoolwork and work environment. But the negative ramifications of not being able to manage our time properly extend way beyond the borders of the office. For those who are not adept at prioritizing tasks, failing to get to grips with managing time properly can lead to a lack of self-esteem, relationship strain, and an overall unhappiness with life that stems from having poor focus. It can even end up affecting our health, if left "untreated". So, have you ever wondered if you're one of the unfortunate victims of your own time management failings? Well, here are some of the telltale symptoms and their inevitable consequences.

Struggling to get there on time

Always late for meetings/dates/catchups with friends? If you find that, no matter how hard you try, you're never on time, you're most definitely not making best use of the time you have.

Poor punctuality can be laughed off, to a point. Particularly in those friendly relationships. But perpetual punctuality issues will eventually eat away at our credibility and cause tempers to fray.

This, of course, is particularly problematic in terms of career, but we need to spare a thought for our loved ones too. Tardiness doesn't just make us late, it impinges on the time of others, if they have to pick up our slack—or the children from school. So, it's vital to learn ways of managing our daily diaries so that we're not falling behind and, by osmosis, causing others to be late for what's important in their lives.

Forever rushing around

This is something of a by-product of punctuality issues but rushing everywhere—in and of itself—can begin to place real mental pressure on us if it happens too frequently. Being late for something triggers our 'flight or fight' response, our adrenaline kicks in, and our stress levels rise.

Whilst a little adrenaline can do us good, in certain circumstances, too much stress response can eventually weaken our immune system and put strain on our vital organs. Not to mention that stress just doesn't feel great!

Lacking patience and feeling irritable

When our minds aren't clear and focused, we have a tendency to become easily riled. Here's an analogy. We're in a supermarket, piling items into our basket—until the handle snaps and the contents spill all over the floor, shooting in every direction.

Now imagine that a wife/husband/friend/boss, comes and throws a couple more items on the floor for us to pick up. What would a normal human reaction be? Anger? Irritability? More than likely! So the trick is not to load our baskets so full that we don't have the facility in place to carry everything.

Hemorrhaging energy

Constantly playing catch-up, plunders our energy resources. Which means we end up falling even further behind because we don't have enough "fuel in the tank" to keep the momentum going.

There's only so long that anyone can keep up with the pressures of life once the tank is empty. And that's where burnout happens.

Failing to set goals

An overstretched mind is a chaotic one. And the more we throw into the mix, the less we're able to be clear about what's important.

Up close, in our day-to-day lives, prioritizing what needs to get done first becomes trickier than it ought to be. Zoom out a little—to the week, month, or year ahead—taking into account the many other burdens that are added to our list, and it soon become impossible to make any kind of sense of the mess in front of us. This can make it nigh on impossible to work out what we want, or need, to achieve in the long run.

Finding it hard to make decisions
Time management is an exercise in prioritizing. And poor time management is the blight of those who find it hard to prioritize. Ultimately, when we can't figure out what needs to happen next, we reach a sort of mental stalemate.

decision can end up placing the burden of judgement onto others just that bit too often, and there are two problems with this. Firstly, we end up giving figurative (or perhaps literal!) power of attorney to someone else. From the incidentals like, "where should we go for dinner?", to the really big stuff like; "should we move house?". And once we're in the cycle, it becomes hard to break.

Secondly, we risk straining relationships by asking the other person to do all of the legwork. Our friends and partners are just that, our friends, and partners. They're not our PAs! And the only person who really knows what you want, is you.

Failing to perform
Rolling on from indecision is incompetence. When we stop taking accountability for our own choices, we start dropping the ball.

To use an exaggerated scenario, consider the military. Military personnel have to make split-second judgements, often, as part of their role. Indecision in a situation like this can mean the difference between life and death. And, OK, so not knowing what to have for dinner isn't going to get anyone killed, but if we can't reach decisions at work—or we can't juggle our priorities at home so that we can spend a weekend with our family—we're failing to deliver as individuals.

Feeling that nothing's ever quite good enough
They might seem juxtaposed, but poor time management and perfectionism share a deep link. Because, whilst perfectionism sounds like a fabulous quality to have, it can undermine our efforts when it's taken to the extreme—resulting in "analysis-paralysis".

According to Psychology Today perfectionists "often get hung up on meaningless details and spend more time on projects than is necessary". By comparison, those who can manage to distinguish between what's really important and what isn't, tend to be far more productive.

Outside of the office, perfectionism can become an insidious force on our close personal relationships. Our loved ones begin to feel unappreciated and alienated, when we constantly set too high an expectation of them.

So that's the symptom checker! If this sounds like you, now's the time to try and get a handle on your time management skills—so that you can have more energy, be more productive, and lead a healthier, happier, life.

Name 5 consequences of poor time management in school

1._____ 2._____

3._____ 4._____

5._____

✏️ Declaration

I_____ Promise to change my time management by

_____

_____

_____

_____

_____

Signature:_____

Signed at_____on the_____

📝 NOTES

_____

_____

_____

_____

_____

_____

MONEY MANAGEMENT

Give your kids an ethical head start on how to handle money, the value of saving and the consequences of wasteful spending habits as soon as he starts getting an allowance. Introduce him to budgeting early on in life. It is vital to indoctrinate the concept of contentment and smart ways of spending.

The earlier teenagers learn about money, savings and investment, the better money managers they will become. Such skills help children to understand the difference between earning, spending, and saving, making them better money managers who're able to budget. It also helps children understand the value of money at an early age and help them make better financial decisions.

Money conversations from childhood help people grow into adults that have a healthy relationship with money. Research shows that money habits as well such as getting an allowance, helping the caregivers in the home budget for household items also teaches the principle of efficiently allocating scarce resources. These all contribute to increasing the growing child's financial sophistication, thus giving them a better financial outcome later in life.

With the high unemployment of the youth and lack of entrepreneurial and financial literacy in our schools, it's important to have such initiatives to make sure that we teach the children skills at a young age. When they grow up, they'll be able to create employment for themselves and make sound financial decisions

Why is Teaching Children Money Matters So Important?

Here are some misconceptions about money:

"Money is the root of all evil."
"Money doesn't grow on trees."
"Show me the money."
"It'll have to wait until payday."
"That money is burning a hole in your pocket."

When and where do children learn about money issues, such as financial responsibility, savings, budgeting, debt, and credit? Perhaps a little in high school, but a majority of children learn money management skills—good or bad—at home. Parents need to be proactive about teaching their children about money, or the world of marketing and advertising will teach them—incorrectly!

A nationwide survey shows that for the first time since 1997, high school students are doing better when it comes to money smarts. However, roughly 65% of those students failed the exam used to measure financial knowledge. (in 2006, 62% failed).

Results of the 2004 Jump$tart Coalition for Personal Financial Literacy study:

♦ 58.3 percent said skills are learned at home, verses 19.5 percent who said they learn such skills at school, and 17.6 percent from experience.

♦ Questions about income and spending were answered more correctly than questions about money management and saving.

♦ 11.4 percent of students use their own credit card.

♦ 15.7 percent use their parents' card and 4.8 percent use both their own and their parents.

♦ Over one third (43.3 percent) of the students have an ATM card.

♦ Nearly 78 percent of the students have a savings and/or checking account with a bank.

♦ The 22.1 percent of the students without any bank account scored lower than those Who have a savings and/or checking account?
So, children in high school are fairly active with money, but not necessarily in a position to make the best decisions.

What type of messages are your parents sending to you?
Remember you have a choose to right, now that you have the knowledge

Day-to-Day Mini-Money
Lessons Money management must be learned and practiced. Consider teaching your own children the following habits in everyday home and family life to better prepare your children for "real" life. These lessons can be included in day-to-day activities and errands, and don't need to take much time out of any schedule.

Discuss with your teens the difference between needs and wants. As basic as it sounds, many financial difficulties could be avoided if people understood that it is merely impossible to have everything you want, and that some things are more important than others.

♦ Teach your children how to prioritize. Prioritizing can help in many day-to-day decisions, beyond those dealing specifically with money.

◆ Help a child understand there is no such thing as a free lunch. If a child wants an item, help them earn and save money to purchase it without going into debt.

◆ Teach the value of working for money, whether by getting a job such as babysitting or a paper route, or by doing extra chores around the house.

◆ Include your children in the process of making a family monthly budget. Make a list of all your income. Then ask the children to come up with a list of expenses, including rent or mortgage, food, insurance, car payments and maintenance, clothing, and so on. Rely on past bank or credit card statements to see how much you spent on these in the past. Have a child find the difference between income and expenses. This monthly activity can effectively prepare a child for building his or her own budget.

◆ Give all family members a personal allowance, whether tied to chores or not, to give everyone an opportunity to manage their own money, no matter how small. If your child wants to buy something not planned in the family budget, give the child the opportunity to buy it or save for it with an allowance. Remember to explain an item can be purchased with saved money, and that the money will not be available to buy anything else the child may want if the money is all spent.

◆ Be patient. It may take a while for children to understand that once the money is spent, they cannot have anything else, but they will eventually learn—if you don't give into cries for more money. Day-to-Day Mini-Money Lessons Money management must be learned and practiced. Consider teaching the following habits in everyday home and family life to better prepare your children for "real" life. These lessons can be included in day-to-day activities and errands, and don't need to take much time out of any schedule.

◆ Resist the urge to rescue your children. Stick to what you have stated about wants verses needs. This may become difficult while surrounded by other shoppers, but it will teach your children plenty about money and control, which will help them avoid unnecessary debt in the future.

◆ Give your children advice but allow them to make their own decisions— good or bad. Children will learn the most from personal experience, perhaps especially mistakes.

◆ Saving is an important habit to begin early— early in life and early in a budget. Teach your children to pay themselves first. This means the first money to come out of a paycheck or allowance goes into savings.

◆ Be sure there is a goal to work toward, such as saving for a trip to Disneyland, a new bike, a college education or simply a new video game. Help the child estimate how much the goal costs and decide how much to save each month to reach that goal.

◆ Consider having children contribute to an overall family goal. Also, consider matching savings funds as an incentive.

◆ While grocery shopping, show your children how to comparison shop, pointing out ways to maximize your dollar, such as reading price labels for price per ounce, or using ads and coupons to plan your menu.

◆ Use play money while making a budget so children can visually see how much money goes to expenses.

◆ Give your children the opportunity to hand money to cashiers, bank tellers, parking attendants, etc.

♦ When writing out checks, show your children how to carry a balance in the check book register. Share your bank, credit card, and investment statements to teach how interest works. Look for opportunities to teach money matters all around you.

♦ Remember that children at different ages conceptualize money matters differently. Gear money lessons around what is understood by the child, giving more responsibility to older children, but never underestimating younger children's ability to observe your habits and attitudes toward money.

♦ Remember that one of the best ways to teach is by example—do your best to practice what you preach.

✎ **Declaration:** From today I choose to make the following changes to my life to better manage my money.

When I am older, and have children of my own, I will instill good values surrounding money, including:

_____

_____

_____

_____

_____

_____

WAYS TEENS CAN EARN CASH

Are you a teen interested in earning some money of your own? You're not alone. Many teens are looking for ways they can make money to cover expenses. I mean, there are things to buy clothes, entertainment costs, electronic gadgets. Plus, it is good to save up for cars, college costs and other big purchases. If you are one of the many teens who needs or wants to earn money to cover these costs, stay on this topic. There is a large list of ways for teens to make money. Choose the ones you think will work best for you and start earning today! There is an almost limitless number of ways that you can rake in some cash if you're a teenager. From online jobs to money-earning apps to in-person jobs, the possibilities are many.

Young entrepreneurs are the lifeblood of the workforce. They can be the group that grows up to create businesses that will employ tens to hundreds to thousands of people looking for jobs.

Check out these ideas for making money under 18. See if you can use one or more to add some cushion to your savings account or to pay for items you want or need.

1. **Searching the Web**

Swagbucks is a legit site where people get paid for browsing the Internet and more. The points you earn are put into a "bank" and can be redeemed for gift cards to be used on Amazon or at local and online stores such as Walmart, Target, and Old Navy. You can also get gift cards to PayPal.

Swagbucks will pay you points to complete small tasks such as:
- Complete surveys
- Play games
- Search the Web

- Watch videos
- Shop online

Using your Swagbucks account in your spare time will allow you to make money to pay for the things you need or want. Best of all, it's free to join, You can Earn points by playing games or watching videos and turn it into cash deposited into your PayPal account. Basically you get paid for browsing the Internet and more the points you earn can be redeemed for gift cards

2. Clean People's Houses

Many people are eager to help keep their homes clean. However, traditional cleaning services can be costly. As a result, people may consider hiring teens who will clean their homes for a reasonable price.

If you like cleaning and are good at being detailed about it, a house cleaning business might be right for you. To get your business started, make a list of what types of cleaning you'll do.

For example, will you clean bathrooms and kitchens? Will you dust? Vacuum? Will you clean windows? Make sure the jobs are jobs you can do well.

Safety Counts

Remember to keep in mind the safety aspect too. For example, you might want to rule out cleaning window exteriors that require the need for a ladder. Next, decide what your hourly rate is. Professional maid cleaning services typically charge between R100 and R135 an hour. Let's say you decide you can do your work quickly, thoroughly and charge R50 an hour. You've just given potential clients a reason to hire you over a traditional maid service. You can get work by advertising your services with family, friends, and neighbors.

3. Sell Your Stuff

Is your closet loaded with items you no longer need? Consider selling them at a garage sale or online.

For instance, do you have video games, DVDs or CDs lying around? See what you can get for them on a site like Declutter which makes it super easy to get rid of a lot of items quickly.

If you don't want to the hassle of selling items one by one, then Declutter can be a great option. You just scan the bar-codes of all the items, put them in a box, and put the free shipping label they provide. To make the most money, selling your items one-by-one will get you the most cash in hand.

The general rule for selling used stuff is to charge 10 percent of the retail cost. You could charge more for larger items such as gaming items, bicycles, or other sports equipment. The better shape the items are in, the more likely you are to get a higher price.

Want to help increase your earnings when you sell your unwanted stuff? Price your items fairly for a quicker sale and be willing to haggle with customers.

Hint: you might be able to talk your parents into letting you sell some of their stuff. Work out a deal where you split the profit with them in exchange for doing the work of selling the items.

4. Make Money Sharing Your Opinion

Companies such as Survey Junkie will help you get paid for your opinion. Brands want to get your feedback and they are willing to pay for it. They have over 10 million members and you can take surveys if you're at least 13 years old.

If you like to give your opinion about things – why not get paid for it?

5. Run a Farmer's Market Stand

Many local farmer's markets charge money when adults set up a stand but allow kids to do so for free. If you've got a small area in your yard, you could grow vegetables to sell at a farmer's market. You could also sell baked goods or specialty foods at a farmer's market.

Farmer's Market vendors sell a variety of items besides fresh fruits and vegetables. Some sell dessert bread, cookies, or muffins. Others sell canned jellies, pickles, and other items they canned from their own fruits or vegetables.

There was a group of teens at our local farmer's market that used to make brick oven pizzas and bread at the local farmer's market.

It's important to check your state's laws about farmer's market foods before selling baked goods or specialty foods. However, many states' food laws don't apply to farmer's market booths.

6. Babysit

Are there young kids in your neighborhood or extended family members who need childcare? If so, you can offer babysitting services and earn some cash that way.
You can offer your babysitting services on nights and weekends during the school year. During the summer you could offer to nanny while parents are at work and kids are out of school.
It's not uncommon for babysitting teens to make R85 an hour, R100 an hour or more. Babysitting is a great job for teens (even 14 and 15-year-olds) who are responsible, mature and enjoy being with kids.
If you want to look outside of your current circle of family, friends, and neighbors for babysitting clients, check out Care.com. Care.com is a database listing available babysitter in specific areas. If you are under 18 years of age, you'll have to have a parent or guardian's permission to be listed on Gumtree.

7. Pet Sit

Another great job for teens involves pet sitting. Some people might want pet care while they're away at work if they don't want the pet to be alone. Others might need pet care while they're on vacation. The amount of time it takes to pet sit depends on the type of pet. Dogs will likely require constant care, either at your own home (get your parents' permission first) or at the pet owner's home. Other pets such as cats or fish may simply require that you just check in on them twice a day. Decide ahead of time which types of pets you'll sit for and which you won't. Set your prices according to how much time you'll spend each day caring for the pet. Hint: We mentioned Care.com above. You can sign up for Care.com as a pet sitter too.

8. Dog Walking

If you're looking to earn money by helping animals but want a less time-intensive job, you could offer dog walking services.

Many people don't have time to walk their dogs but want their dogs to get exercise. These people will pay a decent hourly rate to have someone else walk their dog a few times a week.

Advertise your services with neighborhood flyers, on Facebook or at local pet stores. You can also consider signing up for Rover where it will they will help connect you with people in your area that need a dog walker.

If you're walking dogs that get along with other dogs, you can walk several at once and increase your income. An organized schedule will help you keep track of your dog walking job commitments.

9. House Sit

If you have a neighbor, friend or family member who is going on vacation, they may want to hire a house sitter to make sure their home isn't vacant while they're away.

Depending on what they want, house-sitting clients may ask you to be there for an hour or two a day. Or maybe they might just want to check in on the house every day. Some homeowners want a house sitter to live in the house for the entire time they're gone.

Make sure you get clear instructions about what type of house sitting they'll want before agreeing to take the job. Negotiate the pay you'll receive with potential clients and get a signed contract.

10. Wash Cars

Busy adults often don't have time to wash their cars, but you can make some serious cash doing it for them. You'll need equipment such as a bucket, soap, rags to wash with and towels to dry with.

If you're cleaning the interior of the cars as well, you'll want to get some window cleaner and paper towels. A portable hand-held vacuum can be a great accessory as well.

Most clients will let you use their hose and water to wash the exterior of the car, Some may lend you their vacuum for vacuuming the interior but be sure to check with them before you take the job.

Go Mobile

It'll be a good selling point if you come to their house to wash their car. This eliminates the need for them to make an extra stop at a car wash service center.

Determine how long it will take you to do the cleaning job and offer an attractive rate that still gives you a good hourly wage. Learn to work quickly and efficiently to improve your hourly rate.

11. Organize Homes or Garages

If you're good at organization, you can start a business organizing people's homes or garages. Many people want organized spaces but just aren't sure where to start.

If you have a knack for that type of work, you could be the answer to their prayers. When offering your services, take a thorough look at the job that needs to be done and determine how many hours it will take you.

Then times the number of hours by your desired hourly rate and make that your offered price for the job. You can advertise your services on Facebook, with flyers or with emails. Contact friends, neighbors and family members and let them know about your organizing services.

12. Sell Food and Water

There are a number of places where you could sell drinks (like lemonade) and snacks (baked goods) to residents. Busy street corners, outside of public baseball parks (if your city allows it) and at garage sales are some ideas.

These types of businesses are especially successful in the summertime or during busy event times. When we go to the local state fairgrounds, there are several vendors on the sidewalk selling bottled water and other packaged snacks.

Cost Matters

The key to success in this type of business boils down to cost. Be sure to charge enough to cover the cost of the items you're selling. Add in an extra cost to make yourself a profit for your hours of work as well.

As an example, you can usually get bottled water for about R1rand per litre at your local store(Mainly Checkers Hyper). If you sell the bottled water for R10 a bottle, you've just made a hefty profit. And because sports, fair and other venues tend to sell water for much more than that, clients will be happy to pay R10 for your water.

13. Work at a Restaurant

Two job that teen can take at a restaurant is working as a cashier at a fast-food place and working as a waitress at a local sit-down restaurant. The fast-food job is great because you can make a guaranteed hourly wage in a fun environment with fries as a side benefit. Waitress/waiter job is great because you can make awesome tips along with your salary. Both jobs experiences would allow you to make serious money as a teen.

If you like the idea of helping serve people food, inquire about jobs at restaurants near you. You could also work as a cook, a busboy/girl, or a cashier at local restaurants.

14. Be an Elderly Helper

An elderly helper is different from a babysitter or nanny. It's different because the parent is typically home most of the time you're there working.

As an elderly helper, you'll likely be asked to do a variety of different jobs to help the household run efficiently.

You might be asked to do the dishes, make lunch, or fold laundry. You might help a child with homework, change a diaper or take a young child out to play.

Being an elderly helper allows you to earn money by helping a family while still having an adult nearby. Check with local families and advertise with flyers to find work. Decide what your hourly wage will be based on the type of work you'll be required to do.

15. Run Errands

Many busy people and families would love to pay a teen who is willing to run errands for them. They might send you to pick up some groceries or to stop at the drug store.

They may have you drop off/pick up dry cleaning or make a run to the post office to mail a package. One tip will help you make the most of your errand running income. Choose to work in neighborhoods where stores and other destinations are close to a lot of homes and apartments.

16. Join a Property Management Team

Working for a property management team is another job you can take as as a teen. Investigate rental property companies in your area.

When tenants vacate head over to the house and paint the interior walls and/or clean the property to get it ready for the next tenant. You will get paid well usually directly after each job is finished.

If you like the idea of doing that type of work, check with property owners you know to see if they need help. Or advertise your services online with your parents' permission.

17. Hold a Class at Your Home

If you have a talent such as singing, drawing, painting, or dancing, you could hold classes for neighborhood kids in your yard or home. The classes can be one-time deals or can be held for several days in a row. For example, you could hold a day camp where kids come to participate in scavenger hunts or other activities. If you're going to teach a class to neighborhood kids, you'll need to create an itinerary. The itinerary should teach them what they want to learn and keep them busy for the entire class time. Be sure to charge a class fee that makes it worth your time and is affordable for parents.

18. Retail Worker

Many clothing and retail store managers are searching out teens to work cash registers and keep shelves stocked. Retail work can be done seasonally, like during the holidays, or you can work at stores all year round.

A professional appearance, a good attitude, and a willingness to be on time count where local retail stores are concerned.

If you have these qualities, you might want to consider a job in retail. Check with clothing, home improvement and big box stores near you for available jobs.

19. Ask Parents for Tasks

It's probably likely that your parents (or grandparents) have a lot of stuff they would like to have done around the house, but they just don't have the time to do it.

Ask your parents if they have a list of jobs, they would be willing to pay you to do. Maybe they'll hire you to deep clean the basement or garage. Or maybe they need help removing clutter in a home office.
They might want you to do a spring-cleaning project such as cleaning windows or washing blankets and comforters.

Have them make a list of jobs they need to be done around the house, along with what they'll pay for each completed job. Decide which jobs are jobs you want to do and finalize the details with your parents.

20. Turn Your Hobbies into Cash
Do you have a hobby that you can make money with? Are you good drawing people or animals? Do you know how to make great videos? Are you gifted at creating logos for businesses?
Are you great at writing stories, songs or poems?
Make a list of the talents you have and offer to hire out for them. You can advertise via local ads or gumtree and Facebook marketplace.
You might start out making less than you'd like to however, if people like your work and your services become more in demand, you'll be able to raise your rates.

21. Sell Your Products
Are you gifted at making crafts, jewelry, artwork, woodworking, or other items? If so, you can open an Etsy shop and sell your products.

You can also sell your products on sites such as Gumtree or Facebook market place or sell them at local fairs and events. Be sure to charge prices that cover your materials as well as your time.

22. Sell Your Designs
One way to make money that costs very little money out-of-pocket is to create designs for t-shirts and other items. You make the design, and then upload the

design to sites such as Redbubble or Cafe press, Redbubble or Cafe Press will print ordered designs on items such as t-shirts, tote bags, and iPad covers.

They even take care of shipping and returns. When someone orders an item with your design or saying on it, you get paid commission from the sale.

23. Grocery Store Employee

Grocery stores have many different job positions available for teens. You could be a cashier, a grocery bagger, a cart handler, or a stock person.

Grocery stores offer jobs that require customer interaction and jobs that don't require customer interaction. Therefore, grocery store work could be a good choice for you whether you love working with customers or would rather work behind the scenes.

24. Lifeguard

If you're a good swimmer and like hanging out at the beach, a lifeguard position might be right for you. Most lifeguard jobs require workers to have or get lifeguard certification through a qualified organization such as the Red Cross. Talk with local beach managers about what the qualifications are. Then see about local lifeguard certification class offerings if you're interested in pursuing a job as a lifeguard. If you're responsible and like being outside, this could be a good job choice for you.

25. Movie Theater Worker

If you love people and like movies, you might enjoy a job as a movie theater worker. Movie theaters offer several different job positions such as ticket sellers, ticket takers, concession stand workers and janitorial positions.

Check with your local theater management to see about putting in an application. Note that you may have to keep late working hours if you work at a theater.

26. Umpire or Referee

Local sports organizations often seek out teens to work umpire and referee jobs for kids' sports teams.

If you love and are good at sports such as baseball, basketball, softball, and football, you could apply to work as an umpire or referee. These types of jobs usually pay well too. In my area, umpires get paid up to $30 an hour. Check with local sports organizations for more details about referee jobs.

27. Get a Paper Route

Contact local papers to see if they have paper delivery routes available in your area. Or, check your local newspaper's employment section for ads seeking out paper delivery workers.

Know that working as a paper delivery person can require you to keep odd working hours. Some newspapers need to be delivered very early in the morning, for instance. However, if you're up early anyway you could get your delivery done before school.

Be sure to check on the days and hours you need to work before you sign on for this job. As with mail deliverers, newspaper deliverers are required to deliver in all types of weather.

28. Help a Senior

Many older people are looking to hire young people for various jobs. They might just want someone to spend time with them. Or they may want a teen to read to them, play cards or other games with them, or just simply talk with them.

Check with local retirement communities to find work. See if they have a job posting board where you can offer your services.

29. Be a Golf Caddy

Public and private golf clubs are often looking to hire teens as golf caddies for members and guests that come to play golf. If you like and know about the game of golf, or if you're willing to learn about it, you could land a job as a golf caddy. Bonus: Golf caddies often get nice tips from the people for whom they caddy.

30. Collect and Resell Golf Balls

Another job you can get working in the golf industry is collecting golf balls. Look for abandoned golf balls near local golf courses. Then, clean them up and resell them to local golfers.

You can search outside of local golf courses for stray balls. Look in tall weeds or shallow ponds. You might even be able to get permission to search on course grounds after hours from local club managers.

You can sell your cleaned-up golf balls outside of the local golf club entrance as long as you're on public property. Or you can ask people you know who play golf if they want to buy the balls you find at a price discounted from the retail price.

31. Be a Call Center Agent

Many companies hire call center agents to work from home instead of having to house them in a central commercial location. Call center reps to perform duties such as scheduling appointments. They also often answer customer service questions and product information questions. Many companies that are in need of customer service reps require applicants to be 18 years of age or older. However, some companies allow teens as young as 16 to work as customer service reps.

Companies in need of customer service reps provide all training for employees. Online customer service reps usually train via an online service manual. They'll send you the manual and you can read to learn about the company and its services and products. If you are polite and like working with people, this job could be a great way for you to earn money.

32. Tutor Kids

Many parents are looking for reasonably priced tutors for their kids in specific school subjects. If you're a teen that excels in a particular subject such as math, reading, or a foreign language, you can offer your tutor services to local parents. Ask neighborhood parents if they are in need of a tutor. Or check local online sites such as Craigslist for parents looking for tutors. Make sure to involve your parents when meeting up with a potential customer for safety reasons.

33. Paint Fences

Wooden fences need to be painted or stained every few years to protect the wood from deteriorating. If you like to paint and have neighbors who have wooden fences that need to be re-coated, ask if they'll hire you to do the job. You'll likely need to do some research on how to properly prepare wooden surfaces for painting. You'll also need to know what types of paints are best to use on outdoor wood surfaces before you start.

34. Boat and Camper Cleaning

You may have family members, friends or neighbors who own boats, campers, or other recreational vehicles. Check with them to see if they'd like to hire you to clean them out after they return from outings. Ask to use their hose and water for rinsing, and their shop vac for vacuuming if needed. Bring all other cleaning supplies from home to make it easier for clients. Charge a rate that allows you to do a thorough job quickly.

35. Grass and Plant Watering

Sometimes people need help with the task of watering their grass, flowers, and plants. Offer the service of coming to their home and watering these items for them. This is a job you'll likely perform once or twice a week to keep their grass and flowers healthy and fresh looking.

36. Doggie Doo-doo Scooper

Homeowners with dogs have to take the time to do the chore of cleaning up dog poo from their yards. Many of your neighbors might be open to considering paying you to do this job for them.

Schedule regular yard cleaning times for each client in order to bring in a steady amount of money for your business. Bring your own scooper and a small garbage bag. Discard the droppings in the outside trash bin or wherever your client tells you to.

37. Rent Out Your Video Games

If you've got a lot of video games or books, you can rent them to friends for a small fee. Charge them a certain amount to rent the item for a week or two, and make sure to tell them there will be a late fee if the item isn't returned to you on time. Keep a notebook listing who has what items and when they're due back so that you don't lose track of your stuff.

38. Do Lawn Work

Help your neighbors with lawn work. Mow the lawn in the spring, summer, and winter, also offer to rake leaves when the season of leaves falling start. Fact is there is some people in your neighborhood could use help maintaining their lawns. Ask your parents if you can use their lawnmower or you can use each client's mower if they have one they are willing to let you use. If you're not interested in mowing lawns, you could offer to rake and bag leaves.

39. Weed Gardens

If your neighbors have flower and vegetable gardens, you might be able to earn some money by offering to pull weeds from the garden for them.
Weeding usually needs to be done on a weekly basis in most gardens and is hard work for older people, so they might appreciate a teen taking this task off of their hands.

40. Collect Aluminum Cans or Bottles

If your neighbors drink a lot of canned drinks such as sodas, consider asking them if you can pick up their discarded soda and other beverage cans once a week. Then bring the cans or bottles to a local recycling center where they'll pay you cash for your aluminum cans and empty bottles.

Ways to Make the Most of Your Income Earning Skills

Anyone can do a job, but it takes certain skills to keep clients coming back. Here are some things you can do to help maximize the amount of money you can make at the jobs you do.

Be on Time
Timeliness is a big deal in the working world. Show your clients or the manager at the job you're working that you appreciate the work by being on time, every time. Show up early if you have to, but avoid being late.

Have a Great Attitude
Workers and business owners with friendly, positive attitudes will go a lot further, work a lot longer and earn a lot more money than those with a downtrodden demeanor and a negative attitude.

Choose to be positive in your work environment and spread happiness to others with a cheerful outlook.

Be Professional
A professional employee or business owner possesses certain characteristics. For instance, they work well with others, they avoid office gossip and they take their job seriously.

Make sure to have a professional attitude about whatever-money making ventures you participate in.

Do Your Job Really Well
To keep clients coming back for more business and help make sure your manager wants to keep you as an employee, be sure to do your job to the best of your ability. Do what is asked of you and follow any directions as stated.

Provide Quality Products
If you're working to make money by selling things you make or own, be sure to provide quality products. Take the time to do your best work when selling things, you make such as jewelry or artwork, and when you're selling products you own, be sure to clean them up and have them in good working order.

Go the Extra Mile
Going the extra mile is especially important when you're running a business such as a car washing or house cleaning business. One way to help ensure clients keep asking you to do more work for them is to go above and beyond. For instance, if you're doing a house cleaning job, organize a small closet as a bonus. If you're cleaning cars, scrub out a carpet stain for free. Make sure your "extra mile" added jobs don't take up too much of your time but will benefit the customer. The added effort you give will help provide them with a reason to use your services again.

Practice Safety While Working
Always put safeguards in place as you work. It might mean keeping cleaning chemicals out of the reach of small children or pets while you're doing a cleaning job, or having a parent escort you to meet a new client or work for someone you don't know very well.

Safety at work is good for clients and for you.

There are many ways you as a teen can put money in your pocket. With a little creativity and some hard work, you can be earning serious cash in no time.

Which of the above jobs you will embark in from today on to earn extra cash?

_____
_____
_____
_____
_____
_____
_____
_____
_____
_____

ENTREPRENEURSHIP

Is the spirit of entrepreneurship at this age important?

Learning about the spirit of entrepreneurship at a young age will allow children to learn all types of concepts focused on starting and operating a company. This can help prepare them for the real world where they'll have to think on their own and come up with solutions to all types of problems. Employers look for candidates who're entrepreneurial, think outside the box and can work on their own with minimal supervision.

Like most developing countries, South Africa desperately needs entrepreneurs to help address the serious socio-economic challenges we face.

52.6% of South Africa's youth are unemployed. That's according to statistics from Good Governance Africa. The youth are the most affected by unemployment.
The challenges that young South African's face in accessing jobs are huge. For starters, South Africa's lackluster growth and strict labor laws are not conducive to job creation. What's more, inexperience makes it harder for young people to get their foot in the door. It goes without saying that being young and unemployed increases the risk of social exclusion, a loss of motivation and mental health problems.

Fortunately, it's not all doom and gloom. As a young South African looking to make your mark in the world all you need are these three ingredients:
- The right advice from an expert.
- Marketable skills; and
- Inspiration and passion for a better future.

Young entrepreneurs creating jobs for a better future

Do you think you're too young to start a business? Think again! Many young people are doing it for themselves and they're excelling.

22-year-old Ludwick Marishane – he's the CEO of 'HeadBoy Industries' and an inventor of DryBath, the world's first bath-substituting solution.

Rupert Bryan, now the chief operating officer at Web Africa. Rupert Bryan ran a web development company from the age of 14!

These young entrepreneurs had a vision to change the world and they didn't stop there; they turned their vision into reality; Their passion and determination propelled them to beat the odds; and they're now successful leaders who all entrepreneurs can aspire to.

These young entrepreneurs and many others prove you're never too young to start a business

 Task

Think about the business you want to start.

Name five business opportunities you see around and, in the world, and start planning on how you will execute them. Remember every business starts small and its starts with an idea and then action:

I _____ will be an entrepreneur. I will be an innovator and a game changer.

Choose two or three methods above suitable for you to make money and start doing it.

I_____ choose to engage in the following activities to earn money.

1._____ 2._____

3._____ 4._____

5._____

Below are the business opportunities I will start.

Give it your own name. Example** Xoliswa Divines Hair Solon

1._____ 2._____

3._____ 4._____

5._____

Start Date: _____ this task will be done at _____

Signature: _____

HONESTY

Life may present many disappointing situations. Accepting failure can be difficult to handle. Parents may wish to coach their child to be a better sport and lose or even win gracefully. They may be inspired to take failures in their stride and look upon them as learning lessons. Children who are actively involved in playing sports and accumulate healthy experiences of winning and losing on the field may be better equipped to deal with failures in life.

1. Lying Takes Energy

Making decisions is mentally taxing. Each time you lie, no matter how small or insignificant, you are spending energy on making a decision of whether to lie or tell the truth. It is well documented that the more decisions we make in the day, the worse our judgement becomes. Matters of financial stupidity, infidelity and substance abuse are all greatest later in the day when our decision-making apparatus is at its most burned out. Last minute ridiculous purchases at the check-out counter are induced by making dozens of prior purchasing decisions. Judge's rulings are deemed less fair later in the day after prior decisions. If you only tell the truth you have eliminated hundreds of decisions from your day. You will make better decisions in all other areas of your life by never choosing to lie.

2. If You Lie to Others you Will Lie to Yourself

No one self-identifies with being a liar. The more you lie the more your ego will convince you didn't do it. Your lies become in conflict with your identity, and as a result you start to believe them. After you have begun to believe your own lies, who will be there to tell you the truth? Blurring the line between truth and lie is at the heart of self-deception. Self-deception is the opposite of the enlightened state we seek.

> The first principle is that you must not fool yourself and you are the easiest person to fool. - *Richard P. Feynman*

3. Lying Subconsciously Produces Anxiety and Fear

When one lies, they constantly have to remain on guard for fear of being discovered. This creates a subconscious state of anxiety where the mind worries about the future. Much of our day-to-day anxiety comes from this worry about being 'found out'.

4. Trust Creates Opportunity

When people are aware of your dishonesty, they cannot completely trust you. People will be more guarded around you. People will share true information less easily. People relax and become more authentic with you when they trust you. Information, opportunity, and relationships are extremely valuable.

> Anyone who doesn't take truth seriously in small matters cannot be trusted in large ones either. - *Albert Einstein*

5. You Will be Surrounded by People Who Accept You

When we are 100% honest about ourselves, we select for people that accept us for who we are. Life is too short to waste time being with people that cannot accept us for being our true authentic selves.

6. Lying, Even with Good Intention, is Disrespect

When we lie to make someone feel better (no, you don't look fat in those jeans) we are disrespecting them by implying they cannot emotionally handle the truth. The truth can always be told in a respectful way. A lie cannot.

7. When People Ask Your Opinion, You Know They Really Value it

If you only tell the truth, and people know this, much of the bullshit gets filtered out. People will only ask you questions when they truly want your opinion. People appreciate it. This eliminates mental and verbal clutter from your life. If someone does not appreciate the truth, then this person is not deserving of your time.

Now don't confuse truth telling with being an asshole. There are ways to tell the truth in any scenario without being hurtful. At the core people crave truth and honesty. Wrap the truth in genuine empathy and understanding. A genuine person is a glass of ice water in the desert of superficiality and lies we normally inhabit.

8. Truth Forces Self-reflection

In order to always tell the truth, you need to know what you believe. When you take this truth telling seriously your responses become less automatic. You start pausing because it is so important to you that what you say is genuine. It can be a little taxing and strenuous at first but creates a deep seeded feeling of agency and ownership. It creates calm.

9. Truth Creates Freedom

Every time you lie to someone you have unknowingly limited your options.
In order to maintain the lie and not be discovered some of your freedom must now be sacrificed.

People think that a liar gains a victory over his victim. What I've learned is that a lie is an act of self-abdication, because one surrenders one's reality to the person to whom one lies, making that person one's master, condemning oneself from then on to faking the sort of reality that person's view requires to be faked…The man who lies to the world, is the world's slave from then on…

> There are no white lies, there is only the blackest of destruction, and a white lie is the blackest of all. - *Ayn Rand*

10. Guilt and Shame are Built From Lies

These are toxic emotions and should be eliminated. Lying creates guilt, and guilt leads to shame. Underneath our guilt and shame oftentimes lies anger, resentment, or fear. Telling the truth will not guarantee freedom from these emotions but lying virtually ensures you will have them. If you lie without guilt and shame you may be a sociopath. If you are a sociopath, the other reasons still apply to you, so don't lie.

11. Truth Diminishes Others' Power Over You

If you are always truthful no one can blackmail you with your lies. When you lie, you are giving people power over you. This is counter intuitive because on the surface lies feel so powerful.

12. Like Attracts Like

Truth is a valuable commodity, and truthful people are highly valued. People that value truth are more often truthful themselves. These people will be attracted to you because you are more valuable to them. You will slowly find yourself surrounded by higher quality people. It is a virtuous circle you should cultivate.

13. Lying Cheapens Your Brand

One of the most valuable things you possess is your integrity. It is also one of the easiest things to lose. Keeping your integrity is much easier than trying to get it back. Once you lie to an honest person, they will remember it forever.

Consequences

Becoming truthful will have consequences; mostly positive but consequences none the less. If you are living a life where lying is common the transition may be painful at first. It takes courage and fortitude to face these lies and accept the consequences. Only you can know if or when you are ready. Start dealing with the small lies first and work up to the big ones. Don't confuse truth with confession. You don't necessarily need to dig up old lies from the past and project them on a billboard and announce them to the world, rather you need to make the conscious decision to be truthful going forward.

Declaration:

I_____ I promise to be honest in all my life dealings, I will tell the truth at all times. Lies will have no part of me.

Signature:_____

Signed at_____on the_____

_____

_____

_____

_____

_____

_____

_____

IF YOU CAN DREAM IT, YOU CAN DO IT

We dream.

We take steps.

Those steps become leaps.

We trip and fall but we get up and dust ourselves off.

We get comfortable with the concept of being uncomfortable.

We push ourselves beyond our perceived limits.

We second guess our abilities.

We get up every day and attempt to kick ass. Some days it is our own ass that gets kicked.

Here are a few tips on how you can go about achieving your dreams.

1. Articulate your 'dream'

The most important step towards realizing your dreams is articulating them. A 'dream' in this case is a professional ambition. For example, a bigger car could be something you wish for but that is not a professional dream. A 'dream' would be to achieve in your startup and begin exporting your products to foreign countries over time. A 'dream' could also be to achieve success as an artist by having your work recognized by the art community and wanting to have your work exhibited in a foreign country. Articulating this kind of professional ambition helps create a sense of enduring motivation in the dreamer and can help them move forward on the path to.

2. Be prepared to work hard

Realizing a vision is often painstaking work. Thomas Edison, the renowned inventor, had explained when asked about his 'genius' that 'genius is one percent inspiration, ninety nine percent perspiration'. The dream or the is the inspiration. The perspiration, or work, will determine whether your idea will ever achieve fruition. A great idea is the beginning and not a recipe for success.

3. Stay positive when faced by failure

Taking failure in your stride will help navigate the peaks and troughs of day to day life that are inevitable in any meaningful endeavor. There will be some dark times on the road, and not letting that affect you adversely is key to ensuring that you continue your path. Having unreasonable expectations for the reward you think you deserve for your efforts today could quite likely lead to you losing motivation. Try to stay positive and learn from the mistakes you might make. Not repeating mistakes is the hallmark of a great.

4. Enjoy your successes

Successes will find their way to you if you keep making the right efforts. Take the time out to savor them. Savoring success can help renew the spirit and provide energy for greater efforts in the future. Enjoying your successes will also make the journey worthwhile. The journey is just as important as the destination. Time that goes by, never returns.

5. Have a support system

Very few, if any, of the greatest achievements in history were achieved by people working in solitude. A support system is invaluable on the path to success. Identify a core group of people who support you and keep them close. Pursuing a dream will involve making sacrifices and communicating with your loved ones and helping them understand your priorities is essential. They will be able to stand by you better if they understand. Also, have a. A source of knowledge and guidance, beyond emotional support, can make a significant impact, especially in the nascent stage of starting a business.

Dreams are a beautiful thing. They inspire us and push us to be better than who we are today. Harness the power of your dreams and use that energy to achieve your professional ambitions.

Declaration:: List your dreams below

_____

_____

_____

_____

_____

_____

_____

_____

_____

_____

_____

_____

SURROUNDING YOURSELF WITH INSPIRATIONAL PEOPLE

Who you spend time with the most is who you will become. It's important that you surround yourself with positive people, be it friends, family members, and work colleagues. People's vibes, mindsets, and beliefs will become your own, as we as humans are like chameleons, so only surround yourself with the best who you will help you to take your life to a new level.

Life is hard enough – we don't always win, and there will always be obstacles and naysayers along our path to success. During those times, nothing feels better than having someone you can share your fears and doubts with friends and mentors that not only listen, but also cheer you on to be the best you can be. "Get back in there and do better! You can do it!" They give you energy and help you propel forward. Find and focus on relationships with those who can share their wins and positive vibes and help you realize that you can do the same. Life is too short for the negativity.

It's widely known that one of the best ways to improve on a skill is to practice it with someone who's better than you. Yes, you will have to work harder, think faster, and learn more fundamentals. You'll sweat and have sore muscles, but after a while, your skills will improve and, eventually, you might even be good enough to teach someone else a thing or two. This idea of playing with someone better than you translate nicely to your personal and career successes as well, and that's why it's important to surround yourself with people who are winners.

Find People Who Are Smarter Than You
Many entrepreneurs and businesspeople aspire to be the smartest person in the room on every topic. But if you're always the smartest person, you're actually

limiting yourself. Famously, Jim Rohn once said, "You're the average of the five people you spend most of your time with." It's common for us to underestimate the importance of the company we keep. We need people, whether they're teachers, mentors, family, or trusted friends, who challenge us and push us to be better. The right circle of influence raises the bar, helping us to set new, loftier expectations of ourselves. Oftentimes, we don't know what we are capable of until we see others achieve. When we surround ourselves with positive, successful people they consciously (and subconsciously) challenge us to be our best selves.

Cultivate "Real Life" Relationships with People Who Have Already Accomplished Your Goals

It's time to rethink how we use our social media and focus on our "real life" relationships. Today's social media feeds can often be reminders of what we can't do, haven't done or don't believe we can accomplish. Seeing someone's online "highlight reel" doesn't truly show you what goes on behind the scenes and how much work it really requires. Spend time on the process of success, not just the results of it.

If You Can't Play Tennis, Watch the Game
Experiencing Summit's LA18 experience was both inspirational and aspirational and I met some "real life" people who have already made an impact on my life, but I realize that attending seminars isn't a possibility for everyone. Or perhaps you can't surround yourself with people who have what you want simply because you don't know them or can't get access to them. (Cohen,Jenn)

My solution is simple: consume their media and make them the "friends in your head." For example, if you want to take your business to the next level, listen to Gary Vaynerchuck's daily podcast. Bring him along on your daily drive to work and school and soak up his tips, tricks, and knowledge. Another amazing speaker from the Summit event was Rich Roll. Rich has written a number of books and also has a podcast. If you think you can't master the wellness game, he will show you how it's done.

If you want to become your best self I challenge you to review, rethink, and cull through your social media and real life "friends" and find the right people and media content that will actually help you get there.

Highly successful people are generally willing to share what it really takes to make things happen. They have the ability to help you learn from the mistakes they've made along the way and the "tricks and tips" to help you reach your goals faster. Seek out leaders of your field and get some real face time with them.

 Complete the below exercise and identify people are inspirational to you

"Show me your friends and I'll show you your future." Mark Ambrose	Who are your Friends?
"You become like the five people you spend the most time with. Choose carefully." Jim Rohn	Who are you Spending time with
"You need to associate with people that inspire you, people that challenge you to rise higher, people that make you better. Don't waste your valuable	Who/ what inspires You

time with people that are not adding to your growth. Your destiny is too important." Joel Osteen	
"Surround yourself with those on the same mission as you." Anonymous	Who is on the same mission as you?
"Bad company corrupts good character." Anonymous	What bad company have you been keeping?
"Surround yourself with those who only lift you higher." Oprah Winfrey	Who encourages you and believes in your dreams?
"You're a product of your environment, surround yourself with the best." Anonymous	Where do you hang out? Where, and with whom, do you spend most of your time?
Walk with the dreamers, the believers, the courageous, the cheerful, the planners, the doers, the successful people with their heads in the clouds and their feet on the ground." Wilfred Peterson	Who are your dreamers?
"Surround yourself with people who have dreams, desire, and ambition; they'll help you push for, and realize your own." Anonymous	Who pushes you
"People inspire you, or they drain you – pick them wisely." Hans F. Hansen	Who drains you? Who inspires you?
"Energy is contagious, positive and negative alike. I will forever be mindful of what and who I am allowing into my space." Alex Elle	Who are you allowing in your space

"Your friends should motivate and inspire you. Your circle should be well rounded and supportive. Keep it tight, quality over quantity." Anonymous	Who are your friends?
"Always surround yourself with people who are better than you. If you're hanging around bad people, they're going to start bringing you down. But if you surround yourself with good people, they're going to be pulling you up." Donny Osmand	Who is pulling you up?
"Keep away from people who try to belittle your ambitions. Small people always do that, but the really great make you feel that you, too can become great." Mark Twain	Is anyone belittling you ambitions? If so, who and how?

I_____ promise to surround myself with the dreamers, and the doers, the believers, and thinkers, but most of all, I will surround myself with those who see the greatness within me, even when I don't see it myself.

Signature:_____

Signed at_____ on the_____

HAVE A SUPPORT SYSTEM

No man is an island — describes the inter-connectedness of the human experience. Nobody can make it alone, their own island in the sea. We need others to help us survive and thrive. We're a society of teachers, doctors, builders, and everything else, and none of us can do it all.

Everyone needs a network of people who provide an individual with practical or emotional support.

What is a support system?
A support system, simply, is an informal network of people you rely on — emotionally or practically. The usual suspects are family members, friends, coworkers, and neighbors. It could also be members of voluntary organizations, religious groups, teammates, or online buddies.

Benefits of a strong support system
- higher self-esteem
- a better ability to cope with stress
- feeling more in-control of your life

Research has proved that having a support system has many positive benefits, such as higher levels of well-being, better coping skills and a longer and healthier life. Studies have also shown that social support can reduce depression and anxiety

Why do we need a personal support system?
When things aren't going well or we're just not feeling that great we all need support and encouragement.

For those who try to tough it alone, it can be a difficult uphill battle. On the other hand, much wisdom, experience, and insight that can be gained from friends, family or colleagues who have been there and have learned what it takes to prevail. Before we get to the point of great difficulty, or in anticipation of life's little setbacks, we should implement strategies or have a support system in place to help us through some of those rough spots.

Here are some tips and strategies:

1. **Turn to family and friends.**

There is no substitute for family and good friends to support and encourage you when the chips are down. Sometimes just talking to someone can lift your spirits and help take the weight off your shoulders. Having someone listen to your concerns helps make you feel supported and understood, which in turn encourages you to look at things differently.

2. **Cultivate a variety of interests.**

Read more, go to the movies or a play, listen to great music, enjoy beautiful art, learn to dance. Engaging in healthy and mind-expanding activities can preoccupy you when you need a healthy distraction. Not only do they preoccupy you, they help you grow and develop, therefore leave less time to brood or stay down for too long.

3. **Exercise and play sports.**

Have an assortment of exercises or fun sports you can draw upon to work out and let off some pent-up energy and steam. There is nothing like a good workout to stimulate your happy hormones (endorphins). The after-effects can last up to three hours and put you in a positive frame of mind.

4. Take a short, affordable trip.

We all have someplace we've always wanted to visit, but just never got around to. Travel to a big city such as New York City, Montreal, Boston, or Toronto and partake of the cultural treasures it has to offer. The experience can expand your horizons and give you that change of scenery you need. If you happen to live in one of these bustling big cities, take a trip to the countryside and enjoy the bucolic surroundings.

5. Create a quiet place or sanctuary for yourself.

Find a quiet place in your home, a corner in your local library, or a park where to can go to meditate, contemplate, or rejuvenate yourself. In your home it could be a nice bubble bath with candles and soft music playing. In the library you could find a secluded corner where you can curl up with a book and be lost to the world. You can go for a stroll in the park and enjoy the flowers, trees and birds and connect with the surroundings.

6. Volunteer at a hospital or a home for the handicapped.

Take a day and volunteer your services to someone who needs your help. Giving support is as important as receiving it. It would put things in perspective. Life is short. Learn to appreciate and make the best of it.

Rather than resorting to unhealthy outlets such as over-eating, alcohol, or other harmful substances when we are down, we can find positive ways of expressing ourselves while at the same time building resilience.

We are here to build our resources, rather than deplete them or bring harm to ourselves.

RAISING YOUR LEVEL OF EXPECTATION

Do you have a winning attitude?
Expand Your Vision, looking up and raising your level of expectation will impact every area of your life. Small thinking and small expectations limit God's ability to work on your behalf, God wants us to lift our eyes beyond being concerned only for our immediate needs and wants and only for those things that seem possible. He wants us to expect mighty things and to bring whole nations into His kingdom.

Don't Limit God
God's will for you is to dream big and receive big, Purpose to live expecting great and exciting things in your life every day. In order to raise your expectations, you must look to God's Word and His promises. Those promises, and nothing less, should be your expectations. Wake up expecting good things to happen. When God says He will do something, we can trust that He will. This is our promise, our hope from Him. Raise your level of expectation today! God is good and His Will for my life and yours is to prosper!

Philippians 4:6 - "Do not be anxious about anything, but in everything by prayer and supplication with thanksgiving let your requests be made known to God."

I admire people who like to "raise the bar" a little when it comes to setting goals. Those are my kind of people. You'd be smart to get into the habit of always setting a target that makes you "reach" a little bit higher. That way you won't be disappointed if you fall a little bit short. That's the way to stay centered on your personal growth and development. Organize a plan of action that keeps you focused on winning. Anyone can achieve modest goals. That's why modest goals always yield modest rewards. Will you be satisfied with that? I was never happy with that.

RAISING THE BAR ON EXPECTATIONS, WILL INCREASE YOUR LEVEL OF ACHIEVEMENT!

I never set a small goals for my life in my life! I always wanted to be the very best I could be, and I organized my efforts to achieve that. And it worked! Yes, I started out with more attainable short-term goals, but they all added up to what I really had my sights set on-becoming the very best I could be in my chosen field! Once I became the best at what I do, the only person left for me to challenge was, well myself. And I did that too. I was never content with staying in the same place. I would reorganize my efforts using every tool I could get my hands on to achieve new goals.

What are your expectations today?
Are you just assuming that today will go as it did yesterday, with nothing out of the ordinary going on? Or, do you expect more out of today than yesterday?
Don't lower your expectations to meet your performance. Raise your level of performance to meet your expectations. Expect the best of yourself, and then do what is necessary to make it a reality.

It is important to note that absolutely everything that has ever been achieved happened because a powerful formula was created between the powerful agents of our expectation, the lens of our expectation and the corresponding action.

I_____ promise to practice the below 5 things right now to raise my level of expectation.

**Choose to expect great things of yourself and write down at least five things you expect from your life today.

1._____   2._____

3._____   4._____

5._____

**Now raise the level of your expectancy. Do not use the past as a yard stick to measure your expectations by do not allow past experiences to dull your dreams. By raising your expectancy allow your perspective of your world and what is possible to be enlarged. Rewrite the five things you are expecting from your life.

**Write yourself affirmations to support your high level of expectation and repeat it to yourself throughout each day.

**Stand in front of the mirror and inform yourself that it is okay to have high expectations and that the past does not have a part to play in the decision-making process.

**Wake up each day and openly declare the day as great day before it really gets started, after all it is a new day fresh with no mistakes so why can't it be a great day?

**Be observant, as you go about your day look around you and begin to acknowledge and see the things around you. You will be amazed at what you see when you are really looking.

**At the end of the day write a gratitude journal and give thanks for at least five things that you have experienced each day.

I am grateful for:

1._____ 2._____

3._____ 4._____

5._____ 6._____

7._____ 8._____

9._____ 10._____

Completed on: _____

Signature: _____

Signed at_____on the_____

NOTES

_____

_____

_____

_____

_____

_____

ELIMINATE "I CAN'T" FROM YOUR VOCABULARY

Can't is a terrible word and it has to be taken out of your vocabulary.

When someone says, "I can't do it . . ." I say to myself, "What do you mean you can't do it?" Maybe you don't want to do it but saying you "can't" do it is a completely different story.

With the right mindset, positive attitude, and a clear vision of what you want to accomplish, the only thing that is holding you back is yourself.
Can't is a terrible word and it has to be taken out of your vocabulary.
By saying you can't do something, you're already doubting yourself, submitting to defeat, and you're making that barrier around your life tighter. We are going to remove this word for good.

From now on there is nothing we can't do.
When you stop saying "I can't" and replace it with "I can" or "I will", you will start achieving more than ever before. Before you know it, what you once thought was impossible becomes possible. Make it your goal this week to eliminate the word "can't" from your vocabulary. You don't need it anymore!

"Attitude is like a Tattoo"
Your attitude is everything; it's your reason, your why and how, your facial expression, emotions, body language, and potentially the end result. How you approach an opportunity, and the result of it, is solely based on you — not friend.
If you enter a business meeting with a sour attitude, that negative energy can spread like wildfire. People can also feel it — maybe even taste it. This is not an impression you want to leave.

We can't always win, but even if the outcome is negative, your attitude and perception can turn it into a positive. The question is: can you do it?

It's much better to be known for your positive attitude — your poise, your energy, the reason why things go so well because you are able to maintain such character. A negative attitude is easy. It's easy to complain, it's easy to be mad, and it's even easier to do nothing to change it.

When I say your "attitude is like a tattoo", it sounds permanent. Tattoos can be removed, but that's not the point. Your attitude is like a tattoo because you wear it. People can see it and sometimes, they will judge you on it. If you maintain a negative attitude, then it is permanent until you change it. Change your attitude and I guarantee the results change as well.

Believe You Can Do It

Do you know why most people say "can't" and doubt themselves before trying anything?

It's our lack of self-confidence and fear on many different levels. The one thing we have to purge from ourselves is fear — fear of bad results, fear of change, fear of denial, fear of loss, the fear that makes us worry and lose sleep. Worrying is the same as going outside with an umbrella, waiting for rain to hit it. Stop worrying and move on.

Confidence is fragile: It builds up slowly but can shatter like glass. Project your confidence and energy into believing in yourself. This is a very important and groundbreaking step — one that is usually the hardest to take. Start telling yourself you can do something, anything, and you will do it the best to your ability. Remove doubt, remove fear, and stick with positive energy.

Be Aware of Your Thoughts

Many times, we don't even realize how negative we are, and how this affects our relationships with the people we love. This needs to change. You need to learn how to "catch" these thoughts as they arise in your head. The moment you realize that you are using the "Can'ts" and "Won'ts", you should immediately stop the thought.

Breathe

Only stopping the thought won't do it. Take a deep breath and focus on that, instead of the negative thought. Give yourself time and space. After a few minutes and a few long breaths, you will feel slightly more relaxed.

Change Your Thoughts

Now, it's time to change the can't to "I can and I will". You can add a "someday" or "soon" to make your thoughts seem more realistic and achievable. However, you need to keep that thought. Our brains need 12 seconds to convey positive experiences to long-term memory. If you don't do this, your brain will quickly dismiss the thought.

Make It a Habit

Our habits shape us as individuals, both mentally and physically. Make this way of positive thinking a habit. Once you master the art of thinking positively and minimize the "Cant's" in your life, you will notice a change in your life.

Surround Yourself with Positive People

As much as your mood can affect the people in your life, in a negative or a positive way, the same goes for them as well. If you are surrounded by quitters, unambitious, negative, or toxic people, you will eventually accept those traits yourself.

The Fear of Failure is Your Biggest Enemy
There are many reasons why people give up or do not try to start a plan or an idea. The fear of failure is an invisible "force" that keeps your mind in constant negation, so the goal that you want to achieve remains imaginary. Keep in mind that whatever you want to start needs effort, not just desire and dreams.

There will be obstacles and there will be crashes. I'd be lying if I said there won't be. The world is stern for power and recognition. The world is full of competition and no one will allow you to easily climb to the top.

It takes a lot of effort to succeed. You will fall, but you will bounce back. Life is a boisterous sea, and you are the captain who needs to spread the sails and sail tirelessly and bravely.

The world is mainly made of extremes. There is a day and there is the night. There is good and there is evil, there is a "CAN", but "CAN'Ts" should not be allowed. Remember that there is nothing like instant success. Regardless of the development of technology and all possibilities, hard work, knowledge, and talent are timeless attributes that will lead you to the desired success.

Every Failure is a New Lesson
Evaluate your every step. Learn from the error, analyze what needs to be corrected and what you want to achieve. The road to success is a continuous process of learning and growing. You can never know what you could do if you don't try. Think about how much the goal you want to achieve, arouses excitement, ambition, and happiness inside you and is valuable for your time and money.

We all say it all the time: I can't.

"It won't work." "It doesn't happen like that." "I can't afford it." "I can't find it." "I can't build that." "We can't finance that!" I'm tired of hearing it! For one week, stop being a negative Nancy and try this:

Instead of saying "I can't," train your brain instead to turn this negative statement into a positive question.

Instead of "I can't," ask "How can I?" It's a subtle change, but a powerful one. If you can eliminate this one simple phrase from your life and replace it with this question, your whole life, both business and personal, can change.

Replacing Negative words with Positive words:

Instead Of…	Try Thinking
I'm not good at this	What am I missing?
I made a mistake	Mistakes help me improve
This is too hard	This may take some time & effect
I can't make this any better	I can always improve & I'll keep trying
I can't do math	I'm going to train my brain in math

Declaration

I_____ promise that from today:

I will change my "I can't" to "I can"

Starting with:

1._____ 2._____

3._____ 4._____

5._____ 6._____

7._____ 8._____

9._____ 10._____

Signature: _____

Signed at_____on the_____

POSITIVE THINKING PHRASES TO CHANGE YOUR LIFE

What are positive thinking phrases?
They are sentences, quotes or sayings that inspire and motivate, and which contain insights and knowledge. They are like doors leading to new thoughts and a wider viewpoint.

Positive thinking phrases can help you change your mindset and help you improve your life. Positive thinking phrases and sayings are similar to affirmations, those positive statements that can affect your subconscious mind and your life in a good and constructive way.

Any sentence, phrase or saying that makes you feel good, happy, and inspired is worth reading over and again, writing it down, and putting it where you can see it often every day. It can be useful in your everyday life, in good times and in difficult times. It energizes, inspires, and empowers you.

Below, you will find a list of positive thinking phrases that I have written, which I hope you will like reading. Don't read them just once, but many times. Each time that you read them attentively.

I promise to replace it with the below phrases:

1. I expect the best, aspire for the best, and do my best.
2. As the sun shines after the night is over, so success appears after problems and failure.
3. If some people achieve success, it means that others can too, including you.
4. It does not cost money to think, feel and act positively, and it does not cost money to think, feel and act negatively, so why not choose to think, feel, and act positively?

5. If you want success, you don't sit down moan and complain. Instead, make plans and carry them out.
6. If you don't like the kind of life you are living now, start making changes. You can live a different lifestyle. All you need is ambition, motivation, a good plan, and perseverance.
7. Every thought, every emotion, and every word you express, affects you and the people around you. Therefore, be careful of what you think, feel, and say.
8. I appreciate the goods things in my life and thank the Universe for them.
9. I can learn new skills and I can improve every area of my life.
10. I believe in myself and in my ability to find love, progress in my work, and achieve success in everything I do.
11. I have the motivation and inner strength to invest all the effort needed in following my dreams and goals and making them come true.
12. I invite happiness, love, peace, and satisfaction into my life.
13. I welcome every day with love and joy.
14. I am open to new experiences, new possibilities, and new opportunities.
15. I have an infinite number of possibilities, and I am going to choose the best ones.
16. I shower love, happiness, and kindness on everyone I meet, and get the same love, happiness, and kindness from them.
17. I send love, happiness and success to my friends and family, and for everyone who loves and likes me, and even for people who do not like me.
18. Day by day, my life is improving in every way.
19. I am learning to accept everything without judgement and without taking anything too personally.
20. There is no use to dwell in the past. Whatever happened in the past belongs to the past, but the past does not exist now. What exists now is the present. Therefore, live in the present, improve the present, and enjoy the present.
21. The sooner you get free of the past, the sooner you will have more control over your present and your future.
22. When you let go of the past you make room for new experiences, new people, and new opportunities.

23. Believe that you can become successful, even when experiencing failure and disappointment. If you keep this mental image in your mind, you will ultimately become successful.
24. A strong belief that you can be successful will take you forward, motivate you, and inspire you to take action and move forward.
25. You can be happy the moment you choose to stop dwelling on hurts, losses, and the things you do not like in your life.
26. When you believe in yourself, you do not need the approval of other people for your beliefs and for your actions.
27. When waking up in the morning, tell yourself how wonderful your day is going to be. Repeat positive phrases a few times and believe the words you are repeating.
28. When you enter bed at night, tell yourself how wonderful is going to be tomorrow.
29. Replace your negative thoughts with positive thoughts and negative feelings with positive feelings. If it is difficult, do not give up. Just continue until this turn into an effortless habit.
30. When you change your mind and open the door to better and happier thoughts, your life would change accordingly.
31. If you are facing difficulties now, take this as a challenge, and with energy and joy start looking for a solution, instead of getting depressed and becoming passive.
32. If you say, "I can't" you close your mind to opportunities and stay where you are. If you say, "I can", you open your mind to opportunities and move forward.
33. If there something I cannot do; I can learn to do.
34. If you expect to find opportunities and you will find them. All you need is to change your mind and start expecting and believing.
35. There are always small things in your everyday, which you can do differently. Making things differently changes your life and makes it more interesting.

🖉 Declaration

I_____ promise to change my vocabulary _____(date)

AFFIRMATION CONTRACT

Daily affirmations are simple, positive statements declaring specific goals in their completed states. Although they sound rather basic at that level, these empowering mantras have profound effects on the conscious and unconscious mind.

Affirmations also hold a key to unlocking the Law of Attraction and creating the life of your dreams!

Successful people, from top salespeople and entrepreneurs to bestselling authors and Olympic athletes, have figured out that using willpower to power their success isn't enough.

You need to let go of any and all negative thoughts and images and bombard your subconscious mind with new thoughts and images that are positive and stated in the present tense.

Every now and then, there are days when you just need a little pick-me-up. You can blame it on the weather, on the wrong side of the bed, that horrible thing that your co-worker said, or That Time of The Month. However, this doesn't mean you should talk down to yourself and allow those negative thoughts to marinate. To combat those not-so-great feels, we curated a healthy list of positive affirmations you should tell yourself and bookmark so you can always come back to remind yourself just how awesome you are.

36 POSITIVE AFFIRMATIONS

1. I'm allowed to take up space.
2. My past is not a reflection of my future.
3. I am smart enough to make my own decisions.
4. I'm in control of how I react to others.
5. I choose peace.
6. I'm courageous and stand up for myself.
7. I will succeed today.
8. I deserve to have joy in my life.
9. I'm worthy of love.
10. I approve of myself and love myself deeply.
11. My body is healthy, and I'm grateful.
12. I'm more at ease every day.
13. I'm calm, happy, and content.
14. My life is a gift and I appreciate everything I have.
15. I'll surround myself with positive people who will help bring out the best in me.
16. I don't need someone else to feel happiness.
17. I'm allowed to take the time to heal.
18. My imperfections make me unique.
19. I'm allowed to make mistakes; they don't make up my whole story.
20. I choose not to criticize myself or others around me.

21. My potential to succeed is limitless.
22. Difficult times are part of my journey and allow me to appreciate the good.
23. I forgive those who have hurt me.
24. I'm in charge of my life and no one will dictate my path besides me.
25. I'm doing my best and that is enough.
26. I have the power to create change.
27. I know exactly what to do to achieve success.
28. I choose to be proud of myself and the things I choose to do.
29. I will not compare myself to strangers on the Internet.
30. I am enough.
31. I let go of all that no longer serves me.
32. I love myself fully, including the way I look.
33. My life becomes richer as I get older.
34. I can absolutely do anything I put my mind to.
35. I'm worthy of respect and acceptance.
36. My contributions to the world are valuable.

NOTES

_____

_____

_____

_____

_____

_____

_____

GROWTH MINDSET

Talent and intelligence can be developed over time and with effort. Those with growth mindsets tend to thrive on challenges and embrace failure as a mechanism for learning and development.

Having a growth mindset opens the playing field for individuals to experiment with, absorb, and immerse themselves in a range of skills that will equip them for a future that requires inquisitive minds and problem-solving approaches.
The following five points provide insight into how a growth mindset can be developed:

1. Shape your experiences
Whilst it may be true that we don't have complete control over all our life experiences, we do have the ability to shape our thoughts and (re)actions. Start by actively engaging in what you do on a daily basis and, if undesirable events occur along the way, take the time and effort to apply yourself to mastering what is within your control.

2. Embrace challenges with "YET"
Challenges need to be viewed as the fundamental steps required towards propelling us to our goals. Challenges provide us with the opportunity to learn, grow and develop skills we never knew existed within ourselves. When next confronted with a challenging situation you would rather run away from (from getting to grips with your new accounting system or pitching an idea to a particularly intimidating group of investors) try focusing on a small but powerful word – "yet". For example, I haven't been able to master the art of my new accounting software yet. Adding 'yet' to the statements we make about ourselves and our abilities has proven to slowly shift a fixed mindset into one of growth.

3. Approach learning with child-like curiosity

Having an almost unapologetic curiosity and ravenous appetite for knowledge shouldn't be reserved for children. These are qualities we all need to embrace, daily. Start by asking more questions, actively listening, and keeping a journal of at least one new thing you've learnt each day. A great question to start with is "why". Use "why" to gain clarity, challenge existing solutions and conventions and gain deeper understanding and insight into every facet of life.

4. Expect setbacks but keep moving

Setbacks will happen, so best you expect them. And, in the wise words of Dory, just keep swimming. Agonizing over what you should have/could have done won't help and will gradually kill self-esteem. A technique I've started using is allowing myself 15 minutes of moping time. After those 15 minutes I need to get over myself, look for the lesson in the process and start moving forward again.

5. Be inspired

Research remains inconclusive but I'm pretty sure jealousy really does make you ugly so take my mom's advice and just be nice. Feeling threatened by the success of others is not going to help you develop a growth mindset and it certainly won't help you develop your business or career. Take inspiration from the success of others, reach out for advice, and share in your experiences. Shifting from one mindset to another is no easy task but it's necessary when we take into consideration the pressing need for more entrepreneurial activity in South Africa – specifically the need for greater self-belief. The consequences of believing in our intelligence and personality as something that can be molded and developed over time are limitless. Transitioning to that shift will understandably take time but if encouraging robust and engaged entrepreneurial thinking opens the door to addressing societal, business, and personal challenges then it's certainly something we should start investing in.

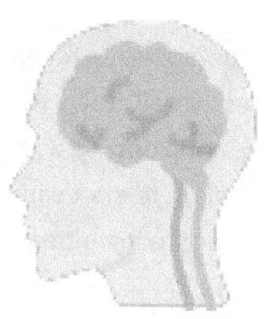

DO THIS

- Ask for help
- Be patient with results
- Make mistakes to learn
- Chance "fail" to "learn"
- List your strengths
- Seek out risks
- Celebrate your progress
- Focus on effort, not speed
- Make short term goals
- List all your options
- Talk back to negative ideas
- Try a new way to learn
- Use the words "yet"
- Try your best
- Understand the brain's muscle grows with effort

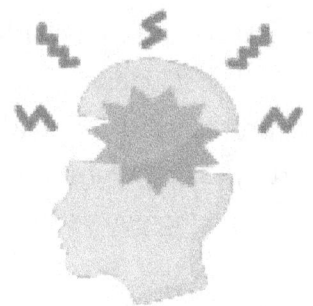

DON'T DO THIS

- Give up
- Don't ask for help
- Not try at all
- Have unrealistic expectations
- Only focus on weaknesses
- Avoid challenges or risks
- Ignore goals
- Only try once
- Focus on speed, not effort
- See grades as your worth
- Believe worry thoughts
- Complete with others
- Choose easy tasks
- Do the bare minimum
- Not have a Plan B, C & D
- Use words like never, can't, stupid, everyone

7 RULES OF LIFE

Life is complicated, but you can make it a bit easier by following these simple tips. The 7 Rules of Life can remind you where to focus and invest your energy, so you can enjoy life more. Sometimes, it can be challenging to follow them, but it is always beneficial.

Here are some tips for making the 7 rules of life work for you.

1: Make Peace with Your Past
The past can affect your present in unhelpful ways. An important aspect of mental health is continuously looking ahead to a bright future full of opportunities. The past is unchangeable. As you keep moving forward each day, you must intentionally move beyond the past. Here are some important components of that journey:

- Forgive other people for offenses or past mistakes.
- Forgive yourself for missteps.
- Let painful memories fade by choosing different thoughts.
- Accept what has happened in your life.
- Make fresh commitments each day.

2: Move Past What Other People Think
This applies to rules #2, #4, and #5. You can never know another person's thoughts. Don't fall into the trap of always worrying how others will react. Instead, be true to yourself, so you can attract the kind of people who truly belong in your life. Do what makes you happy and the right people will stick around. Then, offer others the same courtesy.

3: Time and Healing

This advice is for rules #3 and #6. Often, you just need to let things sit. Life may seem difficult right now, but by following rule #1 and not dwelling on the past, you can move forward to find happiness. Acknowledge your suffering, but don't let it take over. When you don't know the right answer or the right thing to do, you can pay attention to what makes you feel better and what makes you feel worse.

4: Smile, or Don't

This may seem a bit contrary, but you don't have to force yourself to be happy all of the time. Absolutely allow yourself to feel your emotions as they are. Happiness is not about burying your feelings. It's about acknowledging them and giving them their appropriate place. Find a balance by not dwelling on problems. Instead, look at them objectively to take away their power and step toward happiness.

5: Stop Comparing Yourself to Others

Comparison is the thief of joy. Measuring your worth or wellbeing against other people is a useless activity that ends in despair. Every day is an opportunity to celebrate who you are and what you have. Choosing contentment and focusing on the good in your life are powerful ways to overcome habits of comparison.

6: Control Your Thoughts

It's important that you feel empowered to dwell on the right ideas. Rehearsing negative interactions, revisiting the past in your mind, and repeating negative ideas are all unhelpful behaviors. Learning to change your thoughts is an important tool. Hone it, and practice whenever you're struggling with unhelpful thoughts.

7: Let Go of Unnecessary Responsibilities

There are things within your control and things outside your control. When people or circumstances are outside of your control, it is important to not hold them too tightly. Imbalanced responsibilities will make you unhappy. Accepting the right level of responsibility will help you function within your limits

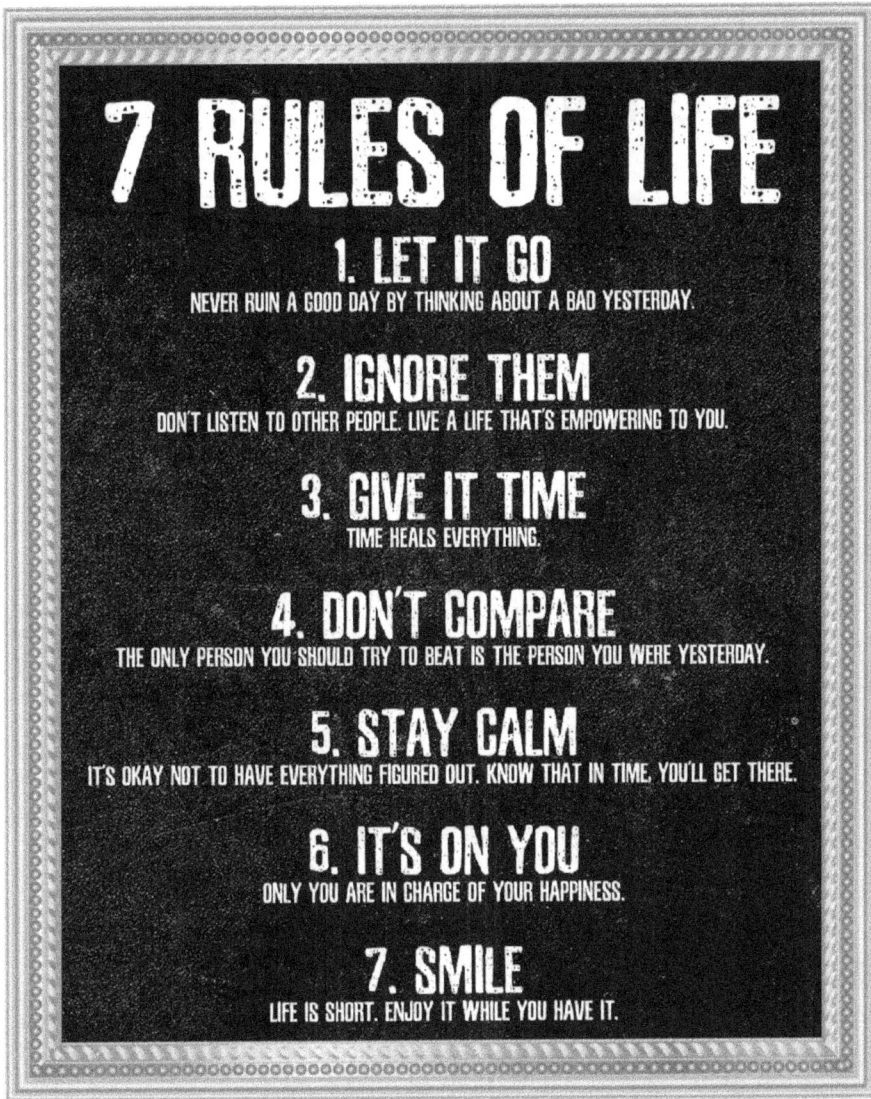

I_____ Promise to live by the 7 rules of life.

Signature: _____

Signed at_____on the_____

GET TO KNOW THE NEW YOU

To know thyself is the beginning of wisdom." This famous quote is often attributed to Socrates. But what exactly do you know when you "know yourself?" six elements of self-knowledge that can help you understand your own identity. As you live your daily life, you can look for clues to these important building blocks of the self.

But first, why is it important to know yourself? What are the Benefits of Self-Knowledge?

Maybe it's obvious, but here in a nutshell are a few reasons why you might want to know your own nature:

Happiness
You will be happier when you can express who you are. Expressing your desires will make it more likely that you get what you want.

Less inner conflict
When your outside actions are in accordance with your inside feelings and values, you will experience less inner conflict.

Better decision-making
When you know yourself, you are able to make better choices about everything, from small decisions like which sweater you'll buy to big decisions like which partner you'll spend your life with. You'll have guidelines you can apply to solve life's varied problems.

Self-control
When you know yourself, you understand what motivates you to resist bad habits and develop good ones. You'll have the insight to know which values and goals activate your willpower.

Resistance to social pressure
When you are grounded in your values and preferences, you are less likely to say "yes" when you want to say "no."

Tolerance and understanding of others
Your awareness of your own foibles and struggles can help you empathize with others.

Vitality and pleasure
Being who you truly are helps you feel more alive and makes your experience of life richer, larger, and more exciting.

Now that you are convinced that self-knowledge is worth having (not that you needed convincing!), we'll move on to those "VITAL Signs" of self-knowledge.

The Building Blocks of Self: Your VITALS
The capital letters in "VITAL Signs" form an acronym for the six building blocks of the self, or VITALS, for short. The letters stand for: Values, Interests, Temperament, Around-the-Clock, Life Mission and Goals, and Strengths/Skills.

V = Values
"Values"—such as "helping others," "being creative," "health," "financial security," and so on—are guides to decision-making and motivators for goals. Research shows that just thinking or writing about your values can make it more likely that you take healthy actions. The motivation provided by worthwhile values can also

keep you going even when you are tired, as shown in many psychology experiments. If you want to self-motivate, know your values!

I = Interests

"Interests" include your passions, hobbies, and anything that draws your attention over a sustained period of time. To figure out your interests, ask yourself these questions: What do you pay attention to? What are you curious about? What concerns you? The focused mental state of being interested in something makes life vivid and may give you clues to your deepest passions. Many people have built a career around a deep interest in something. For example, a friend of mine broke his leg when he was 11 years old and was so fascinated by the emergency room that he decided to become an emergency physician.

T = Temperament

"Temperament" describes your inborn preferences. Do you restore your energy from being alone (introvert) or from being with people (extrovert)? Are you a planner or go-with-the-flow type of person? Do you make decisions more on the basis of feelings or thoughts and facts? Do you prefer details or big Ideas? Knowing the answers to temperament questions like these could help you gravitate toward situations in which you could flourish and avoid situations in which you could wilt.

In the 60s, spontaneity was valued over planning. I tried hard to go with the flow, but it seemed to me that I wasted a lot of time that way. Going against the grain of my own personality turned out to be a daunting task that wasn't really worth it.

A = Around-the-Clock Activities

The "around-the-clock" category refers to when you like to do things—your biorhythms. Are you a morning person or a night person, for example? At what time of day does your energy peak? If you schedule activities when you are at your best, you are respecting your innate biology. As I look back on my life, I realize I've always been a night person since birth.

Your daily life is more pleasant when you are in sync with your biology. In every area, it's easier to enjoy life when you don't waste energy pretending to be someone you aren't.

L = Life Mission and Meaningful Goals

"What have been the most meaningful events of your life?" This was a question I like to ask when students who I coach .Its import to know and note the meaningful events in your life, I have had many meaningful events which have shaped the person that I am today.

Ask yourself the same question: "What have been the most meaningful events of your life?" You may discover clues to your hidden identity, to your career, and to life satisfaction.

S = Strengths

"Strengths" can include not only abilities, skills, and talents, but also character strengths such as loyalty, respect for others, love of learning, emotional intelligence, fairness, and more. Knowing your strengths is one of the foundations of self-confidence; not being able to acknowledge your own superpowers could put you on the path to low self-esteem. Become a person who takes in the good listening for compliments and noticing skills that could be clues to your strengths. Here's an example: A friend tells you that she loves the soothing sound of your voice. What could you do with that knowledge? Likewise, knowing your weaknesses can help you be honest with yourself and others about what you are not good at. You might decide either to work on those weaknesses or try to make them a smaller part of your personal or professional life.

Being True to You

Even if you know your "VITAL Signs," it's hard to remain true to yourself because you are constantly changing and because society's values often conflict with your own.

I love this quote from fellow habits author Gretchen Rubin:

"My first commandment is to "Be Gretchen"—yet it's very hard to know myself. I get so distracted by the way I wish I were, or the way I assume I am, that I lose sight of what's actually true."

For all of us, being yourself sounds easier than it actually is.
But there are a few signposts.
When you've made a discovery about one of your "VITAL Signs," you'll feel a sense of excitement.
Acting on self-knowledge will give you energy and save you energy.
You'll feel freer and stronger because you no longer conform to how you "should" feel, think, or act.

I_____ promise to learn about myself.
I promise to be true to myself so I can bring forth the best version of myself to the world.

Signature: _____

Signed at_____on the_____

PERSONAL VALUES & BELIEFS

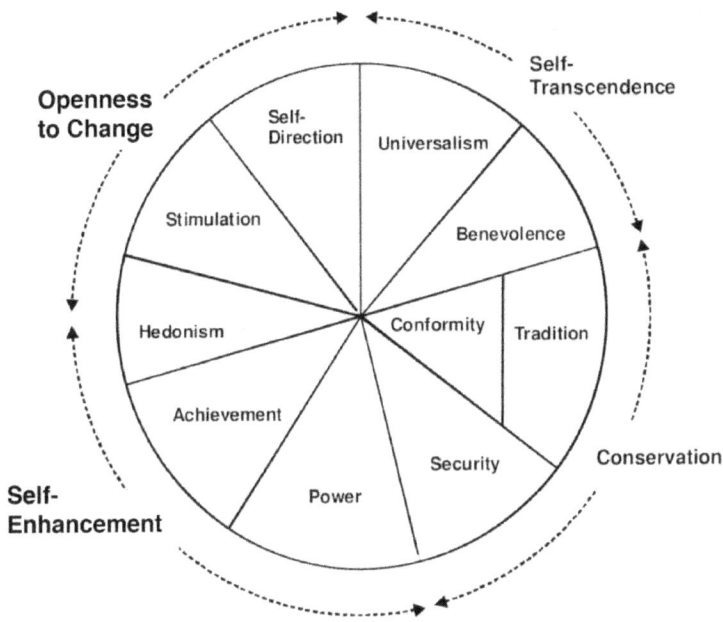

Schwartz Theory Of Basic Values

Personal Values are "broad desirable goals that motivate people's actions and serve as guiding principles in their lives"

Personal values are desirable to an individual and represent what is important to someone. The same value in different people can elicit different behaviors, e.g. if someone values success one person may work very hard to gain success in their career whereas someone else may take advantage of others to climb the career ladder.

A person can have many values with an individual assigning more importance to some values over others. It has been shown that the values that are most important to you often guide your decision making in all aspects of your life such as career, religion, social circles, self-identity etc.

Values	
<ul><li>Self-direction e.g. freedom, creativity</li><li>Stimulation e.g. exciting life, daring</li><li>Hedonism e.g. pleasure, self-indulgent</li><li>Achievement e.g. ambitious, successful</li><li>Power e.g. wealth, authority</li><li>Security e.g. social order, family security, cleanliness</li><li>Conformity e.g. politeness, self-discipline, respect</li><li>Tradition e.g. respect for traditions, modest, humble, devout</li><li>Benevolence e.g. loyal, responsible, helpful, forgiving</li><li>Universalism e.g. equality, wisdom, world of peace, social justice, protecting the environment</li></ul>	

Personal Beliefs

Definition:
Core beliefs are defined as fundamental, inflexible, absolute, and generalized beliefs that people hold about themselves, others, the world, and/or the future.
We use beliefs to help us understand the world around us. A person's beliefs will guide them in their decision making and response to situations. Beliefs are usually formed in childhood or any other significant formative experience.

Sources of Beliefs

- Evidence - logical and rational formation of belief based on evidence that proves causation
- Tradition - family and societal traditions

- Authority - normally developed from a parent but could also be a religious leader, teacher, or any other person in authority
- Association - beliefs can be formed through people or groups we associate with
- Revelation - beliefs that are formed through 'divine intervention" a hunch, inkling or sixth sense

Types of Beliefs – Enabling and Limiting
Beliefs can be seen as enabling (positive) or limiting (negative).
Enabling beliefs are ones that are optimistic and show good self-efficacy or the belief in yourself that you can achieve something.

Examples of enabling/ positive beliefs
- I am intelligent
- I am worthy
- I always try my best
- I am hardworking

Negative beliefs are thought as limiting and they often hold one back in life. Limiting beliefs are often seen in absolutes and are often inaccurate and unhelpful. People with limiting beliefs can often be judgmental of oneself or of others.

Examples of limiting/ negative beliefs
- I am weak
- I am boring
- I am stupid
- I always fail
- I am worthless

Beliefs, positive or negative, are not always true and this can lead a person to make poor decisions based on inaccurate beliefs. Research shows that people with inaccurate negative beliefs about themselves can present with symptoms of anxiety and depression.

Categories of Beliefs

Beliefs can be categorized into beliefs about oneself, about others, about the world and the future. These beliefs can either be positive (enabling) or negative (limiting).

Self
"I am worthy of love and happiness"
"I am flawed and unlovable"

Others
"Others like me and value my opinion"
"People are generally hurtful and disloyal"

The World
"The world is my oyster!"
"The world is a dangerous place"

The Future
"The future is bright, and opportunity awaits"
"There is no hope – things will never get better"

Identification of Beliefs
It is not always an easy task to identify one's core beliefs. It can require a great amount of introspection and some people may need the facilitation from a therapist to unlock their core beliefs.

Modification of Core Beliefs
Once limiting beliefs have been identified modification of these beliefs will help to reframe them into enabling beliefs. Reframing beliefs is not a simple task as negative beliefs are often deeply rooted. Again, the need for psychological therapy may be necessary for deeply ingrained beliefs.

- Define the core belief
- Explore how the belief fits into every aspect of your life
- Examine the evidence

- Critical examination of the evidence that led you to develop the initial belief.
- Advantages – Disadvantages analysis
- Review the advantages and disadvantages of a belief to help see the usefulness of the belief in one's life
- Behavioral experiments

Beliefs result in particular behavior e.g. if you believe "people don't care what I think" you may not contribute when asked about a project at work. By changing your behavior e.g. contributing to a discussion, you may change your belief by discovering that people do care about what you think.

Behavioral experiments are used in Pain management programes where you would use graded exposure in someone with fear avoidance to show them that their belief that movement will make them worse may not be true.

Acting "as if" - Similar to a behavioral experiment, you would act in opposition to your negative belief.

Cognitive continuum - Critical analysis of reframing all or nothing beliefs by using a comparative scale with regards to other people

Historical tests - Examine past incidents where one has implemented a negative core belief and re-evaluate what actually happened. for example, if a belief was "I am unimportant" you may look back at a time when your parents prioritized your sibling over yourself, but on critical evaluation, you realize that at that stage in life your sibling needed more help from your parent rather than you are less important to them.

- Restructuring early memories - Psychologists can be helpful in restructuring early memories to reframe beliefs
- Defining the "new self"- Identify who they would like to be
- Soliciting social support and consensus - Use social support to help them
- Time Projection -Imagine what life will be like if with their "new" beliefs

COUNT YOUR BLESSINGS INSTEAD OF YOUR STRUGGLES

If you are focused on the many problems in your life, chances are you will not be very successful. You might have a decent job but the prospects for you to advance are limited. Those who focus on problems are usually not as happy.

You see, when you focus on problems, you'll have more problems. If you are focused on the blessings in your life, you will probably enjoy more successful. You might be a business owner or an employee with lots of potential for advancement. Those who focus on their blessings are usually much happier. When you focus on the positive, you focus on possibilities, and you'll have more opportunities in your life.

I believe we should all strive to practice this every day. If we are thinking about all the good in our lives it means we are focusing on the good and not the bad. The more we focus on the good, the more our minds will help us see the good. Count your blessings, not your problems.

When we count our blessings, we note all the wonderful things in our lives. This helps us to appreciate how good life is.

Counting your blessings is important. It shows that you are grateful. Gratitude is a feeling of appreciation or thanks. When people count their blessings, they can say it like this: "I am thankful for my family. I am thankful for my friends. I am thankful for my health."

It is better to be grateful for our blessings than to take them for granted. When we take something for granted, we do not appreciate it. Sometimes we are not appreciative of our good fortune and blessings until they are gone.

Now, when we want to show our recognition of all the little things that prove helpful, we sometimes say give thanks for small blessings. We often say this expression in the middle of a troubling or difficult time.

Let's say a friend of yours is angry about a flat tire on his car. But then he stops and thinks for a minute and says, "Well, at least I have a car. I should count myself lucky and give thanks for small blessings."

Count Your Blessings
- Hear the Music
- Snog. Canoodle. Get It On.
- Nurture Your Spirituality
- Move Your Body
- Laugh Big
- Do Something Nice for Someone Else
- Make More Money Than Your Peers
- Seek Positive Emotion as a Path to Success
- Use a Happy Memory as a Guide
- Play the Part of an Optimist
- Try New Things
- Tell Your Story to Someone
- Balance Work and Home
- Be Like the Danes: Keep Expectations Realistic
- Make Time
- Visualize Happiness
- Smile
- Marry Happy

Declaration

I_____ choose to be grateful for my parents, my siblings, my family, my friends, and my home. I am grateful for the good health of our family; for our food;our clothing; our educational opportunities; our freedom of religion; our unlimited opportunities for success, our unlimited opportunities for advancement; our democratic way of life. I am grateful for our form of government; all the good friends we have; the beauty of this day; my comforts and conveniences.

WORDS OF HOPE

"Whenever you find yourself doubting how far you can go, just remember how far you have come. Remember everything you have faced, all the battles you have won, and all the fears you have overcome." — **N.R. Walker, The Weight of It All**

"Growth is painful. Change is painful. But nothing is as painful as staying stuck somewhere you don't belong." - **Mandy Hale**

"Never apologize for being sensitive or emotional. Let this be a sign that you've got a big heart and aren't afraid to let others see it. showing your emotions is a sign of strength."- **Brigitte Nicole**

"Sometimes you face difficulties not because you're doing something wrong, but because you're doing something right." - **Joel Osteen**

"Before you start to judge me, step into my shoes and walk the life I'm living, and if you get far as I am, maybe you will see how strong I really am." - **Unknown**

"Work for a cause, not for applause. Live life to express, not to impress. Don't strive to make your presence noticed, just make your absence felt. " - **Unknown**

"Go ahead tell me that I'm not good enough tell me I can't do it because I will show you over and over that I can. " - **Unknown**

"When you start seeing your worth, you'll find it harder to stay around people who don't." - **Mandy Hale**

"The woman (individual)who does not require validation from anyone is the most feared individual on the planet." — **Mohadesa Najumi**

"The strongest action for a woman is to love herself, be herself and shine amongst those who never believed she could." — **Unknown**

"You were given this life because you are strong enough to live it" - *Ain Eineziz*

"I am not what happened to me, I am what I choose to become."
- Carl Gustav Jung

"Forget Your Past, Forgive Yourself, And Begin Again Right Now." – Unknown

"I don't want you to save me I want you to stand by my side as I save myself"
- Sushil, The Flexible Enterprise

"Hope is the only thing stronger than fear." - *Suzanne Collins*

"Let yourself be gutted. Let it open you. Start here" - *Cheryl Strayed*

"I'll Find Strength in Pain" – *Unknown*

"Being deeply loved by someone gives you strength, while loving someone deeply gives you courage." - *Lao Tzu*

"You attract what you are, not what you want. So if you want it then reflect it!"
— *Tony Gaskins*

"You are allowed to scream. You are allowed to cry. But do not give up."
- *Unknown*

"If you're lucky enough to be different, don't ever change." - Taylor Swift.

"I'm strong because I've been weak. I'm fearless because I've been afraid. I'm wise because I've been foolish." - *Anonumous*

"Wake Up With Determination. Go To Bed With Satisfaction"
- *George Horace Lorimer.*

"Do Not Judge her. You don't know what storm I've asked her to walk through."
- *God #CwG.*

KEEP MOVING

When Life Gets Hard: Keep Moving Forward, One Step at a Time

"You just do it. You force yourself to get up. You force yourself to put one foot before the other, and darn it, you refuse to let it get to you. You fight. You cry. You curse. Then you go about the business of living. That's how I've done it. There's no other way." **- Elizabeth Taylor**

Most of us will experience hard choices, stressful events, and difficult situations that will impact us in one way or another for the rest of our lives.

Hard times happen. They teach us lessons, make us stronger, and give us a deeper sense of self. After all, would sitting in the sun mean as much if you hadn't of experienced the storm first?

1. Confront your struggles head on.
We want to bury our heads in the sand and pretend everything is fine, as if these bad things aren't happening to us. We try to numb ourselves from the pain and reality of the situation. I know I do this. But eventually, you have to face it head on. There is no other way.

There will be times of great heartache when you are forced to make life-altering decisions in which your mind and emotions will play opposing roles. With some of what I have faced, I had to make logical, sound decisions based on the facts available to me at the time. I certainly didn't discount my emotions, but I moved through them with my eyes wide open.

2. Realize it's a process, and the process takes time.
Nothing will happen right away. It will take time, and you will travel from one emotion to another and then back again. And it takes as long as it takes. These things cannot be rushed.

Also, we have to remember to take it easy on ourselves throughout the process. For me, this goes back to self-medicating or numbing. I quite often stumble back into old, self-destructive habits. I'm human, not Wonder Woman. Although I like to think that maybe Wonder Woman wouldn't have survived everything I have.

3. Kick, scream, get your groove on, and then get spiritual with it.
Realize that it's okay to be angry. Find constructive, creative ways to let your feelings flow out of you.

Climb a hill and once you get to the top, scream until your heart is content. Paint something. Beat up your bedding. It'll only make it more comfortable. Get in some serious cardio, if you can—try dance. Make yourself really sweat. Then try yoga and/or meditation to even you out.

Dig down deep and take a look inside yourself for what you believe. Whatever higher power, spiritual path, or religious belief gives your soul comfort—whether it's at home, out in nature, in a church, encircled by loved ones, or in solitude—take a look at finding out what that is.

4. Play out your fears about a situation.
With any given situation, play out the scenarios and then ask yourself, "and then what?" What will I do if this happens next? Keep asking what you'll do next, how you'll continue moving forward. This will move you from a fearful, stuck mindset into a more active, productive mindset.

5. Accept that not everyone will have your back.
This may be the hardest lesson to learn. I found out, most painfully, that some people kept their distance; or better yet, were willing to take advantage and kick me when I was down.

Surprisingly, these are often people you thought you could count on the most. Still, others will not only step up, but they will hold you up through the worst of it. While this can be an incredibly painful lesson, I believe it is a very necessary one. Interpersonal relationships, like life, are fluid. People will come and go. Some people are around to play with us in the sun, while others will weather through storms and seasons with us.

I don't think it's meant for us to know who's who ahead of time, only that this is a fact of life and that you will be okay. Maybe this also teaches us to be more grateful for each relationship, past and present, good, and bad. Some of these people will be your greatest teachers in life, whether you or they know it or not.

The best lesson I learned is that you have to keep your focus on the people who stick around instead of the ones who bail.

6. Change your perspective.
I now choose to believe that adversity is meant to knock us on course, not the other way round. Focus on looking at the situation differently. I can say from my experience as a cancer patient, you often have to find humor in the small things. This helps get you through each day.

Even recently, I beat myself up over not yet becoming the perfect picture of optimal health after cancer. I had to realize, with everything I've been going through, the fact that I'm still standing at all is true testament to my ability to overcome. This has to be enough for now. Just as I am, I am enough.

7. Look forward to the sunshine.
After every storm there is calm, and then the sun shines. If you keep remembering that, you will make it through.

Give yourself the opportunity to feel and process every thought and emotion. This is what the experience calls for. We all know what happens if we bypass or bury our emotions. We must allow the process to happen and give ourselves the space and time to feel everything. Eventually, hopefully, we find ourselves grateful for those hard times, which in turn may make us appreciate the good times even more. I am continually working on all of this, but then again, isn't that the point?

LOOK FOR GOOD IN EVERYTHING

There is a glass half-filled with water. Do you see a glass that is half full?

There is a glass half-filled with water, do you see a glass that is half full or half empty? If you see the glass as half empty, then I doubt that you can see the good in everything. You will have to learn to look at life more positively. It's not easy, and it takes a lot of self-control to drive away all the negative feelings, but it is worth it.

Everything happens for a reason. If something doesn't go your way, instead of agonizing over it, try to accept it and think on ways on how you make your situation better. Things could have been far worse.

1: Realize that success takes time -- and it's totally OK to be bored in the process
Something weird happens in our brains when we're bored with our goals. First, we experience the irritating feeling of listlessness -- which is uncomfortable in and of itself. But that feeling of listlessness is usually followed by aggravation. We're bored with our lives. Then we get mad at ourselves for getting bored. Then we get we try to think of a way to get un-bored, and the only thing we can think of doing are the things that bored us in the first place.

Try this mental reframe: From now on, I want you to begin viewing boredom not as a sign of stagnation, but as a sign of consistent, steady progress.

As long as you're doing the little things that you need to do every single day in order to succeed, then success is inevitable. It's ok to be bored from Point A to Point B. Just don't stop.

2: Create a system to start tracking your progress
The biggest reason why we fail to see the good in everyday situations is because we lose perspective on how far we've come. You're missing the forest for the trees.

Remember coming back from summer vacation and seeing the people who'd grown six inches? You didn't see them for months -- so their growth was quite apparent. But to them, the growth probably didn't feel noticeable.

Point being, you have to start taking notice of the little, day-to-day improvements that you make. Over time, this will allow you to see how far you've come, and it will give you a reference point for where you want to go.

Using a system like this will slowly train your mind to start thinking more positively about the little wins you have on a daily basis.

3: Remember that you can still make it -- even when others discourage you

It's hard to pursue your dreams when your family, friends and coworkers don't believe in you. It feels good to have people that you care about support your vision. But whenever someone tells you that you can't do something, that a goal is "impossible" or downright laughs in your face, don't get frustrated.

Instead, train your mind to see their disbelief as a challenge.

Instead of saying, "They're probably right. I can't do it" -- train yourself to think, "Okay. Now, I'll SHOW you what I can do."

Every time someone disparages you in an opportunity to show them how strong your vision is. Turn their negative energy into your rocket fuel and blast off.

✎ Declaration:

I_____ choose to see the good in all situations. When life hands me lemons, I will make lemonade. I choose to think positively on a daily basis.

What will you do tomorrow when you fail to see good in situations?

_____

_____

_____

_____

Signature: _____

Signed at_____on the_____

📝 NOTES

_____

_____

_____

_____

_____

_____

_____

_____

BE AN ANSWER TO SOMEONE ELSE'S PRAYER

> "If you want others to be happy, practice compassion. If you want to be happy, practice compassion." – *Dalai Lama*

Strike back against the selfishness and greed of our modern world and help out a fellow human being today.
Take just a few minutes today and do a kindness for another person.
It can be something small, or the start of something big.
Ask them to pay it forward.
Put a smile on someone's face.
Don't know where to start?

Here's is a list of ideas to get you thinking. You can come up with thousands more if you think about it.

1. Smile and be friendly. Sometimes a simple little thing like this can put a smile and warm feeling in someone else's heart and make their day a little better. They might then do the same for others.
2. Call a charity to volunteer. You don't have to go to a soup kitchen today. Just look up the number, make the call, and make an appointment to volunteer sometime in the next month. It can be whatever charity you like. Volunteering is one of the most amazing things you can do.
3. Donate something you don't use. Or a whole box of somethings. Drop them off at a charity — others can put your clutter to good use.
4. Make a donation. There are lots of ways to donate to charities online, or in your local community. Instead of buying yourself a new gadget or outfit, spend that money in a more positive way.

5. Redirect gifts. Instead of having people give you birthday or Christmas gifts, ask them to donate gifts or money to a certain charity.
6. Stop to help. The next time you see someone pulled over with a flat tire, or somehow in need of help, stop and ask how you can help. Sometimes all they need is a push, or the use of your cell phone.
7. Teach. Take the time to teach someone a skill you know. This could be teaching your grandma to use email, teaching your child to ride a bike, teaching your co-worker a valuable computer skill, teaching your spouse how to clean the darn toilet. OK, that last one doesn't count.
8. Comfort someone in grief. Often a hug, a helpful hand, a kind word, a listening ear, will go a long way when someone has lost a loved one or suffered some similar loss or tragedy.
9. Help them take action. If someone in grief seems to be lost and doesn't know what to do, help them do something. It could be making funeral arrangements, it could be making a doctor's appointment, it could be making phone calls. Don't do it all yourself — let them take action too, because it helps in the healing process.
10. Buy food for a homeless person. Cash is often a bad idea if it's going to be used for drugs but buying a sandwich and chips or something like that is a good gesture. Be respectful and friendly.
11. Lend your ear. Often someone who is sad, depressed, angry, or frustrated just needs someone who will listen. Venting and talking through an issue is a huge help.
12. Help someone on the edge. If someone is suicidal, urge them to get help. If they don't, call a suicide hotline or doctor yourself to get advice.
13. Help someone get active. A person in your life who wants to get healthy might need a helping hand — offer to go walking or running together, to join a gym together. Once they get started, it can have profound effects.
14. Do a chore. Something small or big, like cleaning up or washing a car or doing the dishes or cutting a lawn.
15. Give a massage. Only when appropriate of course. But a massage can go a long way to making someone feel better.
16. Send a nice email. Just a quick note telling someone how much you appreciate them, or how proud you are of them, or just saying thank you for something they did.

17. Show appreciation, publicly. Praising someone on a blog, in front of coworkers, in front of family, or in some other public way, is a great way to make them feel better about themselves.
18. Donate food. Clean out your cupboard of canned goods, or buy a couple bags of groceries, and donate them to a homeless shelter.
19. Just be there. When someone you know is in need, sometimes it's just good to be there. Sit with them. Talk. Help out if you can.
20. Be patient. Sometimes people can have difficulty understanding things or learning to do something right. Learn to be patient with them.
21. Tutor a child. This might be difficult to do today, but often parents can't afford to hire a tutor for their child in need of help. Call a school and volunteer your tutoring services.
22. Create a care package. Soup, reading material, tea, chocolate ... anything you think the person might need or enjoy. Good for someone who is sick or otherwise in need of a pick-me-up.
23. Lend your voice. Often the powerless, the homeless, the neglected in our world need someone to speak up for them. You don't have to take on that cause by yourself, but join others in signing a petition, speaking up a council meeting, writing letters, and otherwise making a need heard.
24. Offer to babysit. Sometimes parents need a break. If a friend or other loved one in your life doesn't get that chance very often, call them and offer to babysit sometime. Set up an appointment. It can make a big difference.
25. Love. Simply finding ways to express your love to others, whether it be your partner, child, other family member, friend, co-worker, or a stranger ... just express your love. A hug, a kind word, spending time, showing little kindnesses, being friendly ... it all matters more than you know.

> "How far that little candle throws his beams!
> So shines a good deed in a weary world." – *William Shakespeare*

Helping a fellow human being, while it can be inconvenient, has a few humble advantages:

- ✓ It makes you feel better about yourself.
- ✓ It connects you with another person, at least for a moment, if not for life.
- ✓ It improves the life of another, at least a little.
- ✓ It makes the world a better place, one little step at a time.
- ✓ And if that kindness is passed on, it can multiply, and multiply.

I_____ promise to be:

- Helpful
- Honorable
- Compassionate
- To make a difference in someone else's life.

List of things/Acts you will do to help others:

_____

_____

_____

_____

_____

Signature: _____

Signed at_____ on the_____

DON'T WAIT FOR TOMORROW

Make tomorrow today

You can't always wait for the perfect time, sometimes. You have to dare to it because life is too short to wonder what could have been. Don't wait until tomorrow to do what you can do today for what you do today can change your tomorrow. Don't wait for things to get easier, simpler or better. Life will always be complicated. Learn to do things right now, otherwise, you will run out of time.

"If not *you* then **who?** If not *now*, then **when?**

- If you wait to do everything until you are sure it's right, you will probably never do much of anything. The only thing you have is now.
- Sometimes later becomes never.
- Stop saying "I wish" start saying" I will"
- You cannot always wait for the perfect time, sometimes you must dare to jump.
- A year from now you will wish had started today.
- Don't wait for tomorrow, make the possible now.
- Don't wait for the time, make the time now.
- In the end, we regret the chances we didn't take and the decisions we waited too long to make.
- Live your life now don't wait for tomorrow.
- Don't wait for the right time because it never comes, just go ahead and do it.
- You don't have to be great to start but you have to start to be great.

Name five things you going to start today, the future is promised to no one:

1._____

2._____

3._____

4._____

5._____

- You are never going to be a 100% ready and it's never going to be just the right time, meaning every moment is the right moment.
- If you want it, you just have to do.
- It's a terrible thing to wait until you are ready, actually no one is ever ready to do anything.
- There is no such thing as ready, there is ONLY NOW.
- There are seven days in a week and someday is not one of them.

Declaration: I_____ promise to never allow waiting to become a habit.

I promise to live my dreams and take rest, life is happening now.
My life begins right now. I promise to start waiting to be better.
I promise to do the things I want to achieve right now.
I promise to make the most of the moment I am in right now.

 **NOTES**

_____
_____
_____
_____
_____
_____
_____
_____
_____
_____

I CAN. I WILL. WATCH ME.

Each one of us are born with a unique set of skills.
Ask yourself, what is that skill you would like to nurture and grow?

I have ONE LIFE. When I have the chance to upskill myself and excel in life, I proudly say, "I can, I will. Watch me!"

You need to develop a can-do attitude to succeed in life.

Attitude is everything.
If you've got a negative attitude, it will taint your entire outlook on life and dramatically decrease your ability to succeed. With a negative attitude, you will make little (if any) progress on the goals and ambitions you set for yourself. Instead of consciously crafting a successful life, your negative disposition will often lead to a passive personality, one in which you shrug your shoulders and let life happen to you, rather than making things happen for you. If that's not the life you imagined for yourself, then it's time to transform your current attitude into a can-do attitude.
Here are some practical ideas you can start using today to make that attitude shift and start an upward cycle of success for yourself that will reverberate into every area of your life.

1. Starts with Your Mindset
Since the early days of boxing, experts relied on what they called the "tales of the tape" to predict how successful an athlete's boxing career may or may-not be. These "tales of the tape" were a series of physical measurements that included the fighter's fist, reach, chest expansion and weight.

Experts thought these measurements could predict which athletes would be most successful in the ring based on how their numbers shook-out against these measurements.

But get this: did you know Muhammad Ali—hailed as one of the greatest boxers of all time and failed every single one of his measurements?

The so-called "experts" called him a failure. They didn't believe he had the skills and talents to succeed. As Dr. Carol Dweck explains in her book, Mindset, Muhammad Ali "was not a natural." Not by a long shot—at least according to the boxing experts of that era.

But nonetheless, against all odds, Ali went down in history as one of the greatest boxers of all time.

What exactly was it about Ali that contributed to his incredible success in boxing? What made him "the greatest," as he often proclaimed? It wasn't his brawn. It was his brain.

Carol Dweck explains Ali's success as follows:
Muhammad Ali was not a natural. He had great speed, but he didn't have the physique of a great fighter, he didn't have the strength, and he didn't have the classical moves. In fact, he boxed all wrong. He didn't block punches with his arms and elbows. He punched in rallies like an amateur. He kept his jaw exposed. He pulled back his torso to evade the impact of oncoming punches, which Jose Torres said was 'like someone in the middle of a train tack trying to avoid being hit by an oncoming train, not by moving to one or the other side of the track, but by running backwards."

Throughout his career, he was constantly matched with athletes that were bigger, stronger, and faster than himself. But he beat them anyway.

It wasn't his physical talent or skill that helped him do succeed over and over again. It was his mental attitude. His can-do attitude to be more precise.

This leads me to believe that in many cases, the critical factor between someone who achieves success vs someone who does not, comes down in large part to your mindset.

Our mindset determines the way we deal with tough situations and setbacks as well as our willingness to deal with and improve ourselves.
A person with a growth-mindset automatically has a can-do attitude because they don't give up when they fail. Instead, they use failure as a learning opportunity that does nothing more than get them closer to success.
Ali helps us understand that developing a growth mindset and by association, a can-do attitude is about rising strong regardless of how lackluster his physical endowments may have been. Instead of looking in the mirror and saying, "I'm not good enough to be a champion;" instead he said, "I'm going to use a different path to achieve greatness."

And that's what he did. He showed everyone that success comes first from the gem between your ears. The same gem that chooses to leave behind negative beliefs and replace them with an attitude that says, "I can do this."

2. Focus on Being Consistent

Your thoughts + actions + feelings are like a three-legged stool. This is similar to people that follow the old self-help advice to just "think positive."
If we THINK positive, but we still FEEL negative, then how will we ACT?
Positive thinking is powerful, but only when we think of it as one of the three necessary legs that reinforces the stool we're sitting on.
If we don't want the stool to wobble or break, we've got to make sure we give each leg the care it needs to keep us from falling and getting hurt.

I believe that the key here, with this idea, is to focus on being as congruent as possible.

Here's how:
a). Remember that the way you think needs to be in alignment with the way you act. When you affirm powerful thoughts to yourself about what you can do rather than what you cannot do, your biochemistry will change for the better. You will stand taller. You will move with confidence.

b). Understand that the way you act is going to have an impact on the way you feel. When you tell yourself that you can do something repeatedly, your mind will begin to believe it and accept it as the truth. This, in return, will make you feel like a winner, like a success.

c). Realize the way you feel is going to help reinforce the way you think.
The way you feel right now has a lot to do with how you're carrying yourself.
Are you hunching forward?
Are you slouching in your seat?
Are your shoulders sloped?
If yes, you probably don't feel like you're at your best.

Now, straighten out your back, tilt your chest upward, and smile (even if you've got no reason to!) Not only will you notice a shift in the way you feel when you do this, but you'll notice a shift in the way you think as well.
You'll go from thinking thoughts that lead to feeling stressed and depressed, to thinking and feeling confident and creative.
You'll have that can do attitude that leads to the success you crave in life.
Which is going to circle right back around into helping you decide the way you choose to act in any given situation. See the feedback loop these three ends up creating?

Bottom line is, It's not about positive thinking alone that drives our success in life, it's about being in positive congruence between the way we think, act, and feel that drives our success in life.

3. Be Mindful of Your Self-Talk
Your self-worth depends upon your self-talk.

An all-star baseball player once decided to visit a prison to inspire the inmates to better themselves. He told them a story about how his father always encouraged him when he was a little boy. His dad always told him, "son, if you keep on hitting' the ball like that, you'll end up in the MLB one day."
Sure enough, he ended up playing professional baseball.
Upon hearing this story, one of the prisoners stood up and said, "hey, my dad told me something similar when I was a little boy. Every time I did something my dad didn't like, he looked at me and said, 'son, if you keep on mis-behaving like this, you'll end up in prison one day."
Sure enough, he ended up in prison.

As it turns out, 90% of male prisoners were treated like dirt by their parents when they were children.
Many of them were spoken to like they were prisoners before they ended up behind bars.
Now, obviously this doesn't mean that our parents determine the future for us in advance.
We all can respond to our circumstances however we want. But it certainly makes things a lot easier if we have a solid foundation to build upon.
Regardless of how your parents spoke to you though, the take-away from this story is simple: the way we speak with ourselves plays a massive role in the way we perceive ourselves.
And the way we perceive ourselves plays a massive role in our ability to develop a can-do attitude and reap the rewards it affords. Our attitude goes a long way

towards determining whether we decide to take on challenges and pursue success in the face of adversity.

Encourage yourself. Believe that you can do it whatever it may be.

- Your self-talk plays a huge role in your self-image.
- Your self-image plays a huge role in your attitude.
- Your attitude plays a huge role in your ability to succeed in the various endeavors you decide to pursue in your life.

Drop whatever limiting attitudes you're holding on to about yourself and replace them with a strong, self-starting can-do attitude.

Become an Activationist

"Excellent ideas are not enough. An only fair idea acted upon, and developed, is 100 percent better than a terrific idea that dies because it isn't followed up." — **David Schwartz, The Magic of Thinking Big**

Plenty of people have excellent ideas, but only a select few can see their idea through to action. There are two types of people on the planet: "activations" and "passivation's."

Activations come up with ideas and execute them without hesitation—the embodiment of a "can-do" attitude. When these people decide to take a vacation, they take it. When they decide to call a client, an old friend, or even a potential romantic interest—they do it.

Activationists decide to become successful, and they will that decision into reality with a can-do attitude.

Passivationists on the other hand, might have just as many ideas as an activationist, but the passivationist executes none of them.

They postpone and procrastinate their dreams and goals continually.
This lack of action, this lack of success, is the result of having a passive mentality about life and neglecting to cultivate a can-do attitude.

What can we do to break ourselves of the passivation's habit?

We can start by breaking the habit of perfectionism.
Perfectionists put things off because they fear doing something wrong. However, the activationist goes ahead and does things, and then deals with any problems that arise along the way.
This also includes waiting for the "perfect" time to do something.
There is no perfect time, and every minute that you wait makes it that much more likely that you will chicken out of the whole thing.
Now is the magic word of achievement.
It's time to get rid of tomorrows, laters, and sometime and replace them with the readiness and urgency of a can-do attitude.

You Can Do This!

1. <u>It all starts with your mindset.</u>
If you want to achieve success in all dimensions of your life, you'll need to get your mental game in check. Ensure your mindset is directed towards growth and progress for most of your waking hours.

2. <u>Positive thinking can only get you so far.</u>
To generate true change, to develop a real can-do attitude that helps you succeed in whatever endeavor you want, you will need to place equal importance on your thoughts, feelings, and actions.

Treat them parts of yourself that are achieve their peak power and potential when they are unified and treated with equal importance. In other words: we cannot simply "positively think" our way to success.
We must combine those positive thoughts with forward-facing action.

3. <u>Your self-worth depends upon your self-talk</u>.
Repeatedly affirm to yourself that you have a can-do attitude. Look yourself in the mirror and literally say it out loud, "I have a can-do attitude! I have a can-do attitude! I have a can-do attitude!" Do this exercise every morning after you brush your teeth. Yes, this will absolutely feel silly at first, but you will find that the benefits of success far outweigh the momentary feelings of embarrassment or self-consciousness you experience as a result of doing this.

4. <u>Become an activationist.</u>
Do not allow fear to freeze you in place and prevent you from achieving your dreams. Embody the habits of an activationist and take consistent action until you achieve what you set out to achieve.
With each achievement, you will find your self-confidence getting stronger and stronger. This then, will lead to more action, which will lead to more success......
And this cycle of success? It never needs to stop.

✎ Declaration:
I_____

- Choose 'I can do it!' as my life motto.
- Think, talk, act, and conduct myself in all of my affairs as the person I wish to become and what my future self will thank me for.
- Do it my way. I develop my self-confidence and self-worth by knowing I can make a difference and being open to trying new things, → learning and growing.

- Look at any failure as a steppingstone to success, and as an opportunity to learn and improve.
- I will venture outside of my comfort zone by trying something different. I will keep trying new things until I succeed.
- I will always be a part of the solution, not a part of the problem. I will see all problems and stressful situations as challenges and opportunities.

Remember life is an adventure. Always be enthusiastic about it and all that it brings.

NOTES

_____
_____
_____
_____
_____
_____
_____

WHAT CONVERSATION ARE YOU HAVING WITH YOUR SELF?

Are your inner thoughts Positive or Negative?

How well you talk to yourself will impact on how you feel and, subsequently, how well you will perform. Research has shown that how you talk to yourself can affect your persistence, concentration, and stress levels.

It's not uncommon for most of us to keep a running dialogue inside our heads. This dialogue can range from giving ourselves instructions while we carry out a task, random observations about our environment or a situation, or it could be what is often referred to as self-talk.
Self-talk is the internal narrative you hold about yourself.

It's your inner voice and you may or may not have spent much time thinking about it or giving it any attention. The truth is, our self-talk can have a much bigger influence on the way we see ourselves, and the world around us than we realize.

Negative thoughts may lead to decreased motivation as well as greater feelings of helplessness. This type of critical inner dialogue has even been linked to depression, so it's definitely something to fix. Those who find themselves frequently engaging in negative self-talk tend to be more stressed.
Negative self-talk can affect us in some pretty damaging ways. One large-scale study found that rumination and self-blame over negative events were linked to an increased risk of mental health problems

Those who find themselves frequently engaging in negative self-talk tend to be more stressed. This is in large part since their reality is altered to create an experience where they don't have the ability to reach the goals, they've set for themselves. This is both due to a lowered ability to see opportunities around them as well as a decreased tendency to capitalize on these opportunities. This means that the heightened perception of stress is due both to mere perception and the changes in behavior that come from them.

The following are more negative consequences of negative self-talk.

Limited Thinking: You tell yourself you can't do something, and the more you hear it, the more you believe it.

Perfectionism: You begin to really believe that "great" isn't as good as "perfect," and that perfection is attainable. (In contrast, mere high achievers tend to do better than their perfectionistic counterparts because they generally less stressed and are happy with a job well-done rather than picking it apart and zeroing in on what could have been better.

Feelings of Depression: Some research has shown that negative self-talk can lead to an exacerbation of feelings of depression.
 If left unchecked, this could be quite damaging.

Relationship Challenges: Whether the constant self-criticism makes you seem needy and insecure or you turn your negative self-talk into more general negative habits that bother others, a lack of communication and even a "playful" amount of criticism can take a toll.

One of the most obvious drawbacks of negative self-talk is that it's not positive. This sounds simplistic, but research has shown that positive self-talk is a great predictor of success.

How to Minimize Negative Self-Talk
There are different ways to reduce the self-talk in your daily life.

- Catch Your Critic

Learn to notice when you're being self-critical so you can begin to stop. For example, notice when you say things to yourself that you wouldn't say to a good friend or a child.

Remember That Thoughts and Feelings Aren't Always Reality
Thinking negative things about yourself may feel like astute observations, but your thoughts and feelings about yourself can not be considered accurate information. Your thoughts can be skewed like everyone else's, subject to biases and the influence of your moods.

- Give Your Inner Critic a Nickname

There was once a Saturday Night Live character known as Debbie Downer. She would find the negative in any situation. If your inner critic has this dubious skill as well, you can tell yourself, "Debbie Downer is doing her thing again."

- When you think of your inner critic as a force outside of yourself and even give it a goofy nickname, it's not only easier to realize that you don't have to agree, but it becomes less threatening and more easy to see how ridiculous some of your critical thoughts can be.

- Contain Your Negativity

If you find yourself engaging in negative self-talk, it helps to contain the damage that a critical inner voice can cause by only allowing it to criticize certain things in your life or be negative for only an hour in your day. This puts a limit on how much negativity can come from the situation.

- Change Negativity to Neutrality

When engaging in negative self-talk, you may be able to catch yourself, but it can sometimes be difficult to force yourself to stop a train of thought in its tracks. It's often far easier to change the intensity of your language. "I can't stand this" becomes, "This is challenging." "I hate..." becomes, "I don't like..." and even, "I don't prefer..." When your self-talk uses more gentle language, much of its negative power is muted as well.

- Cross-Examine Your Inner Critic

One of the damaging aspects of negative self-talk is that it often goes unchallenged. After all, if it's a running commentary going on in your head, others may not be aware of what you're saying to yourself and thus can't tell you how wrong you are. It's far better to catch your negative self-talk and ask yourself how true it is. Most of the negative self-talk is an exaggeration and calling yourself on this can help to take away the damaging influence of negative self-talk.

- Think Like a Friend

When our inner critic is at its worst, it can sound like our worst enemy. Often, we'll say things to ourselves in our heads that we'd never say to a friend. Why not reverse this and--when you catch yourself speaking negatively in your head--make it a point to imagine yourself saying this to a treasured friend. If you know you wouldn't say it this way, think of how you'd share your thoughts with a good friend or what you'd like a good friend to say to you. This is a great way to shift your self-talk in general.

- Shift Your Perspective

Sometimes looking at things in the long term can help you to realize that you may be placing too great an emphasis on something. For example, you may ask yourself if something you're upset by will really matter in five years or ten. Another way to shift perspective is to imagine that you are panning out and looking at your problems from a great distance. Even thinking of the world as a globe and of yourself as a tiny, tiny person on this globe can remind you that most of your worries aren't as big as they seem. This can often minimize the negativity, fear, and urgency in negative self-talk.

- Say It Aloud

Sometimes when you catch yourself thinking negative thoughts in your mind, simply saying them aloud can help. Telling a trusted friend what you're thinking about can often lead to a good laugh and shine a light on how ridiculous some of our negative self-talk can be. Other times, it can at least bring support. Even saying some negative self-talk phrases around under your breath can remind you how unreasonable and unrealistic they sound and remind you to give yourself a break.

- Stop That Thought

For some, simply stopping negative thoughts in their tracks can be helpful. This, unsurprisingly, is known as "thought-stopping" and can take the form of snapping a rubber band on your wrist, visualizing a stop sign, or simply changing to another thought when a negative train of thought enters your mind. This can be helpful with repetitive or extremely critical thoughts like, "I'm no good," or, "I'll never be able to do this," for example.

- Replace the Bad with Some Good

This is one of the best routes to combating negative self-talk: replacing it with something better. Take a negative thought and change it to something encouraging that's also accurate. Repeat until you find yourself needing to do it less and less often. This works well with most bad habits: replacing unhealthy food with healthy food, for example, and it's a great way to develop a more positive way of thinking about yourself and about life.

Name thoughts which are negative in your head:

1._____

2._____

3._____

4._____

5._____

Declaration: I_____ chose to speak kindly and positively with myself _____(date)

I choose to:

1._____

2._____

3._____

4._____

5._____

Signature:_____

Signed at_____on the_____

POSITIVE SELF-TALK

Positive self-talk is the flip of negative self-talk. It's not about narcissism, or deceiving ourselves into thinking things that are inaccurate. It's more about showing yourself some self-compassion and understanding for who you are and what you've been through.

Positive self-talk sees our internal narrative switching to ideas like 'I can do better next time' or 'I choose to learn from my mistakes, not be held back by them'.

The Importance and Benefits of Positive Self-Talk, As the research suggests, positive self-talk is important for a number of reasons. From helping to overcome body dysmorphia to sports performance, mediating anxiety, and depression, to more effective learning: positive self-talk can make a world of difference.

Three additional benefits include:

1. **Helps to Reduce Stress**

Research has shown that people who are more inclined towards thinking optimistically, are also more inclined towards positive self-talk and utilize more active coping strategies when faced with stressful situations and challenges (Iwanaga, Yokoyama, and Seiwa, 2004).

Positive self-talk helps you reframe the way you look at stressful situations, understanding that you will approach challenges with the best of your ability and that whatever the outcome – you did the best you could. Tackling these situations with an 'I can do this' mindset rather than a negative 'This is too hard' one, opens new ways of thinking and problem-solving.

2. Boosts Confidence and Resilience

Approaching life with a positive self-talk approach can help to boost your self-confidence. Individuals who score highly for optimism and positive self-esteem are more likely to achieve their goals, score good grades and recover quickly from surgery (Lyubormisky, 2008).

Regular positive self-talk can help you to feel more confident in the face of achieving your goals, as you instill yourself with the belief that the things you want are achievable, and when problems do arise, you find workarounds.

3. Helps to Build Better Relationships

You're probably aware of what it feels like to be around someone who is positive, self-assured, and content in who they are as a person. They exude confidence, and it reflects positively on those around them. Research found that couples who were more optimistic cited higher levels of cooperation and positive outcomes.

People who utilize positive self-talk are also extremely capable of picking up on the positive traits of those around them.

Make 5 positive statement about yourself:

1._____

2._____

3._____

4._____

5._____

✏️ **Declaration:** Say the below statement daily, every morning before the start of the day.

I have the power to change my mind.

Attempting to do this took courage and I am proud of myself for trying.

Even though it wasn't the outcome I hoped for, I learned a lot about myself.

I might still have a way to go, but I am proud of how far I have already come.

I am capable and strong; I can get through this.

Tomorrow is a chance to try again, with the lessons learned from today.

I will give it my all to make this work.

I can't control what other people think, say, or do. I can only control me.

This is an opportunity for me to try something new.

I can learn from this situation and grow as a person

ARE YOU TRYING TO FIT IN?

The pressure to Fit In.
All teens want to be accepted, but today they face more and more pressure to be part of the crowd. Fitting in might mean having the latest cell phone or the "coolest" jeans or hanging out with the right people. It could even mean using tobacco, alcohol, drugs, or prescription drugs.

Pressure to Be Perfect.
It's no surprise that many teens have unrealistic expectations about appearance. For some, this focus on perfection may lead to extreme measures, such as eating disorders, drug use to lose weight or steroids to strengthen or improve body image. Other teens just feel stressed trying to keep up with the prettiest, thinnest, or most fashionable kids at school.

Pressure to Be Sexually Active.
Have you noticed that many 15-year-olds today could pass for 21? In part due to sex in popular culture, teens face much more pressure today to be "sexy" and sexually active at an earlier age. Both boys and girls report feeling these pressures. Television and movies decide the physical appearance and style of most teens… the most important influence comes from the opposite sex. Basically, most decisions high school students make come down to TV and sex."

Pressure to Pick on Others.
There have always been bullies, but the taunting and teasing in high schools is at a troubling level. And increasingly it involves aggressive adolescent girls. Many girls often say that putting other people down makes them feel more included in a

group, even if they know it's wrong or hurtful behavior. New forms of teasing, such as cyberbullying, are also putting pressure on teens to take part in this hurtful behavior.

Pressure to Be Successful.
Teens face huge stress around academics, athletic performance, and other areas. Competition for college is tighter than ever, and teens are pressured early on to do "everything right" to get into the best school. Often teens feel they must Times have changed a lot since you were a teenager. Sure, every teen is worried about being popular, but for today's teens, that's just the tip of the iceberg. Take a closer look at some of the pressures your teen faces today and learn how you can help. excel in sports, extracurricular, volunteer, and other activities to be competitive for the best schools. Many parents push their teens without even realizing it. In some cases, the stress may lead teens to use drugs or alcohol to escape from their pressured lives.

Declaration:
I choose not to be pressured to fit in by doing the following:

_____

_____

_____

_____

_____

_____

IMPORTANCE OF JOURNALING

Keeping a personal journal, a daily in-depth analysis and evaluation of your experiences is a high-leverage activity that increases self-awareness and enhances all the endowments and the synergy among them.

Journaling daily is the most potent and powerful keystone habit you can acquire. If done correctly, you will show up better in every area of your life — every area! Without question, journaling has by far been the number one factor to everything I've done well in my life.

There are many benefits of keeping a journal.

Here are 8 reasons why you should be starting a journal today:

1. Keep your thoughts organized.
Diaries help us to organize our thoughts and make them apprehensible. You can record daily events, thoughts and feelings about certain experience or opinions. Journey allows you to tag and archive your diary entries.

2. Improve your writing.
Journaling helps you to train your writing. If you want to practice or improve your writing, the best thing to do is to start a journal. You may not have the perfect topic. All you need is to start writing your thoughts in Journey. The more you write, the more your writing improves.

3. Set & achieve your goals.
A journal is a good place to write your goals, ambitions, aspirations, and new year resolutions. By keeping them in a diary, you can monitor your progress and continue to focus on the next milestone.

4. Record ideas on-the-go.
The benefits of keeping a journal is that you can record all your ideas in one place anytime and at anywhere. Whenever an idea comes to your mind, you can write it down in your journal. Later on, you can revisit these ideas to look for new links, form conclusions or even lead to a fresh idea!

5. Relieve stress.
Writing down your feelings help you to "brain-dump" your anxieties, frustrations, and pains on a journal. This can help you to reduce and release stress which you have harbored overtime. A good way to relive stress is to write in the stream of consciousness style first thing in the morning called "Morning pages". You can also use the mood tracker found in Journey to indicate your sentiment level. Overall, expressing yourself in a diary is a good way to free up any tension that prevents you from feeling happy.

6. Allow yourself to self-reflect.
It is true that Life moves pretty fast but If you don't stop and look around occasionally and smell the rose, you could miss it. The fast-moving pace in our life makes us easily caught up with the day-to-day. Our life can become very hectic as we shoulder more responsibilities and have higher expectations that are required from us.

Journaling is a good way to help us to stop, take a step back and reflect on ourselves. We can self-reflect on gratitude or what we did today and write it in our diary. Daily reflection can be done at night before bed. We can look back at our life in a journal and think about how we've changed and what we can do to improve ourselves.

7. Boost your memory.
Your brain is likely to store information that you have wrote down in your diary. If you learn something new and write it down in a diary, your brain will make stronger connections with the information. You'll have an easier time to recall them in the future.

8. Inspire creativity.
Writing a journal is a great way to unleash your creativity. Everyone has the potential to be creative, just that most of us haven't discovered it yet. Your journal is the best place to start exploring your inner creativity. Write down anything that comes to your mind. Let your imaginations run wild and record it in Journey.

Declaration

I_____

- Will buy a journal/ or make a journal
- Will commit to writing in my journal daily.

HAVE FUN, LIFE IS SHORT

Don't Rush to be an adult, enjoy this phase of your life, You won't get It back!

Life is too short. Enjoy and have fun. Forgive your friends. Love by heart. Laugh out loud. Do everything that makes you smile.

Do you know how many years you have left? Weeks, days, minutes? Neither do I. This is not a tragedy, nor is death itself. Nay, this is an opportunity. If life were permanent, we'd never appreciate it fully.

We are given a short time here on Earth to love, learn, and enjoy. Working hard and pushing past our limits is essential for our survival and evolution, individually and collectively. But it is also crucial that we take time to have fun in life.

It's so easy to take our jobs, our responsibilities, and ourselves too seriously. And it's perfectly fine to do so when there are important tasks to perform. But when the stress piles on to the point we feel our insides may spew out of our ears, let's take five minutes to contemplate the impermanence of life and how precious every minute is truly is.

Now, we don't have to completely throw in the towel, quit our lives, hop on a sailboat, and live at sea while porting to various islands for exotic fruits and rums and listening to ancient parables, gathering up bits of wisdom from all the world.

Having fun in life doesn't have to be epic. It can be little things like humming your favorite song while walking to school, noticing how cute the flowers are on the side of the road or laughing after an awkward high-five.

Rather than setting sail on an epic voyage to discover all the fun life has to offer, let's simply increase our awareness of the little joys tucked in the crevices of our daily lives.

Let's smile at the silly stuff and hum to the tune. Let's wiggle and beebop and let all the bad jokes rip.

Because life is just too short to not have fun.

In life, goodbyes are a gift. When certain people walk away from you, and certain opportunities close their doors on you, there is no need to hold onto them or pray to keep them present in your life. If they close you out, take it as a direct indication that these people, circumstances, and opportunities are not part of the plan for the next step of your life. It's a hint that your personal growth requires someone different and something more, and life is simply making room. So, embrace your goodbyes, because every "goodbye" you receive sets you up for an even better "hello".

Declaration

I _____ declare today _____ (date)
that I will enjoy every moment of my life. Life is too short, time is fast, no replay, no rewind, I vow to enjoy every moment as it comes.

Signature:_____

Signed at_____on the_____

> In life, you will fall out with people that you never thought you would. Get betrayed by people you trusted with all of your heart. And get used by people you would do anything for.
>
> **But life also has a beautiful side to it.**
>
> You will get loved by someone you never thought you would have. Form never friendships with people that will establish more meaningful and stronger relationships. And overcome things you never thought you would get over.
>
> We all have chapters that end with people at some point in life. But take pride in knowing that **the very best part of your book is still being written.**

VALIDATE YOURSELF, BE GOOD ENOUGH FOR YOU

There's nothing wrong with being validated by others.

In fact, it's actually pretty great it just becomes problematic when that's your only source of being affirmed.

Instead, it's important to strengthen your ability to give yourself all the love and confidence you need.

Here are some ways to do it.

1. Increase your self-awareness.
When you're more aware of what's going on for you, it's easier to provide sincere validation for yourself. You can be honest with yourself about your shortcomings as well as your successes. During the whole journey, you can be mindful of what you brought to the table. Then you can pat yourself on the back, knowing you're OK and you can keep your eyes open to the truth.

2. Start speaking to yourself kindly.
I know this sounds easier said than done. It's possible, though! Start with small mantras to feel better about yourself that feel genuine to you. How about "you're good enough as you are" or "you're doing the best you can"? These are ways to provide validation to yourself. With practice, they become more and more believable and even often become your first response.

3. let your emotions and feelings be what.

It's so easy to want to change feelings, especially if you're feeling sad you may try to cover it in positivity. While being positive is a good thing, it's not good when you're doing so at the expense of truly feeling what's going. So, let your emotions and feelings be what they are. Give them space to breathe and run their course. All things shift.

4. ask yourself what you need.

At any given time, what do you need? You can treat yourself like a child if that's helpful. Speak to yourself as lovingly as you would a small human. Make sure you're giving yourself the space to answer this question, though, don't just stay super busy all the time. Slow down enough to look inward in this way. Then go ahead and give yourself what you need.

5. celebrate your victories.

When you do something well, be sure to celebrate that! You're awesome and you're deserving of your own celebration. In doing this, it helps you build up self-esteem and belief in the capable human that you are. No victory is too small to celebrate. You can get yourself a small gift, play your favorite song, or go out to eat with a friend. Celebrate how you want!

6. Read inspirational things.

Whether it's a simple quote on Instagram or a book from one of your favorite authors, dive into what inspires you. That feeling when you read a quote that just hits the spot is a great one. It's one way to validate yourself with the help of someone else. It's not cheating! Use their spark to ignite yours. You're still doing the work.

7. Surround yourself with inspirational people.

When you surround yourself with inspirational people, you're more likely to be inspired yourself. They'll remind you to validate yourself because they're validating themselves. Positive folks around you will keep you doing healthy habits like remembering to care for yourself.

8. Good self-care.
Practicing self-care is a way of validating yourself because you're saying in essence that you deserve to be taken care of. Then you're taking that action. It's confirming that you're a worthwhile human being who loves themselves. Performing self-care can come in all forms like the traditional bathtub with a bath bomb or just cooking yourself a nice meal.

9. Turn to praise not shame.
It's so easy for most people to jump right to shaming themselves. You're bad, stupid, and a messed-up person. This is not the kind of language you want to use when you're trying to validate yourself. Instead of that, try praising yourself for what you did do right and the fact that you tried. Tell yourself you're actually doing just fine.

10. Practice acceptance.
Life happens. Things often turn out ways we don't plan and maybe didn't ask for. In this case, practicing acceptance is a way of telling yourself, "OK, your feelings are valid, and we're going to have to take this for what it is." Acceptance isn't about giving up, rather it's about surrendering to things you can't control and not letting them control you.

HOW TO FIGURE OUT WHAT YOU WANT IN LIFE

Knowing what you want is the first and most important step in creating a better future. But how do you make this important decision? Trying to decide what you want in a world full of so many choices can seem overwhelming.

Most people have a very good idea of what they don't want in life. We look around and see all the terrible things happening in the world, and we realize we don't want war, we don't want poverty, we don't want sickness.

Good news is if you can identify what you don't want, knowing what you do want is within your reach. To perceive anything, there must be a contrast between the two states.

To know that something is unwanted, we must know that something else is wanted instead. One serves as the reference point for the other.
For example, we could not identify the wanted state of happiness if we did not know what it was like to experience the unwanted state of being unhappy.

The reason you can identify what you don't want is that you are aware some other, preferable state exists, otherwise you wouldn't know it was unwanted. You simply have to give more of your attention to the wanted state and give it some clarity.

Once you have identified what you don't want, see if you can flip it over and find the contrasting wanted state. If you don't want to live in the city, perhaps it is because you prefer a slower country pace.

If you don't want to work in a retail job, but you aren't sure what kind of job you would like, write down as many details as you can about what you don't like in retail.

For example, "I don't like retail because it's exhausting to stand on my feet all day. Instead, I would like a job where I could spend more time at a desk."

Once you have identified what you don't want, ask yourself: What would I like to see instead?

Examples:
Don't want: I don't want a spouse who doesn't appreciate me.
Want: I want a spouse who adores me and treats me with respect.

Don't want: I don't want to work at this lousy job.
Want: I want a job that stimulates me intellectually and allows me to be creative.

How to Figure Out Your Purpose.

Step 1: Forget Money and Forget Reason
When the voice in your head is telling you that you need to get the hell out of a certain situation, listen to it. damn the money and damn reason. Trust yourself.

Step 2: Do Things That Scares the Hell Out of You
Doing stuff that scares you is always horrible in the moment. There's no getting around it. You feel awkward and weird and unnatural but trust me these are good feelings to have.

Step 3: Honestly Believe That You Can Do This

Facing fears is hard, but it does something awesome to you. It helps you see that your fears aren't that big and scary after all. Then when you surmount them, you feel

Step 4: Do Not Get Comfortable, Continue to Innovate

I choose to innovate everyday, I want to tell stories. I want to inspire. I want to help people live a life that they want.

How to Figure Out Exactly What You Want

Because I am capable of making only small moves toward personal improvement, I find it helpful to break down the process of clarifying desire into steps. I call them the four Ps: Pushback, Possibilities, Preferences, and Pinpointing. Let's consider them.

Step 1: Pushback	Step 2: Possibilities
While visiting China, I heard a story of a wise man there who taught his acolytes by holding a little songbird on his finger. When the bird tried to leave, he'd drop his hand so it couldn't get enough lift to fly away. Lesson: The ability to soar often depends on pushing back against something you don't want. My feminist friends and I did lots of this; every time we identified things that felt wrong to us in a	Once you've complained yourself into a nice high dudgeon, release the energy of finding fault and take up the energy of imagination. Holding in your mind the situation that leads to the strongest Pushback, begin mentally playing out ways it might change. Emphasis on playing. If you feel confined in your tiny office, imagine working in Cinderella's castle, at the beach, on the moon. As Arthur C. Clarke wrote,

deeply authentic, visceral way, we were articulating the Pushback.

Since most humans are expert complainers, I'll bet you're feeling some level of Pushback right now. Somewhere in your life there's a sense of resistance, resentment, discomfort. When babies feel this way about pureed liver, they clamp their mouths closed, shake their heads, hurl spoons. Though I doubt you do this at business meetings or parent-teacher conferences, maybe you should. Inwardly, I mean. Outwardly, you can nod and smile the way you always do, while noticing the feeling of Pushback.

And when you're ready to start complaining—to your spouse, a cabdriver, the pope—don't just bitch and moan. Bitch and moan about precisely the things that bother you. Find the central flaw in the boardroom strategy session. Figure out what exactly about the teacher's condescending attitude makes you want to punch her in the kidneys. The more specific you are about what upsets you, and why, the clearer you can make your desires.

"The only way of discovering the limits of the possible is to venture a little way past them into the impossible." Each time you feel your Pushback, ride that energy and use it to imagine outrageously awesome Possibilities.

Step 3: Preferences	Step 4: Pinpoints
If you stay loose and relaxed as you're conjuring Possibilities, you'll notice that some of them leave you feeling intrigued, curious, a bit lighter. These are your Preferences. Let them tiptoe into your consciousness. Don't think; just allow. (If you could already think about your Preferences clearly, you'd be creating, not complaining. As T.S. Eliot wrote, "Wait without thought, for you are not ready for thought.") Let yourself form a vague impression, then go for a bit more specificity, as if you're slowly bringing a camera into focus. Allow, and watch.	If you're playful and patient, the Preferences forming in your consciousness will eventually become clear enough to describe in words. You'll begin articulating exactly what bothers you and scenarios you'd prefer to see. Don't jump the gun; hold on a bit longer and get maximum specificity by Pinpointing your desires. Thinking of a solution you'd like to see, ask yourself, What would be even better? After allowing an answer to come into focus, ask, What would be even better than that? Repeat this until you've got an image of a situation so perfect you literally can't imagine a way to top it. This is Pinpoint clarity. Now you're telling the waiter, "Please bring me two free-range eggs boiled for exactly three minutes, seasoned with a dash of sea salt and coarsely ground Tellicherry pepper." That kind of clarity may raise eyebrows, but guess what? It lets everyone and everything around you deliver exactly what you want.

YOUR PATH, YOUR PURPOSE

Do you know what your true purpose is, and are you pursuing it in your life?

Most of us have no clue what we want to do with our lives. Even after we finish school. Even after we get a job. Even after we're making money. Chances are you're more like me and have no clue what you want to do. It's a struggle almost every adult goes through. "What do I want to do with my life?" "What am I passionate about?"

Asking ourselves the following five questions, we can align our life's purpose with what we do and pursue our authentic life's work:

1. What is success?
The definition of success is different for each one of us. Some measure success in terms of the amount of money they make or the possessions they own, while others measure it by the positive impact they have on the world, and on those around them. And while some may define success as spending more time with their loved ones, they may spend so much time at work -- or bringing work home with them on the weekend -- that they don't have the opportunity to achieve the success they so desperately crave. Instead of work-life balance, Nicholas Pearce suggests the pursuit of whole-life integration, where your spiritual self, your physical self, your professional self, and your family self are all integrated. Ultimately, success is faithfulness to your calling.

2. Who am I?
How do you see yourself, what is your identity? Do you define your identity just by your physical body and your mind, or is there something more? According to

Pearce, we are much more than our bodies and our minds. There is something much longer lasting and eternal about the soul within each of us, and figuring out how you wrap your mind around who you are -- independent of what you possess and what people say you are -- is fundamental. Your identity determines your character, and when you adopt a particular character, you take on the persona and value system that goes along with it. This self-discovery is an essential pre-condition to demonstrating vocational courage.

3. Why am I here?

If it's true that there is something more substantial to us as humans than flesh and bones -- that we should have some type of enduring impact on the world around us -- then our presence here on this earth should have some bearing on others' quality of life, just as others' presence should have some bearing on our quality of life. You are not an island, but at the same time there are so many ways that we can each be of benefit to others. What is your unique reason for being, and how do you determine it? Consider this example: If there's a part in your car that you don't understand, you don't go ask 1,000 different people, "What do you think this part is for?" Instead, you ask the company that made the car. In the same way, we look to our maker for the answer to the question, "Why am I here?

4. Am I running the right race?

Each of us has our own race to run, and one of the most important keys to success is to make sure you're running the right race. You might look at others and see that they're full of joy in the race they are running. But don't think you're going to get the same joy by copying what they are doing. You will find your greatest joy and fulfilment in life when you pursue your calling -- what you are uniquely meant to do. This is where your values really come into play. When you have clarity about what your highest values are, you'll understand in what race you should be. This is where courage comes in, because you have to run your own race -- not your parents' or your boss's or your spouse's, friend's, or neighbor's.

5. Am I running the race well?

Running your race is not a competition against someone else, it is a competition against your best self. On this race, the destination is not as important as the journey. If you run the race well and finish, you've won. Running your race well requires figuring out who you really are, understanding what your values are, and then living out your values as you run the race. If you decide to become an investment banker, and you make a habit of cheating others and violating your values, then you are not running the race well. In other words, impact does not excuse disintegrity on the journey. Demonstrating vocational courage is not just about which path you've chosen, but also about the integrity with which you walk the path.

If you knew you were going to die one year from today, what would you do and how would you want to be remembered?	Discovering one's "purpose" in life essentially boils down to finding those one or two things that are bigger than yourself, and bigger than those around you. It's not about some great achievement, but merely finding a way to spend your limited amount of time well. And to do that you must get off your couch and act, and take the time to think beyond yourself, to think greater than yourself, and paradoxically,	

	to imagine a world without yourself.	
How are you going to save the world?	So pick a problem and start saving the world. There are plenty to choose from. Our screwed-up education systems, economic development, domestic violence, mental health care, governmental issues. Find a problem you care about and start solving it. Obviously, you're not going to fix the world's problems by yourself. But you can contribute and make a difference. And that feeling of making a difference is ultimately what's most important for your own happiness and fulfillment. And importance equals purpose.	

FAILING FORWARD

"Forward ever, backwards never"

- Use failure as fuel for the growth.
- Failure isn't fatal it is needed for innovation success—as long as you don't freak out, make catastrophic mistakes or fail to learn from it.
- You need to accept the fact that you are going to fail if you are going to do your best work, and you need to make sure that everyone on your team and, indeed, in your entire company understands it, as well.
- You need to be free them from the innovation-limiting shackles of perfection; don't let them ruin good with perfect.
- Albert Einstein, whose very name we use as a shorthand for describing someone as a genius, was a lousy student. He literally failed his way through academics.
- Great innovation, like great people, typically are not born; it is the result of trial and error.

The phrase, "Be patient, God isn't finished with me yet" is a healthy mantra for most of us and most of our new ventures.

One reason that's true, is that in order to make a product or service everything it can be, it needs to be repeatedly soft launched with both internal stakeholders and external customers. This means literally sending the idea—be it a product or a service—into a limited part of the marketplace with the full understanding that it will be modified (perhaps extensively) based on how customers and consumers react.

For successful launches to happen, you must be OK with the premise that they are starting with what some may consider a half-baked idea—one that very well may fail as constituted.

You must make this OK.

Tell yourself that the real failure is fear of launching an idea until it is perfect.

1. Have no regrets.
Life is too short to live with regret. We will all die one day and wouldn't it be a great tragedy for all of your best ideas to die with you? Or worse, to leave Earth, regretting never having tried?

Did you know that our total time on this planet averages 30,000 days an alarmingly small number that made me become a bit fixated on counting them. Value each day and am determined to make every second count. It's surprising how something as simple as focusing on time or lack of it can reignite your commitment to achieving your goals, big or small.

Go after what you want. Take risks calculated, ones of course; be aware that with every risk could come failure, but without great risk there is no reward.

2. Accept reality.
The hard part of failure can be admitting to yourself that you have failed. When I lost my first business—the moment I made the decision that I couldn't fix it—and I had to sell all the metered taxis I owned.

Acceptance made it easier to move forward; it brought completion to the life cycle of that company so that I could be free to discover what would be next.

3. Don't be a victim, be a strategist.
When you try something and it doesn't work, it can be easy to wring your hands and adopt a woe-is-me attitude, but that won't help you move forward. You have to correct your strategy.

Examine where you went wrong and get systems in place to prevent those errors from occurring again. Have a coach/ family or close friend to provide input on your strategy and spend at least 10 hours a week fine-tuning your strategy. Get ducks in the row.

4. Approach every day as a school day.
Fail forward and fail fast, and every day will be a school day there is always a lesson to be had and failure is one of our greatest teachers.

You have to be open to every experience as an opportunity to learn something new. The faster and harder you fail, the less and less afraid you become of it because you have come out on the other side of it and are usually stronger and better equipped for it.

Declaration

Dear_____

Failing is just part of the journey and a step toward figuring things out.
Embrace Failure to Launch Forward.
I promise to Foster a Growth Mindset.
The art of failing forward will drive sustainability, empowerment, and resilience.

NOTES

_____

_____

_____

_____

WHICH RAT ARE YOU CHASING?

Education rat v/s Fun rat (shiny objects)

Delayed gratification is the ability to postpone an immediate gain in favor of greater and later reward; it is the ability to postpone an immediate reward for the sake of more distant long-term gains.

One of the most important challenges we face in life is the need to delay gratification. The ability to either forgo immediate temptation or to persist in an undesirable activity, in order to reach a later goal, is a key component to success in many life tasks, such as preparing for exams. Delay of gratification is not a capability we are born with, but one achieved throughout development

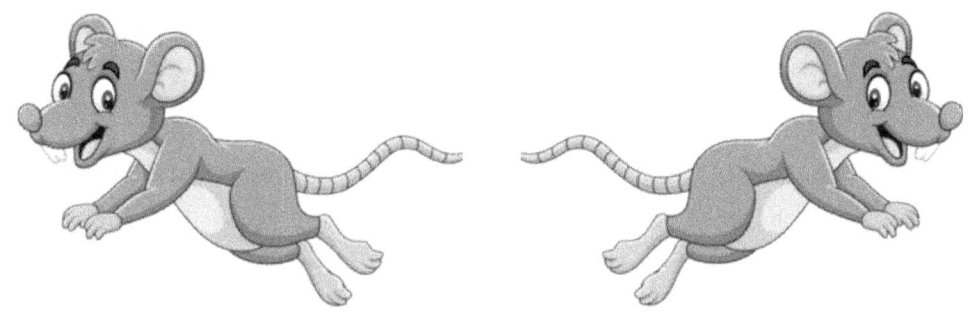

EDUCATION   **FUN**

Education is a fundamental driver of personal, national and global development. Investing in your education is extremely important. It is only through education that people are able to improve themselves. One of the most important factors for escaping from poverty is education. Investing in education is not just the right thing to do, it is smart economics because upon graduation, the end result will certainly pay out in dividends.

It is important to prepare yourself to become productive members of the economy and become responsible and active members of our society. Investing in their education should never be underestimated, think of the long term benefits you will enjoy upon completing a proper course of education.

The truth is, that in life, we have two courses of action.

Play now and pay later. Or, pay now and play later.

The latter simply means that while others are enjoying outings, spending time at nightclubs, and other social activities, you are delaying that gratification by sacrificing your social time to invest in your studies. This will pay dividends later.

If we invest (pay) properly and productively on the front end, we can play on the back end.

One way of looking at this, is looking at those who, in their mid-thirties, can afford holidays, time off, fancy cars and big houses- have paid with their sacrificed time and delayed their gratification. Now they can enjoy the finer things in life.

Those who didn't- who went out partying and enjoyed all the frivolities of youth without sparing a thought for tomorrow, are the ones who now are working fulltime jobs, living paycheck-to-paycheck, and who have to answer to a boss regarding any time off.

PAY NOW AND PLAY LATER OR PLAY NOW AND PAY LATER

IF YOU DON'T STAND FOR SOMETHING, YOU WILL FALL FOR EVERYTHING

When you stand for nothing, you fall for everything

What exactly does it mean to stand for something?
It means to hold firmly to an opinion or belief.
To stand for something means you give it your support.

It's impossible to make everyone happy, Nor should you.
We interact with every kind of person you can imagine, it's impossible to make everyone happy.

All you can really do is make yourself happy, and hope both your happiness and your genuine strength of character are enough to touch the lives of others who will see you for you, and who will respect that version of you. Not for someone whose image is so confused that they are basically a combination of everyone else, not a whole version of who they are.
Don't be the person who lives for everyone else, and in the process loses who they are.
Yes, it's honorable and admirable to try to make everyone around you happy, but what about your own happiness?
Isn't there something to say for that?
And where does trying to make everyone else happy leave you and who does that leave you with?

People who stick around only because you're constantly and consistently making them happy by giving in to their wishes and helping them pursue their own self-interests and agenda?

These aren't the kind of people you want by your side to go through life with. They're not making you a better person, they're just taking away from the person you are, making you less of the person you are.

There's always going to be those people who don't agree with you, with what you say or with what you do. Those people who challenge you and your beliefs. And that's okay. Because they're there to do just that, to challenge you.
Everyone is entitled to their own opinions and their own judgments.
How some people use these opinions and judgments is sometimes questionable.

But that's a whole different story.

Having unique opinions and voices is what makes us so special and different and helps us grow and move toward solutions and answers and progress and change. We're who we are for a reason and we're the only one of us. Yes, we're meant to change and evolve over time, but we should be the catalysts for those changes. That kind of judgment call should come from us. After all, we are the ones who are changing.

We all have these personal philosophies and beliefs and values and opinions that differentiate us, that make us unique. And as a result, we have a duty to ourselves and to those we share our lives with to share each of these unique qualities. Because who would want to be someone they're not and surround themselves by those who really don't know them for who they are? And who would want to be friends with someone who isn't genuine and doesn't share these unique things?

Imagine a world in which everyone was the same. Looked the same, acted the same, said the same things, did the same things and thought the same way. Can you imagine?

Sometimes our differences are what drive us crazy, but we'd be crazier if everyone was just another one of us, an exact replica of who we are.

At the end of the day, all you can do is stand strong for what you believe in and use your voice for the better good. Don't be easily swayed. People will hate you at some point in time throughout your life for one thing or another because of something you did or said. But people will also respect those who have a strong sense of who they are, who stand up for what they believe in no matter how many people are on their team or on their side, who figured themselves out and who love the person they figured out.

Those who don't know who they are yet or what they stand for are easily swayed. They want to make everyone happy. And in those moments, they do. But that's no way to earn someone's respect. Don't let anyone take advantage of you, because you'll lose yourself, and the things you once knew and stood for. Those aren't the people you were meant to grow beside.

Don't define yourself based off anyone else but yourself.

If you don't stand for something, you'll fall for anything.
Again, cliché.

But you have to ask yourself, if it's been said so many times across time, people, and space, then it has to have some meaning to it, right?
Earning someone's respect isn't the easiest task, but once it's earned, it's an unbreakable bond. It's something worth working toward and fighting for.

You shouldn't have to prove or feel like you have to prove yourself to someone else. Be who you are, never falter, always stand strong. People will look up to you, they'll respect you.

It just takes time.

Time, something we tend to have a lot of, but also something we tend to not know what to do with.
We're so impatient, always looking for immediate progress and results. Always focusing on the here and now, never really doing or saying something with the long run-in mind.

Always focusing on going through the motions, doing one thing to get to the next. We focus on short term goals, things that will pay off immediately, things that don't require as much effort or time. We expect things to go our way almost instantaneously.

Our lives could last for decades, maybe even a century.
What you do with that time is up to you.
Use this time to form thoughts, opinions, actions and relationships that are lasting and meaningful.

Sure, your life could be comprised of individual moments that really have no relationship whatsoever. Or your life could be composed of one entire moment, evolving, and growing from start to finish. Supported by everyone and everything that makes you who you are.

Declaration

I_____ promise to define myself by no one else but myself. I will stand firm in my personal philosophies, beliefs, values and opinions.

BE OF SERVICE TO OTHERS

Are you using your ability to change someone's life?

The amazing thing about serving others and giving is that it positively affects the giver. You can't give to others without also reaping benefits yourself. When you see yourself as a servant leader, you will never lack for an audience to help. Always remember that wherever you are in life, there is always someone you can help in some way.

When you look for ways to help others, you'll find that you are constantly blessed with things.

Service is an important part of life by exemplifying in my life. Our words can never speak more loudly than our actions.

Encourage others, stop to hear what people are saying to you, put yourself in the other person's shoes, think before you speak, and above all, put on love as the supreme ethic whenever you interact with others.

The big misconception about giving back is that it requires a substantial investment of time or significant contribution of money. I once thought this same thing, but have since realized that there are many ways, I can serve others without breaking the bank or taking time off.

The options are endless, but just to get you started, here are seven ways you can easily serve others. Many of these anecdotes are from people in my circles who have inspired me to make service a priority in my life. You can use them as inspiration to find ways to give back in your own way.

1. Donate
2. Feed the hungry
3. Donate your product
4. Mentor
5. Volunteer your services
6. Make service a company mission
7. Share the passion your talent brings

Serving people is easy when we know who we are and what we are about. I believe our true purpose in life is to give our lives away to others, and that we receive happiness, fulfillment, and meaning in return

 **Task**

Take a moment and think about what you can do each day to be a servant to others. Before you begin each day, ask yourself, "How will I serve another today?"

_____
_____
_____
_____
_____
_____
_____

VISION

This requires that we have vision or a picture of what is perceived as being possible in life. To improve vision, you really need to imagine it, to picture it. Imagining better is the beginning of finding better in the lives of people. To imagine better requires that we change the stereotypes and assumptions that have surrounded the lives of people with disabilities. That we place our focus on the competencies and abilities that people have rather than placing our emphasis on the struggles and challenges.

Just imagine, if instead of presuming incompetence we were always to presume competence in people.

By presuming competence and providing supports, encouragement and opportunities for people to demonstrate what they are capable of, we create different expectations within themselves and their families about what they are capable of doing and being and create different expectations in others about what might be possible for their lives.

After all, people will live up to the expectations that others hold of them, if you hold low or no expectations then don't be surprised that people will live up to that. By holding few expectations, we deny people the opportunity to take up those life opportunities that not only enable them to demonstrate their competencies but also provide them the bridge to relationships and real participation in the valued fabric of social life.

However, the opposite of course can also be true. If we are not clear, or do not struggle to become clear about what could be possible, if we hold no vision or a very weak vision, then it is very easy for us to be driven this way and that depending on what is happening at the time, who is advising us and our energy for engaging in the challenges. That is, if you stand for nothing, you will fall for anything. Indeed, the reason that we have already come so far is because there have been people, largely families, such as we have heard from most of our speakers today, who have refused to accept reality as it is, or as it is presented to us.

So, you can see that holding onto a vision is not a trivial act. If your vision passes the test you will have a powerful tool that will change lives. Vision is key in keeping hope alive, and we must never let hope for what could be better die. Indeed, hope is more important and powerful than money.

Whenever we hold a powerful vision for a life that is better, we embrace hope, we look beyond the moment, to the promise of what life might yet offer. We begin to embrace a true realism, a realism that is life enhancing rather than life denying.

To pursue the vision, we must have clarity of the underlying values:

1. Recognizing the Humanity and Dignity of People; No Matter What Their Impairments
2. The Dignity Of all people being able to express their Human Will, Freedom and autonomy
3. People Will Thrive Best When the Fullness of Community Is Available to Them
4. Growth Is Ever Possible and Brings Greater Life

So much of what is important in life requires vision, values and faith. As many people with disabilities have demonstrated for us, it often requires that we believe in something before it comes true. If we don't have faith then we won't do any of the great things that need to be done, because we do not believe; we will not put ourselves out there; we won't take a risk. We must be sincerely convinced within ourselves or we will always defer committed action, and when it is the hopes and dreams of life that become deferred or ignored, then life itself and its potentials will fade.

MY VISION:

_____

_____

_____

_____

_____

_____

_____

_____

_____

_____

_____

_____

_____

SELF-DOUBT

> "Our doubts are traitors, and make us lose the good we oft might win, by fearing the attempt" - *William Shakespeare*

Self-doubt is natural, and something we ought not to shame ourselves for, often we are much closer to a breakthrough than we realize, every day we are building on not only what we've done, but how we've thought. We have the ability and capacity to change, however, the level of desire is up to you.

Self-Doubt Destroys the Heart, Mind, Body and Soul.
Self-doubt is one of the major obstacles to living the life you truly deserve. This unhealthy food for the soul drags down your spirit, crushes your ambitions, and prevents you from achieving all that you can.

We all have those inner voices inside our heads that tell us we are not good enough, not strong enough and incapable of doing the things we dream of. Often, these feelings of weakness or incompetence stem from childhood and become ingrained in our very being. Over time, self-doubt can lead to problems with anxiety and depression, which in turn can lead to serious physical ailments like weight gain, high blood pressure, chronic fatigue, and even increased mortality rates among those with heart disease. It is important not only to be aware of the destructive nature of these feelings, but to incorporate methods to counteract this negativity so that you can enjoy a joyful, productive, and fulfilling life.

Tips for Dealing with Self-Doubt

1. Live in the Present
Most of the time, feelings of self-doubt are attached to memories of times in the past when you failed to achieve something or when somebody else told you that you were not good enough. Don't dwell on those moments. Try to ground yourself and think about the now. Just because you couldn't accomplish something before doesn't mean you can't do it again. Every day is a new start and a new chance to go for what you really want.

2. Trust in Yourself
Sometimes we can be our own worst enemies. If you tell yourself that you cannot do something, then you probably won't even try it in the first place. Have faith in yourself, tell yourself that you are just as capable as the next person of achieving your dreams, and stop listening to the voice inside that keeps saying, "I can't." As Norman Vincent Peale famously said, "What the mind can conceive and believe, and the heart desire, you can achieve."

3. Counteract the Negative
At times it may seem as though the negative voices in your head are stronger than the positive voices. Try to be aware of this when it happens and make a concerted effort to counteract these negative thoughts with positive energy. When you feel a negative thought coming on, simply remind yourself about the things you like about yourself, your strengths, and all the things you have achieved in your life and are proud of. Try reciting empowering affirmations.

4. Find the Source of Your Self-Doubt
If you find yourself constantly telling yourself you are not good enough, you may want to delve into the root of the problem. Where did these feelings originate? Was there a specific event that has caused you to harbor such feelings? You can choose to do this on your own or with the help of a professional therapist. Once

you identify and understand the source of the problem, you can begin to work toward eliminating those negative thought patterns.

5. Spend Time with Others

Friends and family are an invaluable source of strength, reassurance, and encouragement. In fact, studies suggest that people who have strong social support have fewer cardiovascular issues and lower levels of cortisol, otherwise known as the stress hormone, when compared to people with fewer friends. Even strangers can be surprisingly positive and helpful when it comes to self-doubt. Simply voicing your self-doubt to others can often put it in perspective and make you realize how illogical this negativity can be. In addition, other people can offer advice and support that will motivate you and give you a huge confidence boost.

✏️ Declaration

I_____ promise to rediscover the genius in me.
I believe in myself and trust the process.
I trust that I will know what to do when the time comes.
I promise to stay in the present moment and won't regret the past or worry about the future.

_____

_____

_____

_____

RELATIONSHIP WITH MONEY

Financial health includes:
Spending money based on your values;
Having low or reasonable debt;
Saving money to meet your goals; and having a safety net, such as an emergency fund or insurance,

Our financial relationship today stems from childhood, which is when we develop "money scripts,". Money Scripts are our beliefs about money, which drive our financial behaviors, usually we're not even aware of them.

Money scripts are shaped by "direct experience, family stories, and parental attitudes"

Research found that there is link between specific money scripts and lower incomes and net worth.

Examples:
- Money avoidance scripts -Money is unimportant or Rich people are greedy'),
- Money worship scripts -More money will make me happier
- Money status scripts -Your self-worth equals your net worth

These are all associated with poor financial outcomes

Improving Your Relationship with Money

1. Shine a spotlight on your scripts.

It is important to make your unconscious money scripts conscious. This way you can begin to challenge your scripts and change them to improve your financial situation. When your money scripts remain unchallenged d, they can influence your behavior in negative ways.

Klontz recommends two practical strategies to explore your scripts.

- Interview family members. Ask your family about their early experiences with money.

Every family has a story around money, and family money scripts all make sense when we know the story

- Recall your earliest money memory.

Ask yourself these questions, what is your most joyful memory around money? What is your most painful money memory? What lessons about money did you learn?"

2. Know thyself.

"Money can serve as an important gateway to a deeper, understanding of ourselves." You can learn more about yourself by paying closer attention to your behaviors around money, then use this knowledge to improve your financial functioning.

For instance, someone who goes to the mall and ends up buying items they don't need might be feeling lonely.

3. Consult reputable resources.

One of many reasons people have a poor relationship with money is misinformation or lack of information. Reading reputable books can help.

4. Consult the experts.

Seek professional help, look for financial advisors and coaches who specialize in finances. Remember asking for help and seeking support is not a sign of weakness, it is a sign of wisdom and an act of courage.

Money is a taboo topic. But once you start exploring those buried beliefs and behaviors, you can build a better relationship with something you previously might've seen as an enemy. And if you need some help to dig deeper, don't hesitate to seek out books, videos or an expert.

Declaration doing the following to change my relationship with money:

_____

_____

_____

_____

_____

_____

_____

_____

RETHINK MONEY

As start, take some time to notice how and when you spend money.

What are your pattern, what motivates you to buy things?
Do you shop spontaneously? What are your triggers?
You might want to start a spending diary to track your habits for a month to get a better idea.

Having a better understanding of how and why you spend money is a good first step to making changes.

Rethink money
While money is essential to meet some of our basic human needs, such as food and safe shelter, it has little to do with other factors that impact our wellbeing.

There are a few fundamental human needs known as subsistence, protection/security, affection, understanding, participation, leisure, creation, identity/meaning, freedom, and transcendence. Think about it, and you will notice that meeting some of these needs requires very little money.

We can meet our deepest needs for affection, understanding, belonging, and identity through our relationships, pursuit of purpose in life, spirituality, and connection with nature. Buying more things or a bigger house simply can't do this.
So, don't look for fulfillment in material, you will be disappointed.

Revise how you spend

As we know, spending money on material goods doesn't bring happiness. But there are ways that money can make you happier.

1. **Spend money on others.**

Experiments show that when people spend "bonus" money on personal items or material goods, it doesn't boost their happiness; but when they spend it on someone else or donate it to charity, they experience a significant increase in their sense of wellbeing.

2. **Buy experiences, not material goods.**

Experiences directly increase your wellbeing and the wellbeing of others you share them with. They can enhance relationships and promote connection to purpose and community. Moreover, we are less likely to have buyer's remorse with experiences, and they don't lose their value over time—instead they can create happy memories.

3. **Spend money to buy time.**

Think about ways that you can create more time in your life for fun and friends. Get a babysitter so you can enjoy an evening with your partner or friends, or just have some down time. Get your groceries delivered. Hire help for the yard or housework.

Avoid comparing

We tend to compare our income to others and only be satisfied if it is relatively higher. If we are offered a raise, but everyone else is too, we are less satisfied.
This is not limited to money, by the way. If we win a race, we will initially be elated, then begin to compare ourselves to someone who is even better, someone who won a bigger race.

Comparing ourselves to others and focusing on income is a never-ending treadmill of dissatisfaction, and it only makes sense to make a deliberate effort to get off.

Set aside time to reflect upon what you like and respect about yourself, without comparing to other people. Focus on how you have improved or grown without worrying about how you rank. Take satisfaction in how hard work and experience develop your skills or speed.

Adjust your goals
Take a good look at your budget. As we said earlier, most of what we need in life is not about money—you can have a good life and spend less. While humans tend to adjust our expectations upward as our income goes up, you can consciously change that. Instead of wanting more expensive things and more of them, you can choose to save new income. Instead of buying things, you can give yourself the security of having enough money.

One way to help yourself change your spending habits is to establish incentives that will motivate you to meet your goals. These can be rewards for meeting goals or punishments when you don't.

Nudge yourself to save
Credit cards can lead us into temptation because they separate the pain of payment from the pleasure of purchasing something new. Saving works the other way—we have the pain of less money to spend right up front, and don't necessarily see the pleasure of having money to live on in the future. So, you need to find ways to increase the incentive to save.

One way to do this is to set up default savings that automatically come out of your salary or bank without you having to choose the "pain."
Furthermore, tell your employer in advance to put any raises that you get in your retirement account or savings if you prefer. That way, your take-home income never goes down, so you aren't losing spending money, but you increase your retirement savings.

How will you spend or save money:

DON'T ENVY OTHERS

Don't envy the lives of others – you don't know the whole story

We rarely see the whole picture of someone else's life. We see small parts that we envy but if we knew the whole story, we'd likely realize that there wasn't really anything to envy. No one knows what another person goes through in their life to live the life they choose. When I find myself comparing myself to another person I try to stop and ask myself "Why?". Why am I comparing myself to them? What is it that they have that I would really want if I could have it? Often, the answer is nothing.

So, what are you looking at? What do you see going on around you that you find yourself envying? Really stop and look at that person, that career, that whatever, and ask yourself if you really had to consider all that comes with that would you really want it?

There's a side that everyone has that they don't show, a side that we keep hidden from the world. No one sees the full life of another, even those who live with that person never really see it all.

Don't envy the lives of others. When you find that you are envious of someone else ask yourself what it is that you really want. What can you really change about yourself? If there's something you can change, then change it. If not, let it go.

> "The reason we struggle with insecurity is because we compare our behind-the-scenes with everyone else's highlight reel." - *Steve Furtick*

It's in our nature to compare ourselves with others. The ability to weigh one situation up against another helps us make decisions and live our lives productively. The downside is that when you constantly compare your own life with those of other people, you will always come up short.

Over-comparing causes envy. Envy is the feeling or sensation we have when we want to get something that someone else has and we can't be happy for them when they have it.

Getting stuck in a cycle of envy is just about the best way to ruin your life. Fortunately, there are several ways to deal with envy that will guide you toward happiness and well-being.

Don't Compare Your Cutting Room Floor With Someone Else's Highlight Reel
Have you ever seen anybody post an unflattering photo on Facebook? Let's face it, you rarely read about someone fighting with their spouse, hating their job, or declaring bankruptcy. Most people show you what they want you to see—a highly edited, glossed-up version of their life.

The next time you feel envious about someone else's life, remember that you're only looking at part of the story, the part they want you to see. Think of something that another person has that you want. For example, maybe someone you know is far more popular than you. On the surface it may appear that they are surrounded with people who look up to them, and that they are well-liked and respected.
But people might have a different view of them behind closed doors. In this case, the actual reality and what we perceive as reality are two very different things.

Even the most enviable lifestyle has downsides. For example, many people covet the glamour and glitz of the rich and famous. But have you ever sat down and thought about what kind of life a famous person has?

Ask yourself if you'd enjoy someone jumping out of a bush and taking a snapshot of you in your grubby tracksuit pants while you're collecting the newspaper from the front lawn. There are always two sides to every coin. What you think you see is not necessarily the reality. So, the next time you get caught up in envy, always remember that unless you are that person you don't really have the whole story.

Do You Really Want What They Have?

If you really want to play the comparison game, remember that if you want someone else's life you have to be willing to do a complete swap; that is, you will have to give up your life as it is and swap over to theirs.

 Here's an exercise that will help you decide if you really want out of your situation and into someone else's:

When you're ready, think of someone you know who has the kind of life that you envy. Then take a piece of paper and in the left-hand column write the heading "What I have that they don't have." Then in the right-hand column, write the heading "What they have that I want." In this column you are going to make a list of all the things this person has that you want. Write down whatever comes to your mind. For example, do they have a lot of money, a nice house, nice clothes, or the perfect partner?

When you've finished doing this, move to the left-hand column. Write down everything that you value in your life. For example, family, friends, pets, and everyone who is important to you.

 Caution: the other person may indeed have friends, family, and pets just like you. But in this case, you're not so much looking at what they have (i.e.: a dog, a child, a husband), but the unique relationship and connection you have with your pets and loved ones. So, remember to write down the names of your family members, friends, and pets. Be as specific as you can. Get clear and what you love about your life. It could be something as simple as being able to finish work early on Thursdays so you can go to the gym.

Now its crunch time; you'll probably find that the list on the left-hand side is much bigger than the list on the right. So, ask yourself, is there anything in this list you would be willing to give up having the life that the other person has?
What you'll likely discover is that everything you have in your list is as valuable as or more valuable than the things that the other person has.

Practice Gratitude
One of the reasons we feel envy is that we often take the good things in our own lives for granted. The happier you are with your lot in life, the better things will come to you. Happiness studies show that truly happy people are not necessarily wealthy, powerful, or famous.
They have simply made a choice to be happy by paying attention to the good things around them. Since whatever you focus on will become the inclination of the mind, this makes perfect sense.

Every night before I go to sleep, I ask myself the following questions:
- What do I take for granted in my life?
- Who are the important people (or animals) in my life?
- Who is in my corner?
- What freedoms do I enjoy?
- What advantages have I been given in life?

This allows me to take stock of what is important and gives me a nice feeling of contentment before I drift off to sleep. Try it for yourself! Our society has conditioned us to believe that your net worth equates to happiness. Accordingly, many people strive to be more, do more, and have more.

But none of those things cause any lasting happiness. They are all impermanent and subject to change. Most importantly, they represent other qualities of heart that can be achieved regardless of net worth.

Ask yourself the question: "What really makes me happy?" Is it the money, possessions, or reputation? Or is it freedom, joy, peace, and serenity?

Happiness is the ultimate currency, and there's no law that says there isn't enough of that to go around.

NOTES

_____

_____

_____

_____

_____

_____

_____

_____

_____

HOW TO STOP BEING ENVIOUS OF OTHER PEOPLE

Being green with envy never feels good. Humans are compelled to compare everything; from the food we eat to the house we own. However, letting these comparisons control your mentality can be harmful. If you spend your days wishing you were living someone else's life, you won't be able to live your own life to the fullest.

1. Figure Out Why You're Envious
If you want to stop being jealous of other people, you must figure out why you're jealous in the first place. What is it that triggers your envy? For example, perhaps you're envious of a co-worker because she can think of unique ideas. Usually, jealousy stems from a feeling of inferiority – so if you want to stop the envy, you need to get to the root of the cause.

2. Focus on the Good
Once you know the reason why you're envious, you can instead focus on the positives in your life. Even if you don't have everything your friends have, you still have something to appreciate. Perhaps you love your smile, or you have some dogs that mean the world to you. Even if it's something as simple as a nice routine each day, being more positive will lead to a better you.

3. Compare Less
It's natural to want to compare, and many times comparisons are not bad. However, if you're a comparison junkie, you may find yourself comparing every little thing. Keeping up with the Joneses comes from constant comparison, and this breeds unending envy. Take a step back when you feel the urge to compare or correct yourself if you catch yourself slipping up.

4. Be Happy for Other People

If you're struggling with jealousy, being happy for other people can be tough. However, being happy for other people's achievements will yield better results than being resentful. If you're jealous, that feeling can be deadweight on your mind and will constantly keep you bitter. Instead, let go and appreciate the work others have completed.

5. Appreciate Yourself More

While it's good to appreciate other people, remember to take care of yourself. Oftentimes, we can feel depressed after comparing ourselves to other people. For example, if you're jealous that you can't play a sport as well as a friend, remind yourself that you have skills in other areas. Perhaps you're a strong musician or you have an excellent memory. Be proud of your strengths.

6. Give What You'd Want from Others

We've all heard the saying "treat others the way you want to be treated." These lessons from elementary school may seem silly, but they still hold true.
Would you rather have someone be genuinely happy for your achievements, or would you prefer receiving a fake smile and a half-hearted congratulations? Instead of letting your resentment and jealousy take over your life, try to remind yourself how you'd want to be treated if the situation was switched around. Taking a walk in another person's shoes can change the way you think.

7. Avoid Other Envious People

When you surround yourself with positivity, you'll have a more optimistic outlook. If you're surrounded by pessimism, then you'll have a more negative demeanor. Each day our peers impact our thoughts. If you're surrounded by people who are petty and say negative comments due to jealousy, you'll be more inclined to do the same. Eliminate these naysayers, and instead, keep company with people who are more willing to let their genuine feelings show.

This won't be an instant change. You'll have to constantly remind yourself and call yourself out on your envy if you want to stop comparing yourself all the time. It takes practice. However, once you get into the habit of being happy for other people first, you'll be able to appreciate your own life even more.

NOTES

POLITELY SAY NO

I like nice! I want to be nice. I want you to think I'm nice. I want to be around nice people.

There's a fine line between being a likeable person and being a people-pleaser.

Not too many of us want to be thought of as the grouch of the family, office, or neighborhood. And most of us think that a good way to achieve niceness, perhaps even a mandatory element for it, is saying yes often. A yes slips off our tongue before we have the chance to stop it even if internally, we're shouting "No!" and slamming on our inner brake pedal trying to stop ourselves from agreeing to something we don't want to do.

And yet, there we go again saying yes to help out on a project, cause, or program that, even though we might care about it, we know is going to add more to our crowded schedules and bulging to-do lists.

It might be saying yes to something that isn't so time consuming but isn't right for you at the moment like: babysitting at the last minute, going out after work with coworkers, entertaining a neighbor who shows up unannounced, or giving free advice to people who are peppering you with questions at a party even though they know the information they're asking for is what you bill your clients for hourly.

Why Is It That We Say Yes So Often?

Part of it is that we're programmed to. It goes back to childhood. When Mama asked us to do something, we were taught to say yes. Later, our friends asked us to join them, and if you wanted to be liked in fourth grade, you said "sure" and ran to play on the monkey bars with the kids who invited you.

Fast-forward fifteen years, and we're saying yes to every request at our new job because we want to be a team player, attract the attention of the boss, and expand our skill set.

Socially, we say yes because we don't want to let people down and sometimes because we feel trapped.
We feel bad that we're not helping when Patty the PTA Nazi assures us everyone else is pitching in their time, money, talents, labor, or whatever the case may be.
We also say yes because it's easier than saying no, and we'd rather deal with our negative feelings than other people's nagging comments, judging stares, and possible gossip if we say no to their request.
So, are we doomed to a life as yes men or women? Is there a way we can nicely say no without feeling guilty or gaining the reputation of grumpy Gertrude or no-help Ned?

Often end up in uncomfortable and messy situations which could totally be avoided if you'd have said NO?
If not said right, saying NO, can often ruin friendships, relationships, and a lot more. But agreeing to do something, that doesn't seem right or is uncomfortable for you isn't also always the right way to go.
So, what should one do in these situations? How to say 'No' politely.
It is tricky but it can avoid you a ton of anxiety.

Here are 10 ways for you to say 'NO' in a polite manner:

1. I'm honored but I can't
2. I wish there were two of me
3. Unfortunately, now is not a good time

4. Sorry, I'm booked into something else right now
5. Damn, not able to fit this one in!
6. Sadly, I have something else
7. No, thank you but it sounds lovely, so next time
8. I'm not taking anything else right now
9. Thank you so much for thinking of me, but I can't!
10. I have another commitment

✏️ Declaration

I_____ promise to Be True to Myself, My Convictions, and My Priorities.

I will not be a people-pleaser.
I will only say YES if I am available, and the task adds value to my life and others.

📝 NOTES

_____

_____

_____

_____

_____

_____

PERSONAL RESPONSIBILITY

Taking personal accountability is a beautiful thing because it gives us complete control of our destinies

Personal responsibility means taking responsibility for your actions, it's being able to take care of one's well-being without expecting or blaming others to do it for you.

Taking responsibility for yourself is both scary and empowering. When things in life don't go well, it's easy to sidestep responsibility. "The dog ate my homework." "I didn't mean to." "You started it." "It's not fair."

It's comforting to have something or someone else to blame or point to circumstances beyond your control that give you an "out." In a way, blaming is a natural reaction to upset or threat. And it is true that life can be unfair; things do happen that are outside of one's control.

There's no shortage of reasons for why you "can't" do something or be somewhere in your life that you want to be. Being your best self and achieving your goals is challenging and there are often roadblocks.
And yet, focusing on what you can't control won't get you anywhere but frustrated, stuck, and feeling helpless.
While it is sometimes true that other people or circumstances that you can't control are interfering with you achieving your goals, it is also true that you still have some things within your own control.

From the definition of responsibility: accountable for something within one's power, control, or management.

We are not responsible for things outside of our own control. We are accountable or responsible for those things within our control, power, or management.

You can control your relationship to the thing outside of your control. You have control over how you respond, react, think about, choose, and act with regard to circumstances or people.

The powers inside of you is sobering, scary, and exciting!

You can control what you think, what you choose, and what you do.
You control how much you believe in yourself and how much effort you make to accomplish your goals.
It's sobering because it's hard to accept responsibility for this.

Bad things happen.
Things don't always go our way.
Challenges are hard.
Procrastination or inaction sometimes are easier, or at least feel better in the moment.

How you respond to the hard challenges in life can affect whether you feel capable and empowered or defeated, and helpless. Owning your own responses and accepting personal responsibility for your choices can feel heavy; it eliminates room for excuses. It can also feel energized by the personal power it offers. You make your best life and your best self by fully owning it. All of it.

The triumphs and challenges, successes, and failures.
What you brought to the hard times, what you didn't do, could have done, did do. How you thought about and reacted to all of it.

When you accept that you are responsible for making something of what you have, then you start figuring out what you can do and learning from all your varied life experiences.

That's where your power lies.

Where to start?
Find a small space in your life where you can effect change; clean out a junk drawer, change a habit, alter a perspective, or thought pattern.

Start small.
Then, decide and commit to what you will do to effect the change.

Do the committed action consistently.
Feel strongly about the commitment you made to yourself and your goal every day to help motivate your consistent action. **Notice what works and what doesn't.** Learn from that and iterate.

Try a new approach.
Feel the power of overseeing yourself and effecting that change in your life!

Notice the outcome and savor the knowledge that you had the power to make a difference in your own life in some small way. Do it again, and again.

The positive feeling will power more momentum and that positive energy is infectious. Notice that in that small corner of your world, you are powerful! Notice also that you have the power to expand that small area of your world just a little bit more. Own your life, one small step and corner of your world at a time.

HOW BIG ARE YOUR DREAMS?

The size of your Dream is as important as the size of your attitude.
In fact, the size of your Dream will determine if you can maintain a positive and high level of attitude. It is well known that your level of attitude determines your level of altitude.

Likewise, the size of your Dream and the altitude of your Dream, will determine the outcome of your success

> Dare to Dream big dreams; only big dreams have the power to move men's souls. - **Marcus Aurelius**

The first secret of self-made millionaires is simple: Dream Big Dreams! Allow yourself to dream. Allow yourself to imagine and fantasize about all your career goals and the kind of life you would like to live. Think about the amount of money you would like to earn and have in your bank account. All self-made millionaires begin with a dream of something wonderful and different from what they have today. You know the song that says, "You have to have a dream if you want to make a dream come true." It's true for you and for everyone else, as well.

All Self-Made Millionaires Started with A Dream
Imagine that you have no limitations on what you can be, have, or do in life. Just for the moment, imagine that you have all the time, all the money, all the education, all the experience, all the friends, all the contacts, all the resources, and everything else you need to achieve anything you want in life. If your potential were completely unlimited, what kind of a life would you want to create for yourself and your family?

Practice "back from the future" thinking.
This is a powerful technique practiced continually by high-performing men and women. This way of thinking has an amazing effect on your mind and on your behavior. Here is how it works: Project yourself forward five years. Imagine that five years have passed and that your life is now perfect in every respect. What does it look like? What are you doing? Where are you working? How much money are you earning? How much do you have in the bank? What kind of a lifestyle do you have?

What Are Your Career Goals? Dare to Dream!
Create a vision for yourself for the long-term future. The clearer your vision of health, happiness, and prosperity, the faster you move toward it and the faster it moves toward you. When you create a clear mental picture of where you are going in life and set clear career goals, you become more positive, more motivated, and more determined to make it a reality. You trigger your natural creativity and come up with idea after idea to help make your vision come true.

You always tend to move in the direction of your dominant career goals, dreams, images, and visions. The very act of allowing yourself to dream big dreams raises your self-esteem and causes you to like and respect yourself more. It improves your self-concept and increases your level of self-confidence. It increases your personal level of self-respect and happiness. There is something about dreams and visions that is exciting and that stimulates you to do better than you ever have before.

Here is a great question for you to ask and answer, repeatedly: What one thing would I dare to dream if I knew I could not fail? If you were absolutely guaranteed of success in any one goal in life, large or small, short-term, or long-term, what would it be? What one great goal would you dare to dream if you knew you could not fail? Whatever it is, write it down and begin imagining that you have achieved this one great goal already. Then, look back to where you are today. What would you have done to get where you want to go? What steps would you have taken? What would you have changed in your life? What would you have started up or abandoned? Who would you be with? Who would you no longer be with? If your life were perfect in every respect, what would it look like? Whatever it is that you would do differently, take the first steps today.

Make Your Dream Come True
Dreaming big dreams is the starting point of achieving your goal of financial independence. The number one reason that people never succeed financially is because it never occurs to them that they can do it. As a result, they never try. They never get started. They continue to go around in financial circles, spending everything they earn and a little bit more besides. But when you begin to dream big dreams about financial success, you begin to change the way you see yourself and your life. You begin to do different things, bit by bit, gradually, until the whole direction of your life changes for the better. Dreaming big dreams is the starting point of financial success and of becoming a self-made millionaire.

Action Exercise: Make a list of everything you would do or attempt if you were absolutely guaranteed of success. Then decide upon one specific action and do it immediately.

List your wildest Dreams below:

1._____

2._____

3._____

4._____

5._____

Action Exercise: Make a list of everything you would do towards your dreams

1. _____

2. _____

3. _____

4. _____

5. _____

SETTING BOUNDARIES

Do you keep adjusting your boundaries to fit others? If so, it's time to review what boundaries mean for you. They are about your relationship with yourself and your own values, after all, so they shouldn't be so fluid.

If you have trouble setting and sticking to healthy boundaries, these six tips should help.

Steps for Setting Good Boundaries & Maintaining Them

1. Know this sad truth: no boundaries = little self-esteem.
Many people don't know what their boundaries are, when in fact they should roll off your tongue like the alphabet. The first step is admitting that your lack of boundaries stems from your lack of self-esteem. After all, what's the point of saying we want to grow if we're not going to be honest with ourselves about where we are now?

2. Decide what your core values are.
Who are you? What do you value? Once you get clear on what matters most to you, then you can take the bigger step of communicating this to others. Instead of creating your boundaries around a difficult relationship in your life, you must make your boundaries about you. For example, I set boundaries around phone time to honor the fact that I tend to get overstimulated by tech. This boundary is to decrease my stress level and not about avoiding others' phone calls or distancing myself from loved ones.

3. You can't change others, so change yourself.
We all want others to change, right? that's part of the human experience. We get into arguments with our spouses, hoping, wishing, demanding even that they stop being difficult. We get mad when our moms call us five times in a day. You want your co-worker—that one who is so negative—to treat you with more respect. The list is long.

We cannot change others. We are not responsible for what comes out of their mouth, the daily choices they make, or their reactions. The bottom line? Since you can't change other people, change how you deal with them.

4. Decide the consequences ahead of time.
So, what do we do once someone inevitably tries to push our boundaries? Decide what the consequences are. The best way to figure out your own boundaries and consequences when people cross them is sitting quietly down with yourself and making this all about you. (Remember: Boundaries are about honoring your needs, not about judging other people's choices.) Write down what you decide so it's on paper somewhere.

5. Let your behavior, not your words, speak for you.
Present your boundaries clearly to people and then let your behavior do the talking. People will test, push, and disrespect your limits. You'll know you're getting healthier when this doesn't get an emotional reaction out of you. When your boundaries are your core beliefs, you will not get riled up if you are tested.

6. Say what you mean and mean what you say.
The biggest part of boundaries is how clearly you communicate them. You can have the healthiest set of boundaries on the planet, but if you do not communicate them clearly, you are going to create some confusing relationships, both for you and everyone else involved.

One way to quickly get someone to question your character or authenticity? Say one thing and do another. Sometimes we're afraid to confront others with truth in love or relationships. We're afraid to tell people what we really want, to admit that we hate going to certain restaurants or have trouble spending time with a friend's toxic cousin or hate when a boss dumps deadline on us at 6 p.m. on a Friday. We conceal our true feelings because we're scared of people's reactions.

The more you ground yourself with your boundaries and values, the more you'll be able to be very clear in your communication.

NOTES

_____

_____

_____

_____

_____

_____

_____

_____

FOCUS ON WHAT YOU CAN DO, STAY IN YOUR LANE

How To Stay In Your Lane (and stop comparing yourself to others)

We all have our own assignments from God, and they are individually unique. We don't need to get caught up in what other people are doing, and we don't need to compare ourselves to others. We need to stay in our lanes. We need to focus on what God is asking us to do. We need to stay focused on our own personal race.

Staying in your own lane does not mean you should not take chances and experiment with new ways of solving business challenges and advancing your career. What it means is that you must remain focused on the immediate task at hand if you want to have the opportunity to take on those new challenges on your terms at a time that is the most favorable to you.

Have confidence that you have done all that you can to do the best that you can, and the results will take care of themselves. You may not always finish first in every race, but if you have given your best and most focused efforts, you have competed against yourself instead of others, and that is the best way to win as many races as you can in your career.

Are you focused on your lane? Are you focused on the best possible version of you? It takes practice. It takes discipline. But you must have that focus to be the best possible version of you no matter what race in life you're competing in.

Social media is a very powerful place. We share every aspect of our lives - from our daily routines to our loved ones, to vacations we take, the homes we live in… the list goes on and on. You can head to a stranger's profile at any time and within minutes know intimate details of their life. Through this access, it's easy to fall into the hole of comparing your own life to others. We may begin to feel less than because such and such person with 500k followers has the greatest skin, clothes, friends, and lives inside a perpetually sunny day. Why can't we look like that? Why can't we have that job, that car, that opportunity?

But the truth is, we are comparing our entire lives to someone else's highlight reel. And even still, the accomplishments that exist on this highlight reel don't take away our own chance to have the life we want to live.
Use your energy productively by narrowing your focus.
five ways to stay in your own lane of self-love, and out of someone else's lane of comparison.

Spend Less Time on Social Media

This is hard. There's no denying it. But it will probably be the best thing you can do for yourself! This also frees up space in your mind to focus on your own brand and your own work -- with less distractions entering your field, you can have a clearer vision of where you want to be.

Cleanse Your Feed

Is there an account you always find yourself stalking wistfully, wondering why your life can't be as glamorous as what they're sharing? Hit that unfollow button. There is a difference between feeling inspired by other accounts and feeling envious. YOU control what you see when you open that app, so use that to your advantage! Choose people and brands that light you up.

Find Your Niche

What's your own mission? What does your brand stand for? Find your niche and hold on tight. If you can become so focused on your own work and making it the absolute best it can be, you'll find a new confidence that won't be affected by other people's content, simply because it doesn't match what you want to put out.

Give, Give, Give

Instead of spending time on social media comparing yourself or your brand to others, spend that time on your own account, brainstorming how you can give more valuable and relevant content. Give, give, and then give some more. Even better --- take that time OFF social media to pour yourself into something that isn't driven by the approval of others

Identify where negative comparisons are coming from

This will not only help you keep a sharper focus on social media but will help elevate your entire life. Comparison, as they say, is the thief of joy, and it can stem from insecurities or our feelings of self-worth. When we come to realize that we are ALL just out there trying to chase our dreams and live our best lives, it makes you see that we are all on a level playing field and are in control of how we approach each day.

Discussion/Reflect: How easy is it for you to get caught up in the comparison game? Challenge: When you get caught up in comparing yourself to someone else, whether it's sport-related, ministry-related or a personal concern, thank God for the talent He has given you, the mission field all around you and for creating you exactly the way He did.

Declaration

I_____ promise to not get caught up with the others in the lanes next to me or the fans in the stands. I will keep my focus on what the Lord laid before me and the work You have called me to do.

Signed at_____on the_____

TRUTH ABOUT DATING

We've all experienced love during our teenage years. We've loved and been loved. This love adds richness and happiness to our lives. It makes us feel important, understood, and secure. It provides us with a chance to discover our own selves as we share it with someone new.

We also learn things — to love ourselves, things we'd like to change and about the qualities and values we look for in a partner. Love and romance teach us self-respect as well as to respect others. Therefore, teen romance should not be discouraged but we must draw some lines.

I believe that teens should be discouraged from a romantic relationship. The only rational thing that they ought to do is to focus on their career and make their life meaningful by pursuing the purpose for which they were sent here on Earth. Each of us has a specific purpose and power of making our dreams come true lies within.

However, we can see many young people indulging in romantic relationship where breakups, matchups are common. The teens have the false belief that they'll be happier if they're able to marry their girlfriend/boyfriend.

But the fact is that they're just trapped in a vicious circle.

A girl commits suicide just because she couldn't marry the guy she wanted, while that guy for sure will fall in love with another girl again. So, sacrificing a beautiful life just for a romantic relationship is a blunder. Instead, they should focus on their career, how they can perform their best in everything they do.

I'm not against true love. However, being in a romantic relationship at such a young age is not rational.

Being in love is not a bad thing. It's just that teenage is not the right age to fall in love. Teenagers should not be allowed to date as there are more disadvantages in teenage love relationship than advantages. I have seen many teenagers blindly fall in love and then face the consequences later. Most teenagers don't act sensibly as they are immature and don't have knowledge of right and wrong. This sometimes leads to wrong activities and decisions.

Children should focus more on their future than on love relationships. Teenagers themselves should try to control their emotions and thoughts for love relationship as far as possible.

Teenagers should maintain friendly relationships, but not romantic.

Having a life partner is a psychological need but waiting for the right time is what makes everything perfect. In addition, opting to date instead of studies will mislead one from the journey of life. Student's priority ought to be their studies, not romance. This doesn't mean students mustn't enjoy life and relationships, but it should be done at the right time.

Therefore, parents fear when their children start to date, neglecting the money invested in their studies.

For many, the teenage years is the most distracting stage of their life. Many lives of teens are permanently changed and subjected to greater responsibilities of a family, having children at tender age while studies become more difficult to pursue. That can happen because of small mistakes made in dating. However, dating is not the dreadful activity many thinks it is. It is certainly a sensitive stage/activity which can twist the path of life. Therefore, teens must be adequately educated to understand the real meaning and purpose of dating. When one does it with a clear understanding about what dating is for, it can render confidence on parents about their children's decision for a meaningful life.

Dangers of dating too early:

The dangers of teen sexual activity
We sadly live in an over-sexualized culture that seems to encourage sexual activity in the teen years, as long as it is practiced safely. Statistics show that by the 12th grade 57 percent of students have had sex. Romantic relationships can lead to sex even for those who don't plan on having sex. Sometimes circumstances, emotions and lack of self-control can lead teens to make spur-of-the-moment decisions they never intended to make.
The fact is that sex has many consequences that can be harmful to a teenager's life and future. Though the "hookup" culture is a part of this problem, teen sexual activity also stems from teens engaging in serious romantic relationships and then not having the self-control to limit those relationships to being solely social and platonic.

The Bible teaches that sexual activity was designed by God to be enjoyed by a husband and wife within the marriage covenant (Genesis 2:24; Hebrews 13:4).
It is also designed for procreation (Genesis 1:28). This law of God is designed to protect, not restrict. Not only are teens not prepared to be effective parents, but teen relationships rarely result in marriage. So, the children born to teenagers often will be raised by a single mother and will not have the benefits of being raised by a mother and father who are lovingly dedicated to each other and to raising the child as a team.

The maturity factors
Research on the human brain has found that it is not fully developed until well after the teenage years. One function of the brain that is not fully developed during the

teen years is the ability to control impulses. Brain imaging has found that the signals from the frontal lobe do not get to the back of the brain fast enough to always regulate emotions. This seems to be a reason risk-taking and impulsive behavior are common among teens.

Because maturity is still developing, it is dangerous for teenagers to put themselves in relationships that tempt them to engage in sexual activity before they are emotionally, physically, or financially prepared to deal with the consequences.

The knowledge that the brain is not fully developed in the teen years also shows that teens' personality, judgment, and wisdom are still in a state of development during their teen years. It is wise for teenagers to focus on their personal development—their education, their personality, their character and their goals—instead of developing temporary romantic relationships that often bring stress and the possibility of temptations and consequences they are simply not ready (nor should they be) to deal with during these formative years.

Doing things in order
Another biblical principle of wisdom that teens should consider is found in Proverbs 24:27: "Prepare your outside work, make it fit for yourself in the field; and afterward build your house."

This simple proverb teaches the wisdom of building one's life in the proper order, one that positions a person for success. Is it wise to pursue romantic relationships in the phase of one's life that should be focused on education and preparing oneself for a career? Could romantic relationships in this phase of life be more of a distraction than a benefit?

The wisdom contained in this proverb supports what has been called the "success sequence," which young people can follow to put themselves in the best position for success in life. The formula follows these steps in order:

Get an education. Education is a key for finding a job that provides financial stability. Without financial stability, life is a whole lot harder. Poverty rates are much lower among those who have pursued and attained an education. Of course, that is not limited to a college education. It also includes various skilled trades and vocational training.

Find work. You need money to function in life, Work is an essential part of life. The Bible teaches that people should work if they can (2 Thessalonians 3:11-12). Consistent employment allows people to be able to afford to marry and have children.

Marriage. Once a person finds work, he or she is better prepared for the financial responsibilities that come with marriage. Marriage is one of the biggest commitments a person can make. God intended marriage to be a lifelong commitment (Matthew 19:3-9).

Have children. One of the worst mistakes a person can make is to have children early and outside of marriage. Teens are woefully unprepared to raise children—emotionally and financially. Children who are born to parents who follow the success sequence are much better positioned for successful lives.

By awakening romantic love during the phase of life that should be focused on personal development and preparation for the future, young people put themselves in danger of breaking the success sequence and making life more difficult for themselves.

Wise teenagers can learn about the opposite sex in their teenage years by developing a variety of friendships with people of the opposite sex, spending time to ether in safe social situations, and observing and learning what traits they prefer in a future spouse.

Declaration

I_____ promise to focus on my schoolwork and goals. I will find the love of my life when I am mature and ready. For now, I choose to wait and enjoy being a child.

Signature:_____

Signed at_____on the_____

NOTES

_____
_____
_____
_____
_____
_____
_____
_____
_____
_____

LET HOPE OVERFLOW

"May the God of hope fill you with all joy and peace as you trust in him, so that you may overflow with hope by the power of the Holy Spirit" **(Romans 15:13)**

Let's be real – things can happen in all our lives that can seem confusing, devastating, or impossible. Whether this be health issues, relational or otherwise.

Whether you count yourself as a Christian or not, I want to encourage you to look in the Bible to see what is written there about challenges that come in life.

The hope that is mentioned here is not a 'may be' or a 'it would be nice if it happened'!
Rather it is something that is definite. It comes from God.
Note also joy and peace being connected to trusting in Him.
Do you know what the rarest and most precious commodity on earth is? No, it's not gold or diamonds, not oil or uranium; it's hope.
Wherever you look today, hope is in short supply. Our world is unstable
The first key to hope is endurance, or steadfastness in faith. We grow in hope as we persevere in believing. Hope comes from trusting God over the long haul.

God uses to build hope. This is the encouragement of the Scriptures. Hope is grounded in the promises of God written in the Word of God. Hope comes into our hearts when we remember the truth of all that the Lord has said in the Bible. One of the major purposes of Scripture is to encourage us by reminding us of what God has already done, and promises still to do, for us, through us, with us, and in us.

Do you have hope, real hope? You could. God gives it to those who trust him and believe in his written Word. It has nothing to do with whether you are optimistic by nature, or your thinking is positive.

May the God of hope fill you with all joy and peace as you trust in him, so that you may overflow with hope.

Prayer:
O God, our hope and trust are in you. Fill us with such joy and peace as we believe that our lives will overflow with hope, and this quality will attract hopeless people around us to you, the source of true hope. Amen

NOTES

_____

_____

_____

_____

_____

_____

_____

YOUNG LADY BE FEARLESS

Be Fearless!
It's about going beyond fear. It's about recognizing fear when it crops up, believe me it will, and then having the courage to set it aside and to move forward, whatever the obstacles. Effective leadership often means stepping into the unknown, disregarding fear and focusing on how you can make an impact.

To go beyond fear is to Be Bold! This goes beyond being fearless – it's proactive, make it happen!
Dream big, be bold, be outrageously collaborative, be unstoppable!'.
Think outside the box and don't be afraid to take risks.
Even if it scares you and you haven't got it all figured out, sometimes you just have made a start and work it out as you go along.
Bold moves demand imagination and determination and I think women have a little bit of an advantage when it comes to those qualities … but then I'm not entirely objective here, as I'm a woman.

Being fearless is also about being your best authentic self. 'don't let the 'gremlins' of self-doubt get in the way'.
Learn from others – there are always ways to do things better – but don't try to emulate someone else to achieve their success.
It doesn't work that way. After all, we're all different – a different mix of skills and life experiences.
So, don't be afraid to be you. Do things that fit with your core values and your essential personality. Be yourself and believe in yourself. There is a CEO in every single one of us. We can all be a leader if we own being the best at what we do.
To be fearless also means to step outside your comfort zone and to embrace change. It's good to have a plan, but in our fast-evolving world, it's also imperative

to stay agile. Just look at the market transitions we are in and how we're changing as a business to make the most of them. Many of our presenters – all people of impact – spoke about how they had adapted to change and made the most of the opportunities it brought. We each build up transferable skills that can be applied to new roles and sometimes even tactical sideways or downwards moves can deliver greater rewards.

Declaration

I_____ declare and affirm that I am fearless, focused, and free of negativity.

I am the best me possible.
I am getting better day by day.
I am emotionally stable and difficult to offend.

NOTES

_____
_____
_____
_____
_____
_____
_____

TRAITS OF A BADASS WOMEN

Most women seem to have it all together and can stand tall and be confident no matter what.

These badass women look fear in the eye and take on the day without worrying about failure or what others think. Here are traits that all badass and fearless women do differently than everyone else. And that's what makes them amazing. Of them. The pillars of women have risen to new heights over the last few decades and now, more than ever, women are standing tall and standing up for what they want in life.

1) They Enjoy Life by Making Fun a Priority
While the rest of us are plugging away at house chores and running errands, they are out there living their lives to the best of their ability.
That doesn't mean spending money they don't have or buying luxury homes in the hills; it means that they see the value in enjoying themselves and make it a priority whenever they can.

2) They Don't Hide
You'll never see a badass woman back down from a challenge – of any kind. Whether it's in the boardroom or in the bedroom, badass women know what they bring to the table and aren't afraid to show it off.

3) They are Assertive
Notice we didn't say aggressive? They are two different things. Assertive women understand that their position is important and that they have lots to offer people. Aggressive women just yell and scream until someone makes things happen. Assertive women take charge and get things done themselves.

4) They are Confident

Confidence is a funny thing that seems to elude most of us on a regular basis. Badass women seem to be oozing confidence at every turn.

They are confident in themselves because they see and know their own value. While most of us are searching social media for acceptance, fearless women are out there living life to the fullest.

5) They are their Own Best Friend

Badass women don't need a man or anyone else dragging them off their path in life. They are comfortable being alone if it means they don't settle for someone not worth their time and effort.

6) They Make Meaning From their Past

Badass women get to be badass because they spend time thinking about how their past impacts their future, but they don't dwell on it.

Regardless of what throws at them, badass women are ready to take charge and make things right. They don't blame others for their situation, and they don't wallow in their sorrows.

7) They Get Things Done

Badass women are badass because they get things done. Period. You better just step aside and let her do her thing.

8) They Don't Care What Everyone Else is Doing

Fearless women don't spend time worrying about how others are shaping up – they are too busy getting their lives in order. Celebrities? Pfft, who cares. Social media? She doesn't have time for that. She's got things to do and people to see.

9) They are Themselves

Above all else, the thing that makes badass women the most badass is that they are themselves all the time. What you see is what you get.

10) They Don't Need to Ask for Attention

A woman worth her weight in gold should not have to ask for any man's attention. If she finds that you are not giving her what she wants, you better believe that she'll be moving on.

11) They Won't Absorb Bad Vibes from a Guy

Toxic relationships are the worst and while they may be hard to get out of, a badass woman isn't even going to get into one in the first place.

When women can hold their own, they no longer need support from men, which means they can pick and choose men to hang out with and spend time with.

That's good news for women and bad news for men who aren't sure how to show up and do more.

12) They Hate People Who Try to Hurt Others

Women with a badass attitude don't set out to hurt others but lift them up.

And they aren't going to put up with others trying to drag down a woman or otherwise. Badass women are strong enough to care for and support one another. You know she's a good woman when she is lifting others up around her.

13) They Hate When Women Don't Support Other Women

It's a pet peeve of many badass women when other women don't support each other. It's hard enough being a woman – they don't need other women cutting them down to size. Be a badass woman by lifting each other up on a regular basis and break down the barriers you face together.

14) They Hate Being Treated like a Child

When a guy assumes, she can't do something because she's a girl, look out! Badass women can do anything, and if they can't do it, they'll find their own help to get the job done. If you want to be on the bad side of a badass woman, tell her she can't do something and then get out of her way as she blazes a trail right next to you.

15) They Know Their Self-Worth
She shouldn't have to make you aware of how amazing she is – you should be paying attention to it all on your own. When a badass woman knows her worth, she is not going to try to make you see it. You need to do that all on your own.

16) They Won't Be Held Back by Men
When men try to hold back a badass woman, she's not going to have it.
She is on her own journey – one that you are lucky enough to be a part of – and she won't put up with people trying to hold her back, especially a man who can't do those kinds of things himself.

17) They Won't Play Small
Don't expect her to be quiet or reserved just because it makes you uncomfortable that she's such a strong, independent woman.
Badass women don't need to be held back or told to be quiet and they won't put up with it at all. Don't make the mistake of thinking that she's lucky to have you: it's the other way around, for sure. The truth is that badass women can make themselves happy and provide for themselves.

Declaration

I am a strong, independent women.
I am capable.
I am unstoppable, I don't play small.
I know my self-worth and I ooze confidence.

Signature:_____

Signed at_____on the_____

BECOME A WOMEN OF IMPACT

Woman is the most amazing creature that God has created. From a homemaker to a successful entrepreneur, this universal creature is influencing the world with her extraordinary skills.

The stats of women's success around the world is sparkling and making the community proud.
- Today there are many women-owned businesses in South Africa and around the world.
- About 60 percent of women earned the master's degrees.
- The number of women-owned firms with more than 10 million in revenue has increased by more than 50% in the decade.

Women are continuously climbing the rank and influencing people with her skills. It is a dream of every girl, who admires those women who are raising the bar and making the whole women community proud to become like them.
So, do you also wish to become one? Get ready to join the campaign by following these tips. This empowering panel cannot be duplicated, but these tips are sure to bring you closer to their goals.

- **Self-Confidence is the key**

Confidence is something that delivers a powerful impact on people. Achieving self-confidence is the first step in your journey to becoming a woman of influence. It can be more comfortable for some women, while others have a tough time remembering how fabulous they are.

If you lack that confidence, try to fake it. "Faking it" doesn't mean that you need to hide your real feelings or being afraid to admit that you don't have the potential to handle everything. But, if you need to cry after a stressful day, let your emotions out in private and come back as strong as ever. The alone time could even be therapeutic that make you feel so overwhelmed.

- **Be Vocal**

Raise your voice to let the world know that you exist. If you have the potential of doing something great, or have some ideas, speak up. The more you speak about your thoughts, the more people will get influenced with your words. If you learn to win the hearts with your words, then congratulations, you have achieved the milestone of becoming a woman of influence.

- **Become a risk taker**

If you want to acquire something big, you must get ready to take risks. No one can become an influencer by playing it safe, and you must follow the rule. Leave your fear of failure on the doormat and push forward as a confident person to achieve your goals.

- **Fuel your potential**

Everyone has some hidden potential to do something great in life. All you need is to feel that potential. Remember that a diamond comes out by rubbing the coal; likewise, you can also shine like a star by polishing your skills or igniting the flame of your passion.

- **Accept Criticism**

Learn the art of using the words of criticism as a tool for your growth. Take it like a stone and pave the path of your success with it. The woman who is now become the icons has mastered in taking the criticism gracefully. If you feel happy by receiving the compliments, then you should also be open to accept the criticism, pay attention to it and learn from it.

Thoughtful feedback can help you guide away from mistakes and toward success. A constructive attitude can transform obstacles into opportunities and encourage others to adopt a similar approach.

- **Aim high**

You will never know how high far you can reach until you try. So, always aim big and then work hard to achieve it. A leader still is the one who knows how to turn your dream into reality and how to overcome the obstacles that blocks the road to your success. Be brave enough to dream big and aim high.

- **Be Positive**

An attitude of positivity can help you achieve significant milestones. How can you become an influencer if you do not have a positive outlook on things? People always admire those who know how to deal with the adverse circumstances without losing your mind. Start your journey to achieve a positive mindset. Think positively, and you will experience that everything starts working out in that way.

- **Never stop learning**

There is no limit to learning. Life is a book of never-ending lessons. You will always have a new page to flip on and learn something new from it. Never try to quench the thirst of knowledge, and you will keep learning new things. Learn new skills, polish them, and use your skills to benefit others. An influencer can be the one who knows how to help people with the expertise they have.

- **Create a path and leave your trail**

Don't try to follow the same way, instead create your path, and leave your trail there. So, people will follow you. If you want to achieve something big things in life, you must learn to walk alone, rely on yourself and become your hero. Give the world the reason to admire you.

Declaration

I Am a woman a creature who can do all the jobs with perfection and dedication. I am Proud to be a woman and I embrace my authenticity.

Signature:_____

Signed at_____on the_____

NOTES

_____

_____

_____

_____

_____

_____

_____

_____

_____

BECOME A MAN OF IMPACT

Men are in the Centre of creating a world that can be secure to live in. The Vision behind Man of Impact is to grow a generation of men who will impact the world Turn your weakness into greatness; re-create yourself as a gentleman. Forge a character even that man's biggest critic can respect: Himself.

I want to tell you about all the ways in which you can be a better man. Some of which only take a little time each day. These reminders will help you achieve what I and many other gentlemen have learned the hard way.

Any man eager to become the master of his life must first take control of his character. It's easier said than done, of course, but you can decide for yourself where life takes you. All that is necessary is knowing how to be a man who progresses with the right intentions.

1. **Wake up early**

Set your alarm clock every single morning, regardless of whether you have anything to do or not. By doing so, you'll prevent yourself from lounging around in bed all day. Consider that most male CEOs wake up at 5:30 am or earlier. In their world, the snooze button doesn't exist. Why should it when life is too exciting to sleep?

2. **Examine your daily habits – drop addictions**

The best habit a man can have is to make right on all his commitments; before rewarding himself.

Consider: Sweets (candy, soda), fats (fast food), smoking, swearing, emotional spending, buying everything on credit, etc.

3. Help other people – be wise about it

When looking for opportunities to be helpful and generous towards others, understand that people will take advantage of these traits.

Where: National parks, animal rescue shelters, food pantries, local libraries, be a sports coach, retirement homes, etc.

4. Worry less about the consequences

Spend time learning the rules first so you know precisely how to break them.

When it comes to the small stuff, don't sweat it. Instead, start focusing on the one big problem ahead of you. Consider that more than often all those little problems that seem to plague you will end up being solved on their own or will turn out to be not such as big deal as you once believed. Doing so will help you better identify your stress triggers too.

5. Be known for finishing, not starting

Keep your word, stick to it. Before making any sort of promise consider a few things first: Perhaps the most important of them all… Understand that your word is a personal guarantee. Be selective with the projects you take on. Determine the amount of time and resourced required before making a commitment. Adjust your time and energy accordingly to meet your goal.

If it is a work document you promised your boss, complete it on time. Should it be a personal objective, don't continually let yourself down.

6. Balance your budget

Grit your teeth, open those bill collector letters, and get them paid down. If you want more freedom, the answer is simple: Reduce your debt. Start learning how to invest and begin saving for the things that matter the most. To figure out how to stop buying things you don't need look at your last five purchases. Evaluate them monthly.

7. Be more productive

Stop sitting around the house all-day binge-watching addictive TV show series. Put down the gaming console. Start working towards your goals today. Take short breaks throughout the day to recharge instead of dedicating full days, weeks, months or even years for pure entertainment.

8. Settle less

Start seeing things as an opportunity and not a challenging obstacle you can't overcome. Avoid settling for less than you want, whether it be a wife, career, or anything else. Stay focused and hungry until you find it.
Go to a Rolls Royce dealer and admire around. Let your dreams run wild.

9. Don't be a liar

The truth is, it's the most dangerous thing a man can become. Live with an honest an intelligent effort if you desire to be successful. It will help keep your mind clear and your judgment sound.

NOTES

_____

_____

_____

_____

_____

_____

PERSONAL DEVELOPMENT

There is an endless amount of benefits to personal development and growth. While the journey can get bumpy and it's not always positive, it can be hard, lengthy, and scary, and sometimes the objective is not always achieved, there are many skills and experiences derived from personal development that lead to a richer, happier, more fulfilled life.

1. **You become happier**

The main goal of personal development is to be happier. Naturally, when you improve yourself, your life, your relationships, achieve your goals, you become happier. This doesn't always happen right away or all the time, but it happens in time with consistent and deliberate personal development.

2. **Your relationships improve both with yourself and others**

Personal development is about improving the relationship with yourself. It at least normally starts there. When you improve the relationship with yourself, people are naturally drawn to you and your relationships you already have with others also improves. The people you attract are also more likely to be better for you. You attract people who are at your level so once you start raising your level, the people who come into your life are going to be at your higher level.

Personal development can also be dedicated to improving relationships with others whether it be intimate relationships, friends and family, work relationships, or relationships to people and communities. Relationships and communication are topics within personal development.

3. You learn new things

A major component of personal development is education, learning, and knowledge. You can not only learn new skills and knowledge and education, but you also learn about yourself, about others, and about the world and humanity. Through learning, you learn about different viewpoints, values, beliefs. You learn skills that aren't taught in school too like how to set goals and how to have healthy relationships.

A great resource I love to learn new skills is Youtube. If you're a visual learner and prefer to learn through watching videos or are interested in learning more technical and creative skills.

If you prefer to learn through books and reading, Kindle Unlimited can help you read more books for free.

4. You live better

With more happiness, better relationships, achievements, and a better you, your quality of life improves. Your life becomes richer in either or both the physical sense and the metaphorical sense.

5. You are better able to adapt to change

When you embrace, accept, and seek change for yourself and your life, you're better at accepting and adapting to unexpected or out of your control change whether good or bad or the change you brought yourself from your personal development. But with a strong foundation, you're more likely to be happy and fulfilled with your achievements, or you're better able to deal with any of the anxiety and negative emotions that may arise.

6. You're able to make decisions and solve problems better

Personal development is meant to help you live more effectively. This helps you become better able at making better sound decisions and being able better and more effectively solve any problems that arise.

7. You're healthier

When you're involved in personal development, you're more likely to value and take care of your health. Better health is also a side effect to many personal development habits. This list shows some habits that help improve your mental and physical health. Happier people are healthier people.

8. You're likely to reach your goals

Setting goals is a major component of personal development. Reaching your goals is one of the main goals of personal development. With knowledge and use of personal development techniques, you're more likely to succeed at reaching your goals.

9. You're more likely to have financial and career success

Because personal development affects all areas of your life and can be applied to the financial and career area of your life, you're more likely to achieve success in that area. How to Win Friends and Influence People is one of the most recommended books by business leaders and CEOs even though it's a self-help book. It can be applied to both personal and work life.

10. You inspire others

When you are personally growing and succeeding, others around you are probably going to notice. Your story, your progress, and your success can inspire others. This is great if you're trying to influence or help others to make a change in themselves which I discussed in this article.

11. It feels goods

When you go after your goals and make progress and achievement, it feels good. It feels a lot better than if you wouldn't have worked on personal development. And the result is a lot stronger feeling that makes everything that made it up that point worth it in 'the end.'

12. It's interesting

A lot of personal development involves psychology which most of us find interesting. There is a science to personal development. Hearing people stories of failure and unexpected success can also be interesting to us. Personal development is always expanding with new discoveries and studies that we didn't know before or expected.

13. It affects all areas of your life

You can use personal development in all areas of your life. Personal development in general also affects all areas of your life even if it just being directly applied to one area. For example, working on and growing your confidence can positively affect and improve the relationship area of your life and the work area of your life.

14. You become more aware

Awareness is necessary for personal growth. It's the first step. Awareness helps you notice and learn things about yourself and your life around you. Awareness is a highly valuable skill that allows you to realize and learn the facts and stay grounded. Many people miss out on learning and growth opportunities because of lack of awareness.

15. You think better and become smarter

Personal development can help you make better and more informed decisions. It also tends to involve reading which does make you smarter. All the things you learn help make you smarter as well.

16. Better society
When more people are happier and more fulfilled with their lives, that makes for a better and happier society. People who are involved in personal development are also more likely to positively influence and inspire others around them.

17. It makes you more interesting
When you expand and grow yourself, you become more interesting because you learn more and you experience more through personal development. You're also more open to different viewpoints and worldviews as well as being more aware both of yourself and others around you.

18. Self-esteem – you like yourself more
Personal development helps you improve your self-esteem and like yourself more because you become the person you want to become. You also learn to respect, accept, and love who you already are. You believe in yourself and know that you are capable of achieving growth and your goals.

19. Greater resilience
Personal development helps you build and develop the skills to better deal with adversity and when times get tough. You have stronger belief in yourself and confidence that you will overcome it as well as motivation to overcome adversity and failure.

19. Sense of direction – find your purpose
Personal development gives you a sense of direction and helps you discover what it is you really want out of life and yourself. It can also help you find your purpose because you become more in tune with yourself and your connection to the world. With successful personal development, you'll want to give and contribute yourself to the world because you begin to value yourself and your ideas.

20. More opportunities and luck

Because you're seeking advancement in your life, personal development opens doors to numerous opportunities. Personal development also helps you make your own luck. One study found that people who considered themselves as lucky were better and faster at completing tasks than people who considered themselves as unlucky. The reason for that was that they were more open to opportunities. The people who considered themselves as unlucky missed more change opportunities to succeed.

21. Overcome fear

A big part of personal growth is doing things that push you out of your comfort and can scare you. Personal development can help you face your fears and gain the courage to overcome them.

22. Overcome things you normally wouldn't have without personal growth

Personal growth can help you overcome and fix problems that you otherwise would have to just live and deal with. This article shows what's possible to be changed and fixed according to psychologists.

23. You don't settle

With personal development, you're continuously growing and improving. You're less likely to stay stuck and stagnant in your life. There is always room for improvement with personal development. You're more likely to achieve more and become greater than just "good" by getting involved with personal development.

24. Discover yourself

Personal development allows you to discover what you love, what you want out of life, your values, and your beliefs. It helps you learn who you want to be and then become that person. When you develop and grow, you learn and discover about yourself.

25. It makes you more creative

Personal development helps you become more creative not only because it helps you have more ideas and develop your artistic abilities and skills, but you're more likely to value and cultivate your ideas. You're also more likely to follow through with your ideas and stories because you have confidence and belief in yourself, and you take more effective initiative with personal development.

With all that said, keep in mind personal development Personal development takes effort, work, and time.

Personal development should be a lifelong mission that is never complete. When we take the time to assess ourselves and think about how we would like to grow, doors start opening. The most successful people aren't people who rely on their raw talent – they are people who continue to grow throughout their careers of their own volition

7 Personal Growth Areas in your life to help you determine which goals to focus on in your life

Personal development plan for_____
Created on_____

Steps to make a personal development plan:

A. Identify what is the goal and purpose of this personal development plan.

1._____

_____

_____

B. Describe the steps of the action plan focusing on those issues that depend solely on you.

1._____

2._____

3._____

4._____

5._____

C. Take an inventory of the resources you are going to use.

1._____

2._____

3. _____

4. _____

5. _____

D. Set short-term goals that are aligned with your main goal.

1. _____

2. _____

3. _____

4. _____

5. _____

E. Create a support network.

1. _____

2. _____

3. _____

4. _____

5. _____

UNLEASH YOUR POTENTIAL

You want to unleash your full potential. You want to unlock your hidden talents and abilities. You want to change the world. One of the toughest parts about starting something new is getting the courage to take that first step. We've all been there, one moment we feel excited, but then the next the voice inside our head creeps up to silence our passions.

1. **Train your brain to learn new things by embracing uncomfortable situations**

Always strive to put yourself in uncomfortable situations and thrive in that uneasiness. Ask yourself 'do I learn better by writing or walking around? Do I study better early in the morning or late at night?' It may take time to find out what works exactly for you, It's a constant trial and error. Through that, you will discover that everyone has different skills, and what works for some might not work for another. You just need to put yourself through these uncomfortable situations to figure it out."

2. **Don't believe what people say you can't do**

Often, you'll find people in your life that can make you feel like you can't achieve certain goals. If I would have listened to my teachers and friends, I don't know what would have happened. People always told me that I couldn't do all these things because I was too much of this or that. The moment I let all of that go was the moment I realized I could really do whatever I set my mind to."

3. **Set small goals to achieve big results**

In order to start believing in your potential, you have to start by setting small goals. By changing little habits, you can start setting yourself up for success. "You can do this with anything. For example, if you are used to playing a particular sport, you can start by trying out a new one and setting small goals to get better at it. In doing this, you'll start to discover new skills and abilities that you might have not known you had before. You can train yourself to have the courage to do more."

By adopting these habits, you can start reaching your full potential. And in the end, it all comes down to believing that nothing can stop you from achieving what you want to do: the only thing holding you back is yourself. "Everything you want to do, everything you want to achieve, you can do it. You are limitless. The only limitation is in our mind. You can listen to different opinions and perspectives, but at the end of the day, you must trust yourself and believe in your own unique capabilities. Once you start doing this– everything can start to change."

Words Are Powerful
Say the following words every night to support your goal to unleash your potential:

I am smart.
I am beautiful.
I am creative.
I am talented.
I am blessed.
I am healthy.
I am loved.
I am confident.
I am strong and courageous.
I am generous.
I am disciplined and focused.
I am a world changer.

CAREFUL WHAT YOU LET IN YOUR MIND

Before you change your thinking, you must change what goes into your heart. The books you read, the movies you watch, the people you associate with and the conversations you engage in. Be careful what you feed your mind. Your mind will always believe everything you tell it. Feed it faith, feed it truth, feed it with love.

To keep our computer safe from attacks, we try to strengthen its defenses. What can be done to ward off computer problems? Install a firewall. A firewall isolates our computer from outside influences like the Internet. It allows the data we consider safe to enter and blocks the data we don't consider safe from corrupting our computer.

It's no different with our mind. We must strengthen our defenses by installing a spiritual firewall to guard our thoughts.

Isn't it true that our thoughts dictate the direction of our lives? The greatest battlefield of life is the mind, and we are constantly at war for its control! If we want to live right, we must put up a spiritual firewall and not allow just anything to affect our thinking.

We must be careful what we let in, and what we allow to influence us. We must keep wrong thoughts and wrong ideas out of our minds, because how we think will affect how we live.

Do you eat decayed food? No, then don't feed your mind with decayed books. Be as careful with the nutrition of your mind as you are with the nutrition of your body.

Declaration:

I chose to read books that will feed my soul and mind.

I chose to watch content that will enrich me and move me to the next level of my life.

I chose to spend time with people will encourage me and push me to my best self.

I choose to engage in activities and conversations that will uplift me and groom me.

My mind is a sacred garden, and my thoughts are the seeds. I chose to protect it.

I chose to be mindful of who and what I allow in and I plant the seeds I want to grow.

Signature: _____

Signed at_____on the_____

NOTES

_____
_____
_____
_____
_____
_____
_____
_____

STARVE YOUR DISTRACTIONS, FEED YOUR FOCUS

We've all been there. Even with the best of intentions to stay on task, we still catch ourselves scrolling through social media when we should be working on a project. We can't help but grab our cell phone the moment we hear a notification. And then there's email! If we aren't checking it every five minutes, we worry we might miss something important.

Distractions can seem impossible to avoid. Statistics show that distractions cause a massive loss in productivity.

Avoiding distraction is tough. You're not alone when it comes to distractions. It's not easy staying on task when you need to work for hours at a time, but some people are able to do it.

The question is: why them and not you?

You were never taught how to focus. It's funny how all throughout our school days we were never taught HOW to learn and be focused, even though that's all we did. It was just assumed, and ultimately it was hit or miss on whether you ended up knowing how to do those things at all.

The tools to help master your ability to focus. Since everyone's left to their own devices, it's up to you to find ways to master your focus ability. That's what these tips are for, so you can finally stay focused and on track with what we want to accomplish for ourselves.

Strategies to keep focus

1. Keep Your Vision and Goals in Mind

First things first, why do you even need to focus? Do you want to become a skilled guitar player? Do you want to write a novel? Do you want to start working from home?

Think about it. Knowing why we need to stay focused can help us push through the tough and tedious parts of accomplishing our goals. That's when our ability to focus is really tested and when it's most needed.

2. Reduce the Chaos of Your Day by Focusing on 2 to 3 Important Tasks

If you have 20 tasks you need done every day how effective do you think your focus ability will be? Terrible, right?

You can't expect to do those things with sophistication if you're too scatterbrained to focus. You need to break it down to the essentials.

Focus on only doing 2-3 important tasks a day (even one is okay), but no more than that. It's all you need to take steps towards accomplishing your goals. Slower is much better than giving up early because you took on too much, too early.

3. Do Those Tasks as Soon as Possible

To make sure you get those 2 to 3 tasks done; you need to do them early. This means as soon as you wake up, you're already plotting how to do them. So, get up, use the bathroom, eat breakfast, and do it.

It's tough but waiting to do them only invites distraction to take over. Those distractions will come, and they will drain your willpower. This makes working on your goals harder to do, so don't wait do work on your goals, do them as early as possible.

4. Focus on Only the Smallest Part of Your Work at a Time

An easy way to kill your focus is to see a goal for the big giant accomplishment that it is. Most goals will at least take a few weeks to months to accomplish and knowing that can make it feel like it'll take forever to do.

This will cause you to do one of two things: You become discouraged because the goal is too big; or you fantasize about what it'll feel like to achieve the goal
Either way is terrible for your focus and always a potential problem when focusing on the big picture or using visualization.

So, what should you do? Focus on doing a very small, minimum amount of work instead.
For example, which seems easier: Writing 200 words per day or writing a minimum of 2 sentences per day?
20 pushups per day or a minimum of 1 pushup per day? The key here is to use minimums. Chances are you'll push past them. Eventually your minimum will increase, and you'll slowly improve your ability to stay focused on the bigger tasks.

5. Visualize Yourself Working

There is a proper way of using visualization, and it's by visualizing yourself working, not as if you've succeeded already.

Champion runners use this technique to great effect, usually by working backwards. They imagine themselves winning at first, then they act out the whole process in reverse, feeling and visualizing each step all the way to the beginning.
A quicker and more relevant way to apply this would be to imagine yourself doing a small part of the task at hand.

For instance, if you need to practice your guitar but it's all the way across the room (let's assume maximum laziness for the sake of this example), what should you do?

First, imagine standing up (really, think of the sensation of getting up and then do it). If you really imagined it, visualized, and felt the act of standing up, then acting on that feeling will be easy.

Then repeat the visualization process with each step till you have that guitar in hand and you're playing it. The process of focusing so intently on each step distracts you from how much you don't want to do something, and the visualizations "ready your body" for each step you need done.

All you need to do is apply this process to whatever it is you need to focus on, just start with the smallest motion you need to do.

6. Control Your Internal Distractions

Internal distractions are one of those problems you can't really run away from. You need to find ways to prepare your mind for work and find simple ways to keep it from straying to non-essential thoughts as well.

A good way to prime your mind for work is to have a dedicated workstation. If you always work in a specific area, then your mind will associate that area with work related thoughts.

When you take breaks make sure to leave your workstation, that way you'll know when you're "allowed" to let your thoughts roam free as well.

Deadlines are useful here also this helps keep your mind from wandering around since you've got that looming deadline coming along.

Ultimately though, silencing those unwanted thoughts is all about getting some traction going. So instead of focusing on what's happening internally, focus getting something done (anything!). Once you do that, you'll see that all your thoughts will be about finishing your task.

7. Remove External Distractions

This tip is straightforward, just get away from things that distract you. Is the television a distraction? Work in another room. Are the kids distracting you? Get up earlier and work before they wake up. Is the Internet distracting? Turn off the modem. It's usually obvious what you should do, but you still shouldn't overlook this piece of advice.

8. Skip What You Don't Know

This is a tip I don't see often enough, if you hit a snag in your work then come back to it later. Focus your attention on what you CAN do, keep working "mindlessly" at all costs. All this means is that you should focus on the easy parts first.
Eventually you can come back to the more difficult parts, and hopefully by then it'll have come to you or you'll have built up enough momentum that it won't break your focus if you work on it.

9. Improve Your Discipline with Focus Practice

There are a few focus exercises you can do to improve your overall discipline. The first one is meditation, which is basically the definition of focus in practice. Think about it, you're literally just sitting there doing nothing. It's a great method for building focus ability, de-stressing, and giving you greater control over your emotions. You should give meditation a shot.

10. Manage Your Momentum

Momentum is like a discipline lubricant, it helps ease the process of sticking with goals. That's why I think it's important that we never take true breaks from our goals; we end up losing momentum and relying on discipline to get back on track not an easy thing to do.

This means each day we need to do something significant to further our. Significant don't necessarily mean a big task–but rather, any task that brings us closer to our goals.

Stop Getting Distracted by things that have nothing to do with your goals

For instance, if your goal is to be a freelance writer, then write one single pitch on a weekend. If your goal is get healthy, then go for a short 5-minute walk every day.

Nothing big, nothing crazy, only stuff that is significant enough to contribute to the success of your overall goal.

Declaration

I promise not to get distracted by useless things that do not add to my growth.
I promise to stay focused on my goals.

I will stop_____and _____,_____

Signature: _____

Signed at_____on the_____

REFERENCES

- thepeakperformancecenter.com
- mindtools.com
- margiewarrell.com
- ctclearinghouse.org
- liberationprograms.org
- goop.com
- courses.lumenlearning.com
- coursehero.com
- ptotoday.com
- alachuafarmandlumber.com
- collegelearners.com
- thoughtcatalog.com
- thriveglobal.com
- smarthustle.com
- huffpost.com
- www.urban.org
- psiloveyou.xyz
- settlement.org
- centerfordiscovery.com
- the-cfya.org
- thetalko.com
- careerindia.com
- hercampus.com
- puresight.com
- theuniguide.co.uk
- practicalmoneyskills.com
- Excerpt from: blind ambition: how to go from victim to visionary by Chad E. Foster.
- agegracefullyamerica.com
- developgoodhabits.com
- libertystaffingusa.com
- nebula.wsimg.com
- careerplanner.com
- whichritual.com/allrituals/visionboard
- entrepreneur.com/article/243218
- goalcast.com
- wikihow.com
- aljazeera.com
- faithfulman.com
- kiis1065.com.au
- yourtango.com
- 80twentynutrition.com
- platia-syosset.com
- mamiverse.com
- goodmenproject.com
- www.boystown.org
- www.forbes.com
- www.highspot.com
- parenting.firstcry.com
- idswater.com

- tweespruitprimary.co.za
- goodchoicesgoodlife.org
- linkedin.com
- zandax.com
- news24.com
- extension.usu.edu
- wellkeptwallet.com
- moneyunder30.com
- whichfranchise.co.za /
- news24.com/truelove/
- parenting.firstcry.com
- jeetbanerjee.com
- thehappyphilosopher.com
- psychologytoday.com
- globallinker.com
- linkedin.com
- forbes.com
- vacounseling.com
- blog.kcm.org
- joegirard.com
- lifehack.org
- medium.com
- successconsciousness.com
- linkedin.com
- theeverygirl.com
- redandyellow.co.za
- betterhelp.com
- psychologytoday.com
- physio-pedia.com/
- learningenglish.voanews.com
- celebrationgoddess.wordpress.com
- tinybuddha.com
- entrepreneur.com/article
- nbcfl.org
- lifehack.org
- success4.com/blog/how-to-develop-a-can-do-attitude-and-succeed-in-whatever-you-want
- positivepsychology.com
- verywellmind.com
- ctclearinghouse.org/
- thomkesslertherapist.com
- journey.cloud/journaling-benefits
- bewellplace.com
- lifelovequotesandsayings.com
- thoughtcatalog.com
- psychologytoday.com
- medium.com
- oprah.com
- From the book: The Purpose Path, by Dr. Nicholas Pearce
- happify.com
- Article by Mark Manson
- forbes.com
- mycontributiontothisplanet.blogpost
- inspiremetoday.com

- andrewpaulthomas.com
- leapireland.com
- huffpost.com
- psychcentral.com/blog
- takingcharge.csh.umn.edu
- sitbreathelove.com
- successconsciousness.com/blog
- etiquetteschoolofamerica.com
- indiatoday.in/education
- ng.opera.news/ng/en/business
- linkedin.com
- facebook.com/
- mindbodygreen.com
- thesilverliningsgroup.com
- thehimalayantimes.com
- gabardi.com
- lifehopeandtruth.com
- woh.org
- blogs.cisco.com
- hackspirit.com
- thriveglobal.com
- nextluxury.com
- reachingself.com
- www.forbes.com
- www.lifehack.org
- clevergirlfinance.com

www.ingramcontent.com/pod-product-compliance
Lightning Source LLC
Chambersburg PA
CBHW081004180426
43194CB00044B/2760